Jill Johnston in Motion

CLARE CROFT

Jill Johnston in Motion

Dance, Writing, and Lesbian Life

Duke University Press *Durham and London* 2024

Project Editor: Livia Tenzer
Designed by Courtney Leigh Richardson
Typeset in Freight and Retail by Copperline Book Services

Library of Congress Cataloging-in-Publication Data
Names: Croft, Clare, author.
Title: Jill Johnston in motion : dance, writing, and lesbian life / Clare Croft.
Description: Durham : Duke University Press, 2024. | Includes bibliographical references and index.
Identifiers: LCCN 2024010784 (print)
LCCN 2024010785 (ebook)
ISBN 9781478026808 (hardcover)
ISBN 9781478031055 (paperback)
ISBN 9781478060017 (ebook)
Subjects: LCSH: Johnston, Jill. | Dance criticism—United States. | Feminist art criticism—United States. | Feminism and the arts—United States. | Lesbian feminist theory—United States. | Authors, American—20th century—Biography. | BISAC: PERFORMING ARTS / Dance / History & Criticism | SOCIAL SCIENCE / LGBTQ Studies / Lesbian Studies
Classification: LCC NX640.5.J55 C76 2024 (print) |
LCC NX640.5.J55 (ebook) | DDC 818/.5409 [B]—dc23/eng/20240620
LC record available at https://lccn.loc.gov/2024010784
LC ebook record available at https://lccn.loc.gov/2024010785

Cover art: Jill Johnston, early 1970s. Photograph by Phyllis Birkby.
Courtesy of the Phyllis Birkby Papers, Sophia Smith Collection of Women's History, Smith College, Northampton, MA.

CONTENTS

PREFACE

She leans.

But there's no falling here. Don't even worry about it. She's not.

This is a secure lean, calculated—a resting, a waiting. One foot is just behind the other, which lets her settle into her hip as her hands press into jean pockets. From this position she can watch for a while, a long while even.

There's a hint of seduction too. It's subtle: her hip doesn't jut out; her eyes don't beckon. They focus, perhaps, on someone beyond the frame. There's a slight yielding in her chest, laughter stretching her mouth wide, almost into a grin. Looking at her, I sense that time can pass, and that will be OK, even pleasurable.

We don't get everything, or even an offer of everything. Her denim jacket functions like a uniform, the hardness of 1970s denim rendering whatever softness lies beneath into edges and lines. The jacket's frame emphasizes that she has squared her shoulders to the camera even though she looks away.

She is approachable, but she will not make the approach. We will come to her. She's not worried about falling. But maybe we should be.

Not many writers put a photo of themselves on their book's front cover, and certainly almost no author puts a full-body photo of themselves on their book's front cover. But Jill Johnston did. The front cover of *Marmalade Me* (1971)—Johnston's first book, a collection of essays mostly from her writing about dance for the New York alternative weekly newspaper, the *Village Voice*—features a leisurely Johnston, seen from head to toe in a photo by Helen Ansell (figure P.1). There is something straightforward in Ansell's framing: an invitation to think of this woman as just *Jill* in addition to the more formal *Johnston,* the widely read critic who introduced New York and the nation to the reinvention of dance for the concert stage now known as *postmodern dance*. By the time Ansell took the photograph that appears on *Marmalade Me*'s cover, Johnston was absolutely an authority on dance, performance, and visual art. Yet in the cover photo, she presents an image of authority that is not, well, authoritative. Instead, her body and relationship to the camera argue for authority as playful, even joyous. I can see what Johnston's friend (and a choreographer whose work she often wrote about) Deborah Hay means when she tells me that Jill was "always obstreperous, and laughed a lot, and made fun of everything she could, in a good way."[1]

Marmalade Me's cover offers a literal snapshot of how Johnston reimagined authority by way of scrambling gender codes—a reminder that 1971 was both the publication year for Johnston's first collection of dance criticism and the year she emphatically came out in the *Village Voice* in a series of columns titled "Lois Lane Is a Lesbian." The play at work in the cover photo connects Johnston's understanding of embodiment, which she learned from dance, to Johnston's attention to how embodiment can be a tool to reimagine categories of gender and sexuality. In the *Marmalade Me* photo, Johnston undoubtedly "reads" as a woman, especially with her long bangs and past-the-shoulder hair. Yet her jacket, her lean, and her nonchalance all borrow from masculinity's repertoire. If we hold all these elements together, Johnston's lean emerges as a lesbian lean, an example of what performance theorist Kemi Adeyemi sees in the action of leaning in public: "a disavow[al] of 90 degrees as the position of authority, asserting instead a new methodology of authority."[2] To lean, to be nonchalantly off-center in public, Adeyemi argues, is "inextricable from the lives and experiences of black women, women of color, queer people, and queer people of color."[3] For Johnston, as a white woman, public (sometimes subtle, sometimes not) assertions of her queerness as difference would certainly not have carried the same level of risk as for the other groups Adeyemi lists. Yet, like all those within queer communities who lean, Johnston slyly sends queer authority into public circulation. Her posture reimagines both what authority can look like and what being a woman can look like.

The cover of *Marmalade Me* is not an outlier among Johnston's many books. Almost every one of her ten single-authored books features a photo of her, usually taken by a woman: Helen Ansell, Roz Gerstein, and Dona Ann McAdams, among others. Contact sheets from these photographic encounters suggest that the images Johnston chose for her book covers were more than just one woman's physical assertions of queerness. These photos document encounters between women and, more often than not, encounters between lesbians. The contact sheets are full of hints of lesbian collectivity—flashes of something just shy of fact. They ripple with images

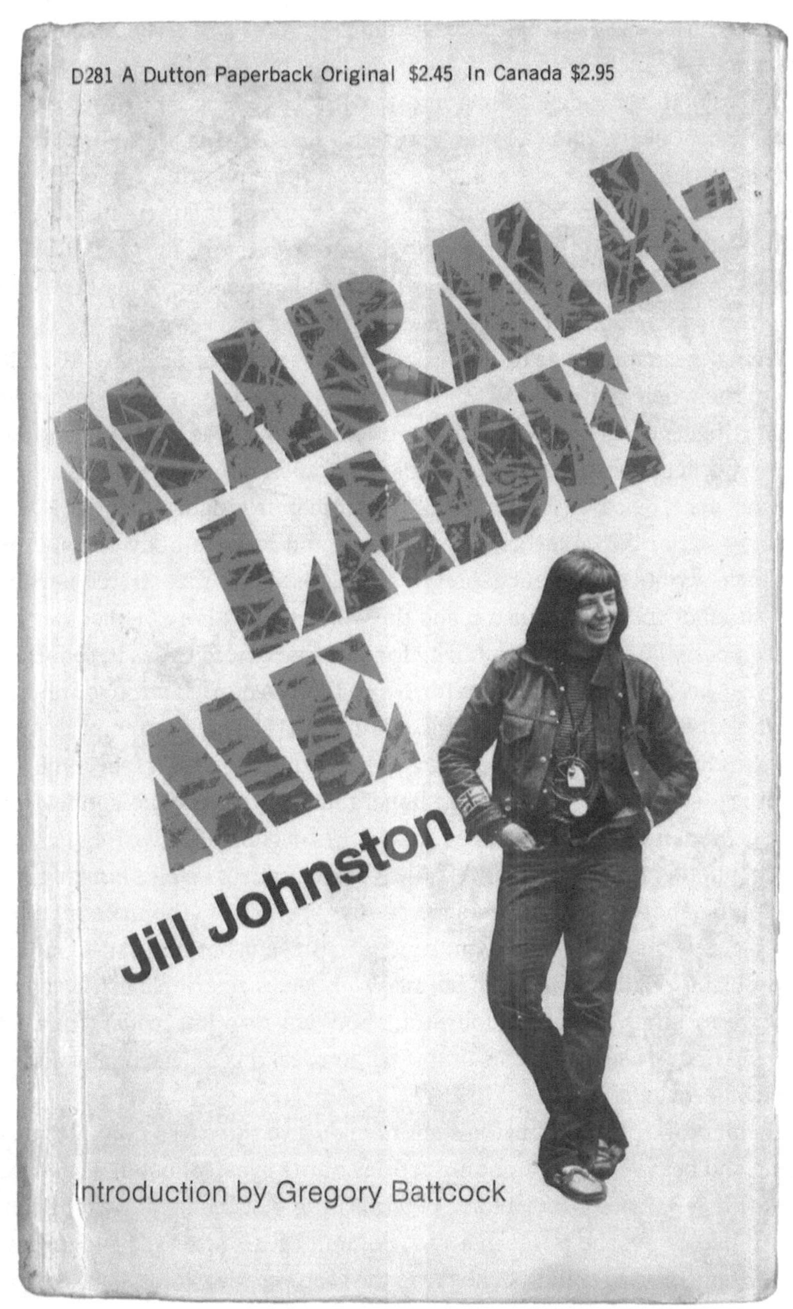

P.1 Cover of *Marmalade Me* (New York: E. P. Dutton, 1971). Photo of Jill Johnston by Helen Ansell. Cover design by Karl W. Stuecklen.

that could be viewed as ones of lesbian life. Images from Ansell's shoot for *Marmalade Me* include a few of Johnston bare-breasted. More than a few feature cats. In almost all, Johnston toys with the photographer's gaze. In a contact sheet likely from Gerstein's session with Johnston for her 1974 book *Gullibles Travels*, Johnston straddles a rooftop while pointing a rifle directly at the camera. Her lanky body stretches over the roof as she trains her eyes forward, just above the gun barrel.[4] No matter the scene or the year, all these photographs present a woman always taking full ownership of her body and often testing the limits of what it means to be seen as a woman.

Seeing these images as ones plucked from early 1970s lesbian life could lead to them being dismissed as mere confirmations of stereotypes, yet they are moving, even as they are mundane. They are records of strong and assertive women, photographer and subject, often in domestic spaces, seeing one another. They are (to borrow a term from performance theorist Diana Taylor) "scenarios" of lesbian life, gestures and body-to-body encounters that form scripts of cultural expression and possibility that stretch beyond the textual or spoken.[5] Johnston and the women who photographed her offer the possibility of lesbian publicity for those who need to see it, to feel it.

A year before the photo shoot for *Marmalade Me*, Ansell wrote of photographing Johnston as "becoming me finding her."[6] Ansell's attempt to capture the charged effect Johnston had on her requires gerunds: "becoming," "finding"—multiple *-ings*. Motion lingers in the images. The connection among women didn't just happen; it's happen*ing*. Ansell's writing echoes lesbian photographer Joan E. Biren/JEB's description of being a lesbian photographing another lesbian, an act JEB says "revers[es] the male myth of the objective observer, seeing but not seen, present but not participating, we [lesbians looking and looked at] allow ourselves emotional involvement while we are photographing."[7] Johnston's book covers prime readers for what they will find in her writing: an almost paradoxical mix of leisure and action borne of lesbian looks.

The photographs of Johnston's entire body also serve as a reminder that seeing and being seen are not only actions of the eyes. Johnston witnessed the world as a dance critic, a form of witnessing that requires paying attention to bodies. As she put it in a 1969 column (years after she supposedly left the dance world behind), she "read the gestures the expressions like the good dance critic I am."[8] Whether dance, lesbian feminism, or what Johnston called the "theatre of life" was her subject, she centered her work in the physical, sometimes focusing on others' bodies and sometimes on her own.

Dance also taught Johnston how to be seen and how to look without giving too much away. Those who need—those who want—to see Johnston's image on her books' covers as a lesbian image have just enough evidence to do so, even as she never fully confirms her identity.[9] The possibility of lesbian arises as one opts in and coauthors the moment's meaning with the photographer and with Jill. The viewer-soon-to-be-reader gets in on Ansell's "becoming me finding her."

Johnston created such effects by being both bold and furtive. In 1965 Peter Hujar, the well-known documentarian of queer life, photographed Johnston in his studio. In the photo Johnston assumes a version of her familiar posture: legs crossed, weight more on one foot than the other, hand in pocket, shoulders squared to the camera (figure P.2). Here, however—unlike in the *Marmalade Me* photo—she looks directly at the camera, but sunglasses disrupt any sense of exchange with the male photographer. She is fully present but refuses full engagement or visibility. The portrait verges on being a parody of her book-cover images photographed by women. She almost seems to be in drag standing in front of Hujar. The signifiers of masculinity sit *on* her body: the drink—dark like Scotch or whiskey—plus vest and tie compete for space with the big metal piece (which Johnston once described as a "kind of a third breast in the center like the better known third eye") that dangles from her neck.[10] Her square metal belt buckle sits just below, dead center in the photograph, so that each half of her body gets a full half of the frame, a structural choice that emphasizes that we are meant to look at her entire body. Johnston—who her longtime partner Ingrid Nyeboe tells me was quite tall, at least five feet nine—takes up the whole picture.[11]

Scholars often laud Hujar for his ability to capture "unusually unguarded" images, but his portrait of Johnston seems anything but.[12] Instead, this is a lean, yes, but a protected one. Johnston pulls slightly away from the camera, sitting into what dancers sometimes call "backspace," and her dark sunglasses further mark her remove. Sure, these observations could be explained by potential drunkenness. The glass is probably not a mere prop: the mid-1960s were, by all accounts, times Johnston saw the avant-garde party scene as of almost equal import to the art that preceded or surrounded the party. Too, the year the photo was taken was perhaps one of Johnston's most difficult: the person in this photo was still recovering from the end of her relationship with choreographer Lucinda Childs and time spent institutionalized in mental health hospitals. But seen amid the book-cover images, the photograph's power supersedes this more melancholic reading. Like the *Marmalade*

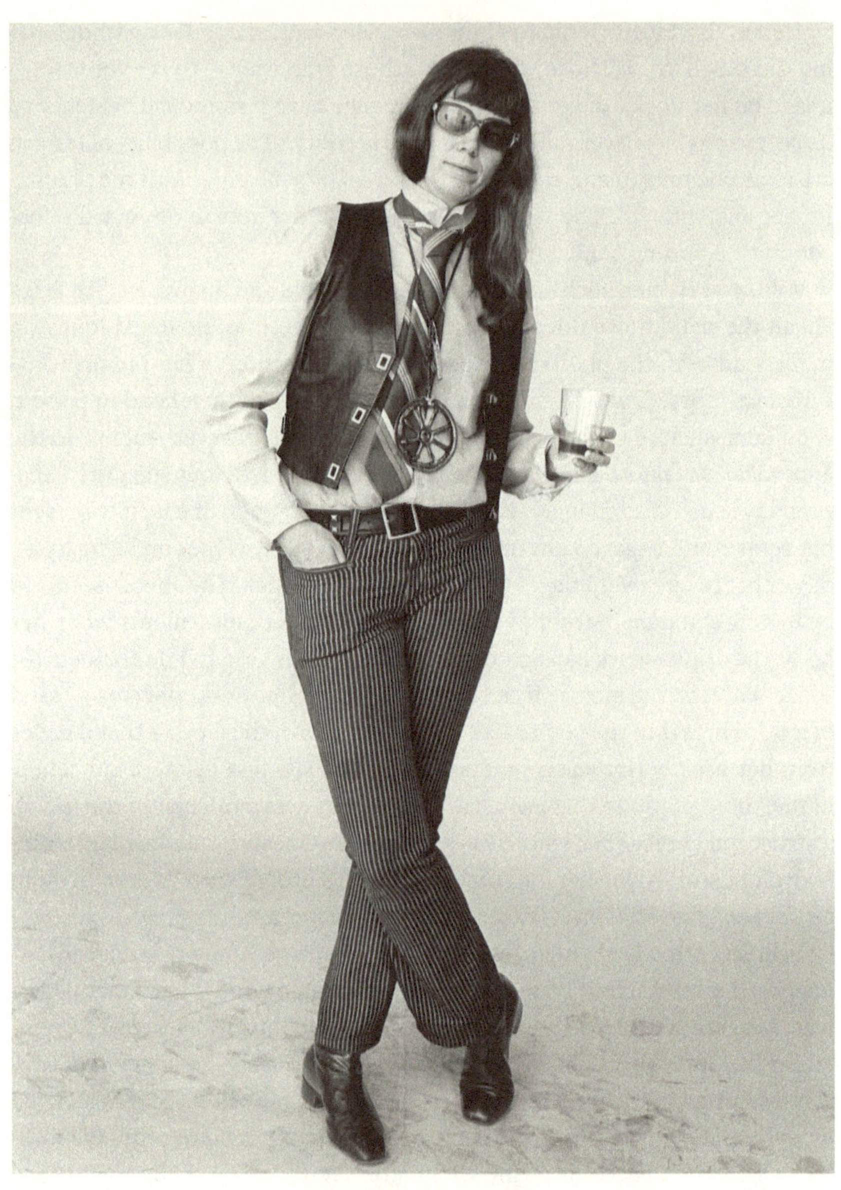

P.2 Jill Johnston, 1965. Photo by Peter Hujar. Courtesy of The Peter Hujar Archive / Artists Rights Society (ARS), New York.

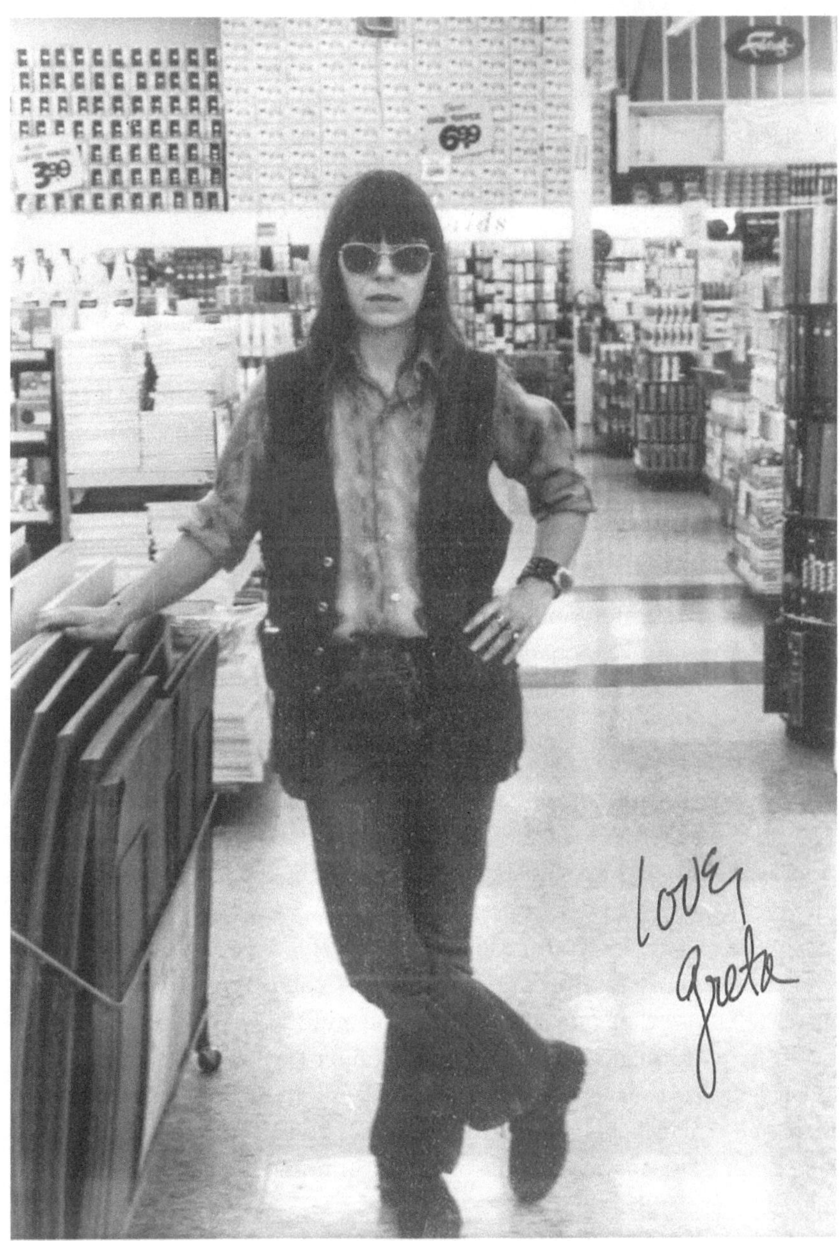

P.3 Fan emulates Jill Johnston, early 1970s. Photographer unknown. Courtesy of the Jill Johnston Literary Archive, New York.

Me photo, Johnston via Hujar issues a sexy challenge to gendered ways of looking, throwing up barriers and invitations all at once.

Johnston demonstrates that being an out lesbian means creating a public place to be at ease with other women, particularly other lesbians, while also crafting protection from misogyny and homophobia. The complexity of Johnston's gendered offering led women to gather on the steps of the *Village Voice* each week, awaiting the appearance of the paper and the latest installment of her column. By putting her lesbian body into public circulation, she made space for others to do the same—and to not feel like they were doing so alone.

Johnston's stance so emboldened her fans that some mimicked it in photographs and then sent those photographs directly to her as accompaniment to their letters of adoration. See, for instance, a photo from a fan who wrote frequently (figure P.3). The inspiration is clear in the posture: tossed-over foot, hand on hip, arm akimbo, and, of course, the clothing and sunglasses. The lean is there but is slight compared to Jill's. This is a lesbian in training. The fan lacks Johnston's nonchalance, but there is reason to hope she'll get there. Her posture demonstrates just how closely she's been watching. She caught all the clues Johnston provided.

Those clues might have been rather intentional. Johnston studied philosophy and art history in college, so she likely knew the stance that she struck in photographs, became known for, and that fans copied was one art historians call the contrapposto stance of Renaissance sculpture, a posture originally associated with masculine strength repurposed by the late nineteenth century into a coded sign of homosexual camp. Think of images of Oscar Wilde leaning, his legs crossed at the ankles and his elbow jutting slightly out. Or Thomas Eakins's painting of nude men in his iconic *Swimming* (1885), each man's weight settling into a back foot, hand on a hip swayed just to the side: a posture performance and art theorist Jennifer Doyle has described as one of a "committed sexual dissident."[13] Johnston gathers these references and more and redistributes them across women's bodies, her own and those of her readers. She answers the question, "How does a sexual dissident committed to lesbianism stand?"

She leans. And she makes me want to read her.

ACKNOWLEDGMENTS

Books often have only one name on the cover, but they emerge from a network of support, intellectual engagement, friendship, and love. Thankfully, this book is no exception.

Funding from the University of Michigan's Institute for the Humanities and from the National Endowment for the Humanities provided me with crucial time to focus on research and writing. Invitations to share work in progress were also critical, including talks at Kenyon College; Northwestern University; the University of Illinois Urbana-Champaign; the University of California, Los Angeles; the University of California, Riverside; and the annual conferences of the American Society of Theatre Research, the American Studies Association, and the Dance Studies Association. The writing in this book also developed through the editorial guidance offered by those who helped publish portions: Gillian Jakab at the *Brooklyn Rail*; editors of *Futures of Dance Studies*, Susan Manning, Rebecca Schneider, and, particularly, Janice Ross; and Melissa Blanco-Borelli, Royona Mitra, and Bryce Lease, editors of a special issue of *Contemporary Theatre Review*. The support of Duke University Press, particularly from Ken Wissoker, Ryan Kendall, two anonymous readers, and the press's faculty advisory board, has generatively challenged the project and cleared the path that brought this book into the world. I owe thanks to all.

I owe a special gratitude to the lesbian adjacencies I had in undertaking the research for this book. I will never be able to fully convey my gratitude to Ingrid Nyeboe and Louise Fishman for their generosity in giving me access to the Jill Johnston Literary Archive—and the gift of their (and Ollie's) company as I worked. I am also indebted to Holly Hughes and Esther Newton for all they did to help me come to know Ingrid and Louise.

I am grateful to the archivists and staff at the Archives of American Art at the Smithsonian, Dick Cavett Show Archives/Cavalier Films, Lesbian Herstory Archives, and the New York Public Library's Jerome Robbins Dance Division. Throughout the entire process, I have been lucky to have excellent research assistance from Alexander Davis, Al Evangelista, Nicole Reehorst, and the incomparable Sophie Allen; without Sophie neither this book nor *The Essential Jill Johnston Reader* would exist. For their help in preparing the manuscript, I thank Eileen Clancy, Shelby Brewster, and the production team at Duke University Press. I am also incredibly grateful for those who wrote letters of recommendation for fellowships, asked provocative questions about the project, and read and gave feedback on drafts: Angie Ahlgren, Mark Clague, Tommy DeFrantz, Susan Foster, Kyle Frisina, Joseph Gamble, Jennifer Harge, Holly Hughes, Omi Osun Joni L. Jones, Hannah Kosstrin, Anthea Kraut, Marjorie Levinson, Peggy McCracken, Patrick McKelvey, Jennifer Monson, Esther Newton, Deborah Paredez, Ramón Rivera-Servera, Valerie Traub, Penny Von Eschen, and Kristen Warner.

I am, as Jill Johnston was, a writer shaped by art and artists. Several artists' work deserves credit for catalyzing and challenging so many of the ideas in this book. I am sure that it would not exist had I not had the opportunity to watch DD Dorvillier and Jennifer Monson's smart and funny, loving and tender *RMW(a) & RMW*. DD introducing me to Pauline Boulba and Aminata Labor proved another happy accident of queer life, and I'm glad this book enters the world alongside their *JJ* trio of performance, film, and the French translation of Johnston's writing. This book has also been forged by the sacred space that is the Agnes Martin Gallery at Taos's Harwood Museum. This book has ridden great artistic coattails—or perhaps, more accurately, wigs, pink shorts, and Levi's; Bowery rooftops; and delicate blue and white stripes.

This book was written during a particularly complicated time, in my life and in the world. I weathered a global pandemic mostly thanks to a California crew that took me in as family. Rachel, Dawn (Tata), Talia, Rich, and Sancho, thanks for being a house where guests can bring guests.

My always and forever family—Mom, Dad, and Johnny—transformed in the years I wrote this book. I didn't know I could love you more, but in April 2023 I learned just how much more I could.

And then there is the family who are my home: Sara and Harper. Sara, my gratitude is as endless as my love. Please keep building the boat with me. Harper's sweet spirit—and the many hours she spent snoring under my chair as I wrote—lives in every page of this book.

Introduction

In 1955 Jill Johnston shifted from one site of dancing to another, moving from spending her days (mostly) in a dance studio to spending her days (mostly) in a dance archive. That year Johnston began what would be a ten-month-long job at the New York Public Library's Dance Collection, one of the largest archives of dance material in the United States.[1] A white woman in her mid-twenties, Johnston had moved to New York City two years prior, "armed with philosophy and geared for dancing," with plans to study the former at Columbia University and the latter at the school of foundational modern dance figure José Limón.[2] A broken foot served as a catalyst for Johnston's departure from the Limón school, where she had been focused on building a life as a dancer and also secretly (or so she thought) falling in love with the women of the Limón company.

Jill Johnston in Motion considers how dance and lesbian desire intertwined and became the most defining aspects of Johnston's life. They were, perhaps, co-occurring in this particular moment, but their entanglement is more related than is usually imagined in accountings of Johnston's life. She has generally been described as, first, a dance critic and, later, a lesbian activist, with her desire for women bracketed away from her early love of dance, and dance left behind as she turned toward feminism, specifically lesbian feminism. In contrast, I argue that dance—with its requisite attention to embodiment—shaped Johnston's life, writing, and activism deeply. Through dance Johnston learned that where one focuses one's body, how one approaches others' bodies, and how one offers their body to others are potent actions that can be used to social and political ends.

As a dance, performance, and visual art critic, Johnston was a poignant, sensual, and humorous writer of bodies in motion. She (mostly) did this work in her cutting-edge column in New York's alternative weekly, the *Village Voice*, where she began writing about dance in 1960. By the end of the 1960s, Johnston had shifted the column's focus from dance to her burgeoning life as an out lesbian, and she focused her writing there for (most of) the rest of her life. Dance, however, never really disappeared from Johnston's writing. In fact, her writing became a kind of dancing.

Postmodern dance's mix of clarity and obscurity drew Johnston's attention and eventually became a key strategy she deployed to imagine and reimagine her identity as a lesbian and the politics thereof. In her writing about her life as a spectator of performance and her life as a lesbian within feminist and gay liberation movements, she taught her readers to read choreographically. In Johnston's writing, postmodern dance's emphasis on formal strategies like rhythm and accumulation became metaphors and practices attuned to how one can find pleasure and meaning in experience rather than searching for full comprehension. Johnston's writerly rendering of what composer and theorist John Cage called *indeterminacy*, an approach to authorship that invites chance into the process of making and an idea that served as a major catalyst for modern dance's transformation into postmodern dance, allowed Johnston to build queer, lesbian theories of mess, excess, and uncertainty. With these ideas in mind, Johnston taught her readers how absence and presence collide, seducing those who want to read and sense differently.

Reading choreographically has much in common with queer approaches to archives, so it seems an auspicious coincidence that Johnston's life as a dance writer began in the Dance Collection. If one is looking in archives for evidence of queer women's lives, particular tools of engagement are needed—tools that clarify what's there, what's not there, and all that might lie in the space between full presence and total absence. It is in this middle space where lesbians often live. I turn to the idea of where lesbians exist in the archive not so much to prove that lesbians exist in (dance) history—I know they do; I'm dancing with Jill already—but rather to find ways to be *with* lesbians across time. This book is not merely an attempt to find queer women in history—what performance theorist Tavia Nyong'o terms a *salvage* project—but rather it is an attempt to write lesbian history as a practice of attachment, adjacency, and even touch.[3] Put more broadly, this book is about imagining ways to keep intimate company with the past.

Looking for Her

Lesbians: felt, not found.

Johnston described the feeling of working in the Dance Collection in 1955 as one of being surrounded by men and their creations. The shelves, full of books and dissertations seemingly all written by men, made her feel literally encircled by men and their ideas.[4] From the same library decades later, musical theater scholar Stacy Wolf wrote of an eerily similar feeling of patriarchal claustrophobia. For Wolf, an overwhelming sense of heterosexual presence further compounded her experience of the archive as inhospitable to even the possibility of lesbians. Working in the collection made her distrust what she knew: of course lesbians had been part of theater history. Yet Wolf found herself wondering "if the lesbian files had been intentionally destroyed . . . if there *ever were* any lesbian files" (emphasis added).[5] Wolf goes on to describe reckoning with her confoundment and then her own desire—need, really—to locate the lesbians in history, lesbians who she knew were there but who had been displaced by the archive's doubled emphasis on patriarchy and heterosexuality. Holding her desire close opened a path forward. Wolf concludes her essay in a different place from where her research quest began, offering that perhaps it is just as important to trace one's desires in the archive as it is to locate the objects one seeks.

I am similarly compelled to examine my desires for lesbian presence and absence in the archive. As a dance researcher, lesbian, and queer person interested in studying women and specifically lesbians in dance history, I deeply sympathize with Wolf's exasperation and also her visceral experience of desire. Too often, wanting what you cannot find (or are told you will not find) summarizes queer life in the archive and beyond. This context makes Johnston a compelling case study. As can often be the case with lesbians in the archive, Jill Johnston is both easy and hard to find. She wrote voluminously in popular platforms about her life and her loves (performance and lesbians) but artfully eschewed easy categorization around either topic. She was one of the most prolific and influential writers in second-wave feminism but has barely been engaged by scholars, artists, or activists—in part because she refused alignments with other writers, activists, or collectives. She has given me (and us) so much to search, while also remaining just beyond reach. In many ways, this book is a documentation of my attempts and failures at finding Jill Johnston.

The lesbians who are looking and the lesbians for whom we look can touch, but how to be open to that touch?

The figure of the lesbian presents a particular quandary but also a unique possibility for historians. Theorist Annamarie Jagose has argued that lesbian figures are almost always configured as "elsewhere," which results in the lesbian being exiled "to the impossible dream of exteriority of normative power."[6] Imagining lesbians as somehow utopically floating outside of power and norms of meaning making obscures both the specificity and multiplicity within the category of lesbian. Relegating women who lived outside the norms of heterosexuality to some imagined elsewhere flattens and disappears from history women-who-love-women's complex refusals of constricting social norms. We lose the provocations of so many: the Black performers Angela Davis calls "blues women"; the radical feminists of the late 1960s who brought Johnston into feminist consciousness, many of whom also fought for space for women within gay liberation movements; Latina lesbian writers, activists, and editors, like Cherríe Moraga and Gloria Anzaldúa; and so many others.[7] To value these women's lives, insights, and labors requires historians and theorists of lesbian life take up Jagose's challenge "not to secure a body or a sexuality beyond networks of power but to understand [the lesbian] body and sexuality, as *incoherently constituted through discourse*" (emphasis added).[8] The lesbian in the archive, the lesbian in history, is a powerful if not always fully comprehensible disruption from within.

Jill Johnston is a fascinating case study for considering how the lesbian is "incoherently constituted through discourse," because she exemplifies a queer lesbian strategy of what I call *recognition without confirmation*. Recognition without confirmation helps me think about how lesbians, because of their overlapping status as women and homosexuals, often work to make their presence known while also resisting too much clarification of their identities—a strategy sometimes deployed for surviving sexism, homophobia, and/or racism, and other times deployed for pleasure. Is this a lesbian gesture? A lesbian dance? Who wants to know? What or how might you need to watch to get an answer?[9]

Johnston's skills at this game are virtually unmatched. Even as she became one of the most prominent voices of lesbian feminism, she often either stopped just short of fully elaborating what that meant for a male and/or straight readership or provided so much elaboration that her lesbian cup spilled over. This is part of why she publicly chafed at the limited ways *lesbian* has been understood, lamenting in a 1973 column that "sometimes I think I'll have to stop using the word lesbian because of its still prevalent exclusively sexual connotation in society at large."[10] She did not intend to displace the sexual connotation of *lesbian* but rather wanted more for *lesbian* as a label. Johnston was not alone in her frustration that *lesbian* had become so associated with its sexual definition that its political dimensions were overlooked. As her fellow *Village Voice* feminist writer Vivian Gornick wrote, in her own complaint about the flattening of lesbian identity within feminist movements, "The point is not that lesbians in the movement are homosexual; the point is that they are feminists."[11] Looking for the lesbian in the archive is not just a matter of looking for a pattern of sameness among women and calling that *lesbian*. Looking for lesbians in the archive requires looking for the loud echo of patriarchy and those who demand to be free of it.

In my case, there are many lesbians in the archive, and one of them is me: a dance theorist and critic born a decade after Stonewall who identifies as queer, as a lesbian, and as a feminist. Jill Johnston would probably run those terms all together—queerlesbianfeminist. She hated commas and avoided them almost entirely. But I like a little breathing room between the words. They all overlap for me, but together, as a list, they help me point in several directions at once: to sexuality, to gender, and to politics. I also know, however, the danger in putting too much space between words. When I realized that the dance critic I knew through *Marmalade Me* (the 1971 collection E. P. Dutton published of Johnston's 1960s dance writing) was also a lesbian feminist activist, I was nothing less than thrilled and intrigued . . . but also more than a little annoyed I'd earned multiple degrees related to dance history without ever being in a classroom where Johnston's prominence as a lesbian had been mentioned.

Studying Jill Johnston has been a dance with my desire to be with a past—maybe *my* past. That desire, however, cannot supplant Johnston as the subject of my research, even as I also cannot dismiss the role desire plays. I want to be with Johnston, not obscure her. Queer theorist Elizabeth Freeman's frame of "erotic historiography" has been a useful guide in this effort. Freeman, drawing heavily on Sigmund Freud, argues that history too often functions as a reclamation project overly focused on the desire of the historian (the figure in the present) for a referential object (a queer figure from the past), imagining that once the researcher obtains her object and brings her into the present through writing, a lack or absence can be ameliorated. In a performance of queering time, Freeman offers that we do not need to search history for these past objects but rather to acknowledge that the past is already with us. For her, erotic historiography is a way to encounter "the present itself as a hybrid" of something called "the past" and something called "the present."[12]

Now there are (at least) three of us here: my desire manifested as fantasy subject (Jill); the writer, theorist, and activist (Johnston); and the historian, audience member/critic/writer, and dancer (me).

Building on ideas of speculation elaborated in Black studies, Nyong'o describes queer archival work as holding the potential for a dynamic relationship between a desiring subject and a desired object, a tension that registers most clearly through sensuality and speculation. He encourages scholars to "enter the archive phenomenologically, to move and be moved by the past . . . encounter[ing] its sensuous fragments, and build[ing] narrative, speculative, and creative accounts accordingly."[13] To approach the past with a willingness to be moved can open a portal for imagination and transformation.

Performance, especially when seen through Johnston's writing, provides a space to practice being open to sensations and collisions of presence and absence. Johnston began her career as critic as much in the visual art world as that of dance, often attending performances, particularly Happenings, in visual art galleries. The sonic, visual, and semiotic mergings of these multimedia events clearly affected her and inspired her first writings. Even in these earliest reviews, Johnston courted readers' full range of senses and sensualities. As she turned more explicitly to dance in the 1960s, her emphasis on the sensorial expanded further, often presenting itself as an experience of excess and overlap. She took readers to the moment of the event and helped *them* experience how *she* had experienced time unfolding, often pleasurably and humorously disorienting her reader (much as performance can do). In her reviews Johnston re-creates the feeling of being close to a performance or performer, rather than positioning the writer or reader as viewing from a distance. Johnston's writing bends time to make proximity possible, provoking affect and connection in a manner that helps avoid mistaking that proximity for comprehension. Getting closer means sensing more, being with the details and the surprises.

Johnston's approach to performance criticism is not dissimilar to what queer theorist Carolyn Dinshaw compels historians of queerness to practice: a "touch across time." Similar to Nyong'o, Dinshaw contends that the work of queer historiography is to make "affective relations," in which histories become "manifest by juxtaposition, by making entities past and present touch."[14] Dinshaw elaborates her argument from her perspective as a medieval historian, denouncing the sedimentation of the premodern into an "eminently obvious monolithic against which modernity and postmodernity groovily emerge."[15] Historians must avoid resigning the past to being only the present's foil and fodder and instead invite encounters with gender and sexuality in the past as "indeterminate and heterogenous" (a phrasing that could just as easily be a way to describe postmodern dance as it is a description of the queer medieval history Dinshaw writes).

One way Johnston created a sense of proximity to performance through writing involved dropping her reader into the middle of a scene or argument, describing—often in dizzying prose—all that was unfolding. There was little explanation or setup. As a reader, I take this as her vote of confidence in me. She's assuring me, "You already know enough to be here." I am a witness, not a detective. The only way to make any sense (if sense is even an aim) of what Johnston writes is to take in as much as possible and let it merge and collide inside and outside of you. With this in mind, this introduction drops into several scenes. In the first set, Johnston builds an archive through her writing; in the second set, I encounter her in the midst of institutional archives. Throughout, I try to keep in mind the lessons Johnston teaches in her writing about what it means to approach the past queerly, to look for what lives between presence and absence, and to read choreographically, attending to rhythm, layers, and the way meaning accumulates through sequence. This is an introduction to this book's ostensible topic, acts of criticism made by one remarkable woman, but more so I intend this to be an introduction to writing as a form of looking and reading as a form of witnessing.

I need to dream to start.

It is 1955, and she—Jill—is sitting and working at a table in the Dance Collection.[16] Up walks a man. The man is Louis Horst: a huge figure in American modern dance at the time. Horst is teacher and collaborator to modern dance matriarch Martha Graham, as well as a member of Juilliard's dance faculty and the managing editor of the New York dance publication *Dance Observer*. From these prominent platforms, particularly *Dance Observer*, Horst argued that modern dance (a category primarily composed, for Horst, of mostly New York–based, mostly white choreographers) must exhibit "structural and dramatic unity."[17] He saw these values in modern dance's earlier generations, notably Graham, as well as Doris Humphrey and José Limón. In his teaching, writing, and public speaking, Horst proclaimed these choreographers' greatness by elaborating how he saw them enact "unity" in their choreography, creating a feedback loop that furthered his aesthetic values and that, by the 1950s, had begun to seem "archaic."[18]

Jill doesn't recognize him. Writing about the encounter decades later, she describes Horst as merely "an old man with white hair."[19] By describing him initially with only a physical description rather than a name, Johnston makes a calculated diminishment of his standing—a dismissal of how he attained power in the dance world. Like so many of midcentury dance's most powerful men, Horst came into power from offstage, as writer, accompanist, editor, and administrator. Describing him via his body rather than his name or titles, Johnston situates him within the milieu most dancers, particularly women, experience: being a body amid bodies. In the moment of hearing his voice, sitting at the table, looking up, Jill would likely have not recognized Horst, at least not initially. Johnston's approach to description lands her readers next to her, hearing a voice and looking up to see "an old man with white hair."

Johnston's writing allows me to sit down beside Jill at that table in 1955. We look at Horst together. We see him as she has created him through her writing: another man in a library full of men.

But Horst knew *her*. He knew her name, and he knew her writing. He knew her because she'd complained. Johnston had recently written to Horst as the editor of *Dance Observer* and, apparently, had gotten his attention. The letter does not exist in either Johnston's or Horst's archives, but given that it led Horst to want to meet Johnston—seemingly enough to seek her out at her place of employment—it was likely well written and persuasive, possibly even intriguing. The letter probably eviscerated Horst and his critical milieu.[20] Shortly after this meeting in the archive, Johnston wrote an essay for the *Dance Observer* (likely drawing on her letter to Horst) in which she accused critics of not "meet[ing] the challenge" presented by a new generation of choreographers.[21] Critics were only writing about what they understood. In contrast, Johnston imagined criticism that charted a path between known and unknown. In an essay the next year, she confronted critics again, writing, "Looking within ourselves and finding nothing to respond with, we attribute to the artist a poverty which is our own."[22] To write about new forms of art, of dance, required new forms of writing.

But in 1955 no essays have yet been written. Jill is looking up at Horst, who is somewhat unaccustomed to having someone disagree with him but is still engaged. This is the beginning of Johnston's career as a dance critic, and one of many times she would confront a powerful figure. In the two decades to come, leaders and celebrities ranging from Norman Mailer to Betty Friedan would find themselves publicly undone by Johnston's often physical, often spectacular antics. She interrupted a Friedan speech by swimming topless in the pool at art gallerists Bob and Edith Scull's Long Island mansion. A few months later, she publicly derailed a Mailer display of blustering masculinity by making out with two other women as Mailer tried to hold court.[23] As Ann Cvetkovich, in her writing about being a lesbian go-go dancer, and Raquel Monroe, in her writing about Black lesbian performers in hip-hop, have shown, these physical interruptions of patriarchy and respectability are a frequent lesbian strategy—insistent insertions of women's existence and sexuality that, as Monroe puts it, "literally and discursively prope[l] lesbian sexuality and fantasy into . . . hyper-masculinist sphere[s]."[24]

This younger Jill at the library (she was twenty-seven in 1955) was still almost twenty years away from the physical interruptions that helped make her a famous lesbian, but I don't think she would have given reverence to the man standing before her. I bet she looked at him just as though he was any other man—not powerful, just one more among so many. Horst tells her who he is—name, title—and invites her to write for his magazine. She remains nonplussed, says *yes* without hesitation or gratitude. Maybe she does an internal eye roll that manifests externally as a slight chuckle or shoulder shrug. Through these subtle actions, she flips the notion of a library "full of men." No longer would the presence of so many men and their scholarship be evidence of power consolidated. Instead, yet another man's appearance would be a sign of how boring having only one perspective can be.

When Johnston's first published writing appeared in the *Dance Observer*, she already sounded like someone who trusted she should have a platform. Reflecting years later on her early days as a critic, she wrote, "I . . . submitted to his publication the first thing I ever wrote besides letters and school essays, and the sight of my name in print at the top of the article when it appeared catalyzed my interest in criticism and writing. I had barely begun, and my ambition was extensive; already I fancied myself America's leading dance critic."[25] Self-appointed as "America's leading dance critic," Johnston unapologetically launched herself to the front of a line full of men. She read and somewhat admired the leading twentieth-century dance critics: Horst, John Martin, Walter Terry, and, particularly, her queer compatriot, poet Edwin Denby.[26] Johnston as line leader, metaphor or otherwise, however, does not quite work. She always felt herself to be an outsider, different from the rest, even as she was aware, as she put it, that to become a dance critic was to "inherit . . . the mantle of several dead or retired old men."[27]

But still, in 1955, Johnston said yes to Horst's offer. In that moment, as I like to imagine it, Jill picks Horst up and swings him over her shoulder, using her tall, lanky body to counterbalance his weight. The seat of Horst's pants replaces his white-haired head as his most visible feature. Male critics were constants, sometimes burdens, sometimes asses. Regularly they were unavoidable gatekeepers. Johnston had to accomplish—and did accomplish—the task of dealing with men in a patriarchal world. In journalism this would be an unending task for her: 1955 was also the year that three men, Ed Fancher, Dan Wolf, and Mailer, founded the *Village Voice*, the publication where Johnston had her most prominent platform and where she would often be condescended to by male editors and owners.[28] In all these male-led publications, however, Johnston exploited men's invitations to create the playful, excessive approach to writing she first brought to dance and visual art and later to her feminist activism.

At least at first, Jill had no choice but to carry all this patriarchal weight. But she also got to work. She started writing, and she never stopped. She became known for crafting sentences so long they steal breath, so long no one can interrupt. Dance writing was her thing, and she would make it a "her thing."

"Sure, 'old man with white hair.' I'll write what I think in your magazine."

Johnston titled her first *Dance Observer* essay "Thoughts on the Present and Future Directions of Modern Dance." As I read Johnston, I frequently think, "Jill, that's a lot to cover in just a column; it's just one essay." But her writing pushes the boundaries of linguistic capacity. For her a dance review is often equal parts performance description, field assessment, plea for critical generosity, and theoretical treatise. In that first essay, there is already the big, capacious mind engaging a wide range of artistic voices, and there is also the focused prose examining philosophical ideas as they relate (and don't) to dance. In this essay her larger concern is what is implied by the term *progress*. There are also early signs of the prosaic genius for which she would become best known, namely, her dizzying, kinetic lists—lists charged with verbs, imagery, and challenges to parallel structure and punctuation. For instance, to capture the energy of the new choreographers, a group she names only as "the rebels," she paints them as a "pot of arm waving, choreography by change, egos in vacuums."[29] This short list contains many types of phrasing that would become her signature: densely physical ("pot of arm waving"), wry ("egos in vacuums"—both a compliment and not), and attentive to how linguistic meaning emerges sonically and rhythmically ("choreography by change"). As is often the case with her lists, if broken down to individual elements, the list does not quite make rational sense. If taken in like one is reading a windstorm, there is a logic to be felt. Johnston teaches me (us?) that writing about dance requires a willingness to play with language and the ways meaning gets made. Sense comes in the experience the writing creates. She did not just demand a new mode of criticism in her writing; she provided one.

Johnston's lists—which grew longer and denser with time—became literally breathtaking features of her twenty-year tenure at the *Voice*. Through this tactic and others, she persistently resisted language as a mechanism to fix bodies, ideas, identities, or relationships into easily digestible or legible categories. Rather than writing sentences, she calibrated them. Using energy and rhythm, she discussed the ambiguities and abstractions central to the dance making she wrote about/with the "rebel group," the group who would eventually become New York's postmodern dance icons: Merce Cunningham (whom Johnston was among the first to champion as a choreographer, not just a vibrant dancer), Yvonne Rainer, Robert Morris, Lucinda Childs, Deborah Hay, and many others (most, but not all, part of the Judson Dance Theater).

In her dance writing, Johnston was practically Horst's opposite, refusing his notion of structural unity as aesthetic triumph. Instead, she reveled in unsettling incongruences and excesses. (And yes, in Johnston's writing, *excess* can be plural.) Take, for instance, the opening to her 1966 review of a Robert Whitman–directed Happening:

> Robert Whitman presented a beautiful happening or theatre thing rather he would prefer maybe (to call it) in East Hampton August 27 and 28. The location was fantastic although I couldn't see it too well. It was a NIGHT TIME event. The location was fantastic. Whitman lit the place up for tripping the lights. I thought I was in a metaphorical paradise. I was. I couldn't find my seat, which was in a field. The field was full of grass and other weeds and there was also a swamp and nobody stepped on it (except the performers). But first of all (and last) I walked through an alley of paper bags glowing candles. They made a curving country path leading from the road where two guides (policemen) led the performing spectators with their flash lights, down to three enormous plexiglass sheets sprayed with copper to make them into mirrors and situated so as to form a kind of room (enclosure). I found myself in the mirrors. I thought I was a clown at a country fair, or an amusement park. I was. Distortions are a riot if it doesn't bother you.[30]

In this passage Johnston plays with time and perspective, tossing her reader among the performance's elements and her myriad impressions. She does much more than note a feeling. Instead, she provides a way to have that feeling, finds new ways to describe how sensations and events shift, change, and overlap. In *Marmalade Me*'s preface, she refers to this Whitman review as a turning point in her career. Encountered within the context of her *Village Voice* contributions across the 1960s, it reads as such. Johnston invites readers to enter a past performance and someone's dream at the same time. Soon after this review's 1966 publication, Johnston began to treat all avant-garde art makers in the visual arts, theater, and dance with the playful zeal she afforded Whitman. What writing genre is this? A performance review? Maybe. Also something more? In the introduction to *Marmalade Me*, art critic Gregory Battcock remarks on Johnston's range, writing, "It is to Johnston's credit that her work is several things all at once."[31]

Johnston's approach to writing—penning prose that was never fully coherent or categorizable but always full, physical, and evocatively excessive—blossomed in the mid-1960s as she pushed her columns further and further. After 1965 she wrote less about dance, and even her reviews that were ostensibly about dance were likely to discuss everyday items (her wallpaper, for instance, as was the case in a May 1966 review of a shared evening by two of her favorites, Rainer and James Waring).[32] As Johnston's writing changed, the *Voice* hired Deborah Jowitt to cover dance in a more traditional form than Johnston had ever really done. Jowitt's writing ran under the column title "Dance," and Johnston's column became "Dance Journal." In this period Johnston's writing transforms from being *about* dance to being a form of dancing itself: a current of events, people, and sound swirling all at once. In 1971 the column gets another name change; "Dance Journal" is now "Jill Johnston." By this point, categorizing Johnston's writing is nearly impossible. Category, genre, and editors were all tested by these expansions. In an undated letter to Johnston, her then editor Diane Fisher begged Johnston to rein in her experiments: "We are, Jill, after all a newspaper!"[33]

There are many reasons to sidestep clarity.

Johnston's refusal of easy meaning or category *is* meaning in her writing. This was clear as she substituted a dancer-ly sensibility for dance as subject and focused that sensibility on daily life, usually her own. Readers had to track how she wrote. Rhythm, energy, and spatial arrangement became as important—perhaps more important—than what she was writing about. Some dismissed her as no longer making sense. Johnston usually acknowledged such dismissals with glee. In a 1968 column, she bragged that "a lady at

Jasper John[s]'s house last night where a black-tie thing was going on . . . told me 'they' didn't understand my writing anymore."[34] Johnston's use of quotation marks—"they"—signals what her column underscored as it evolved: making sense of avant-garde performance and bohemian life for a heteropatriarchal readership (aka the New York elite who attended black-tie art functions) was not her goal.

Johnston's refusal to make her writing broadly comprehensible became so widely apparent that the *Voice* made a joke (and marketing ploy) of it. In 1969 the paper ran a cleverly designed ad in the *New York Times*, listing what portions of the *Voice* would be most compelling across readers' astrological signs. Under Taurus, the ad copy laments the sign's preference for being "ordered, systematic, [and] stable" and names Johnston's column as the ultimate test for the Taurus reader: "Jill Johnston's disdain for order in her Dance Journal (which never mentions the Dance) will challenge and perhaps confound your inherent inflexibility."[35] Elsewhere *Voice* editors treated Johnston's writing with derision, including frequently publishing homophobic and misogynist letters to the editor about her on the paper's famous opinion pages, but they also kept increasing the space she had in the newspaper. Her column got longer and longer and was frequently teased on the paper's front page. Editors did not know what to make of her, but they knew readers wanted her.

She had latitude because she had a following. Letters to her, both those published in the *Voice* and those in her archive, confirm I am not the only reader of Johnston's column who has used her writing to create a fantasy—a Jill of our own. As her own newspaper made fun of her prose (albeit to advertise the paper), Jill's dis-order reached and inspired a wide audience. By the early 1970s, groups of fans, mostly women, could be found outside the *Voice*'s office each week waiting for Johnston's next installment. With a just-published paper in their hands, these women walked away with more and more hints about Johnston's sexual identity. In 1969 Johnston began to use the phrase *the collaboration* as a euphemistic reference to her lesbian relationships. There were also references to Gertrude Stein and Alice Toklas. A "friend" (read: girlfriend), Polly, traveled with her on trips she chronicled.[36] Jill Johnston came out as a lesbian by way of a choreography of accumulation.

Women began putting the pieces together, even if they weren't quite sure what they added up to. The hundreds of letters in Johnston's personal archive, examined in print for the first time in this book, were sent by everyone from housewives fantasizing about living as lesbians to young queers newly arrived in New York. Those who needed new ways to categorize their lives found Jill's "disdain for order" not just legible but necessary, inspirational, and, in some cases, hot.[37] Take for instance, a letter sent to Johnston in March 1971, penned by J. of Jamaica, New York, who writes about the effect Johnston's writing has on her: "Remember what you said in the March 4th article '. . . you have to perpetuate the illusion that it means something to somebody beside yourself.' That's no illusion! That's reality. Do you know that for two weeks now [since reading the March 4 article] I've been confused, frightened, and thoroughly unhappy! because for the first time in my life, MISS STRAIGHT (me) has been seriously question[ing] if this is really what I am. If being straight is really what anybody is."[38] The way Johnston wrote about her sexuality brought into question the value or use of categories of sexuality. Was being straight as ubiquitous as it seemed? If the answer might be no, then what excitements might be found in categories beyond the supposed norm?

Another admirer could feel that potential, telling Johnston in a letter that her column was "stimulating . . . [capable of doing] something to you that is indefinable you get a certain feeling like falling into a whirlpool or at times a cesspool."[39] Johnston's prose appealed to these letter writers because it created a space to be sexy and sensual, a misfit, outsider, and/or provocateur. Johnston charted a path for herself and others not defined by patriarchy and heteronormativity. As she put it in a 1971 column, she hoped to "educat[e] all the members of ourselves," a phrase that beautifully combines individual and collective, acknowledging the task of making lesbian identity a reality across many sites, groups, and individuals.[40] She makes *lesbian* into an aspiration, a horizon, or, to return to Jagose, an idea "incoherently constituted through discourse." In her writing Johnston always refused to reduce the sign of *lesbian* to coherent legibility, doing everything she could to inject possibility into the word.

There were, however, limits to the possibilities Johnston could imagine for *lesbian*. Questions of race were largely not part of her reckoning. By the time she published *Lesbian Nation* in 1973, she was aware of those limits, describing herself as having come into her political consciousness in the late 1960s after being one of the "completely unconscious active ablebodied privileged white middle class women of amerika."[41] This social position was further sedimented by the arts and Village bohemian worlds in which she moved in the 1960s, where she remembers Black culture, "the cultural revolution of hip and beat and black jazz and the twist and the drugs," being all around her, even as very few Black people were.[42] This local context meant that the New York white avant-garde was perfectly situated to engage in appropriation, which dance historian Imani Kai Johnson defines, in her essay "Black Culture without Black People," as "something being taken and . . . being taken up in a certain kind of way: with the power to do so uncritically and unethically."[43] Seeing Black culture as available, even important, but Black people and racism at a distance was a theme in the communities in which Johnston moved throughout her life. She thought of racism as a thing of the South, where, while studying for an MFA at the University of North Carolina Greensboro, she had seen "whites only" signs everywhere.[44] American racism, of course, was not confined to one region. Johnston moved into downtown Manhattan in the early 1960s, just as a number of infrastructure projects (many led by the infamous Robert Moses, others explicitly focused on the arts) pushed Black and Brown residents out of New York's central borough.[45] It was not just the case that Johnston moved in a variety of predominantly white New York scenes of the 1960s; she moved in locales that were actively being whitened.

Johnston's racial consciousness expanded as she became more involved in activism in the late 1960s and early 1970s. Her attention shifted from Black culture more generally to Black politics, with Black nationalism becoming a key inspiration for what she termed *dyke nationalism*.[46] But, still, these ideas were just that—ideas—not deep engagement with Black thought or the Black people authoring and enacting them. Beyond a few instances at feminist rallies, Johnston seems to have had little to no engagement with the work or writing of the many lesbians of color—Black, Latina, Asian American, and/or Indigenous women—who were actively organizing in the 1960s and 1970s. These leaders penned their own experiments in writing, work first made widely available in 1981 with the publication of the watershed text *This Bridge Called My Back: Writings by Radical Women of Color*, edited by feminist, lesbian Latina writers Cherríe Moraga and Gloria Anzaldúa. That volume included Moraga's call for what she termed "theory of the flesh," which spoke to how truly revolutionary politics must be born of lived experience, including what it felt like to be "often the lesbians among the straight" *and* "the colored in a white feminist movement."[47] In the former, being "lesbians among the straight," Moraga and Johnston overlap in their concerns, but the latter, what it meant to be "the colored in a white feminist movement," Johnston never addressed and likely never really considered.

This critical hole in Johnston's perspective on feminism, an absence of attention to race and ethnicity, cannot be overstated, nor is a simple marking of the gap sufficient for considering her relationship to race. Reckoning with Johnston's racial formation requires a three-tiered analysis that focuses, first, on the production of whiteness; second, on the dynamics that have perpetually yoked *lesbian* to whiteness, particularly in the wake of the feminist movements of the early 1970s; and, third, on the role of racial difference. The production of whiteness is perhaps the most constant element in Johnston's approach to race. Both in her work in the arts and in her lesbian feminist activism, Johnston was a white woman among, almost exclusively, other white people, which shaped her writing in each of these arenas. Whiteness is so present and so the norm that it is almost always unmarked and unremarked on by Johnston. As dance scholars Susan Manning and Rebecca Chaleff have outlined, the modern dance world in which Johnston first studied and the postmodern dance she championed naturalized whiteness as norm, albeit in different ways. Johnston's period of study at the Limón school, her entrée into New York dance, was shaped by what Manning describes as "mythic abstraction," a commitment to universalizing all dancers' bodies, thus leaving racial differences unmarked.[48] As Johnston became a dance critic, whiteness was again rendered invisible to the largely white group within and around Judson through an emphasis on the "ordinary," which was, as Chaleff has demonstrated, a new regime for forwarding whiteness as norm.[49] The whitening of the Manhattan neighborhoods where Johnston lived and saw performance, plus her enmeshment in New York's modern and postmodern dance scenes, schooled Johnston in how *not* to see the whiteness all around her.

This persistent whiteness contributes, then, to the naturalization of lesbian as white, a phenomenon Victoria Hesford has located within US culture in the early 1970s. Just as Johnston came to national prominence as a spokesperson for lesbian feminism, the national media, through its coverage of women's liberation, created and circulated a caricature of feminist activists that Hesford calls the "feminist-as-lesbian," a figure insistently deemed white, middle class, and dour. The rapidly circulating caricature erased all difference among feminist activists and, as Hesford argues, manifested the lesbian "as a boundary figure between white respectability and class and racial otherness."[50] Lesbians of color became even more invisible to the larger public, and the white lesbian emerged as feminism's abject figure. Johnston could be seen as the ultimate example of the lesbian as boundary figure, served by her white privilege but ostracized by straight feminists because she was a lesbian.

Racial difference might be the most obvious of the three layers of racial formation in Jill Johnston's life: of course her whiteness made her experience of being a lesbian different from that of lesbians of color. Yet still the question lingers: how to describe racial difference when whiteness is so ever-present that, for some, it erased all other points of view? This book's answer to this question comes in what I call *lesbian adjacencies*. In each chapter I place Johnston alongside—adjacent to—other lesbian thinkers, artists, and writers, a conscious revising of Jagose's observation of how often literature renders lesbians as always adjacent to the categories of *woman* and *gay man*.[51] In this book lesbians are adjacent to one another. Lesbians see one another and think together. Some of these pairings have to do with overlaps in both life and thought, and these tend to put white lesbian alongside white lesbian: Johnston and contemporary critic and writer Susan Sontag in chapter 1, and Johnston's writing about lesbian and queer artists Gertrude Stein, Yvonne Rainer, and Agnes Martin in chapter 4. Other lesbian adjacencies are more uneasy fits, particularly as they attempt to hold the possibility of lesbian adjacency and racial difference together. For instance, Johnston and Audre Lorde overlap in both chapters 1 and 2, first as I consider how Sontag, Johnston, and Lorde all grappled with the erotic possibilities of writing, and then as I consider how writing lists, as Lorraine Hansberry, Johnston, and Lorde often did, create what I call the lesbian genre of *powerlisting*. Sometimes these pairings feel forced, and I have avoided erasing that discomfort. The circumstances through which these lesbian writers arrived at these overlapping theories and genres were very different. Yet, too, I want there to be possibility in this book for lesbians of color to take up space as something other than what historian Kimberly Springer has described as the usual way women of color appear in historical narratives of white feminism, recognized only when they have to "react . . . to racism in the women's movement."[52]

In Johnston's writing and thinking, the word *lesbian* is meant to vibrate. For those who know how to read with an eye toward inhabiting *lesbian*'s possibilities, it invites what Dinshaw says a "touch across time" can manifest: "imitation and caress."[53] But for all the pleasure that these touches, these adjacencies, might offer, it's not all pleasure. The greatest potential for what *lesbian* can mean for women, for queer community, and for coalition building lies in recognizing both pleasure and discomfort.

Choreographing the Archive

Acts of reading that arrive as imitation, caress, and discomfort turn me from Johnston's writing to my experiences of the archives in which I've sought Jill, moments that have vibrated with experiences of past-in-the-present (à la Freeman), as I feel the reverberations of Johnston's reimaginings of both *woman* and *lesbian*.

This is not a dream.

"This is the women's bathroom. Are you a woman?"

I hear his voice from inside the stall of the women's bathroom at NYPL's Dance Division, the same library where Johnston encountered Horst and where I am researching Johnston. The voice belongs to the security guard I passed in the hall on my way to the women's bathroom. I am crouched above the toilet in the position my mother taught me was how women should use public toilets. From this position in the stall, I have listened to the door squeak and his feet as they crossed the linoleum floor. He bangs the heel of his hand against the metal stall door that separates us, almost shouting, "This is the women's bathroom. Are you a woman?"

It's 2016, and the US public, in legislation and in private acts of surveillance, is consumed with policing how people express their genders in public. Bathrooms have become a battleground for those whose visual presentation does not signify their gender "correctly." Against this cultural background, I've become accustomed to disapproving looks in bathroom lines, little taps on my shoulder that precede a supposedly gentle whisper, "This is the women's bathroom." The moment in this bathroom, in this dance library, feels different, though, somehow elevated. He bangs on the door again. "This is the women's bathroom." The performative force of the statement and his physical choices render my gender suspect and out of place. I wish I had thought—or said—"Well, if this is the women's bathroom, then you're the one who doesn't seem to belong."

I am not quick enough in the moment to make my fantasy response real. Instead, my reality looks and feels like this. A mix of fear and frustration hits my stomach. My quads give out. My ass hits the toilet. I have been taught that women should never sit on a public toilet seat. My gendered failures mount, overwhelming the pleasure I usually find in my queer, lesbian self-presentation. I tilt my head up and imagine his face on the other side of the metal door, looking down at me. I'm not interested in proving anything to this person, but offering proof seems the only way forward. I want to channel Jill, to refuse legibility or reinvent a label. I manage nothing like that. I don't know what I said to him.

All I know is that he left. His footsteps tapped away from me and out the door. I was scared in the moment, but given the numerous vectors of privilege I enjoy as a white, middle-class woman, it's unlikely the interaction would have ever resulted in anything more than me feeling uncomfortable. I wasn't really worried he'd return. So there I sat, on the verboten toilet seat, thinking about Jill. Thinking about her helps me remember that categories can be revised toward ends other than sameness or legibility to dominant norms. A year later I'll read in her journal an entry from August 1974, where she recounts answering an attendant in a Parisian bathroom who questioned whether she was a "man or a woman." Jill's response: "I'm a horse."[54]

One of Jill Johnston's central gifts as a writer was inserting a range of femininities, a range of lesbian sensibilities, into scenes where others think they (we) don't exist. This expansiveness was a common feature of her writing, perhaps most famously so in the essay she first shared in 1971 as part of the panel that eventually led to her standoff with Norman Mailer. She began her speech by announcing that every woman is a lesbian; "she just doesn't know it yet."[55] Like any good journalist, she knew this first sentence, the lede as it is called, could cut an idea wide open. With her lede, Johnston made a provocation intended to expand and reimagine the category of lesbian. In the speech that followed (analyzed in detail in chapter 3), she continued, in luscious, often humorous prose, imagining how lesbianism might offer a site for women to unite across difference and against patriarchy and hierarchies. When Mailer tried to silence her, saying she had used all her allotted time, Johnston called two women onto the stage for a fierce make-out session and then departed as Mailer blustered. For the rest of the night, Mailer was left to refer to Johnston only as an absent presence, an example of what I describe later in this book as a "lesbian echo," a tactic central to Johnston's strategic manipulation of taking space in public as a lesbian.[56]

Right now, however, I am more interested in where Johnston *is* present, and I suspect she's in the bathroom, the space where, as dance scholar Cindy Garcia has argued in her writing about Latina solidarity in salsa clubs, women often go to find camaraderie and space to strategize. Garcia describes the women's bathroom as a place where women work together to "navigate" and collectively "undo" patriarchal codes.[57] In male-centered spaces, as institutional archives can be, looking to such offstage spaces of negotiation is key. So I am now in this little bathroom stall, offstage, at least temporarily out of sight to the guard, strategizing with Jill. We think together about how a lesbian, a butch, and/or a queer might claim *woman* and be recognized as such, if that's what they desire. (And that's what I desire.)

In 1993 queer theorists Wayne Koestenbaum and Terry Castle published books theorizing how queerness, particularly queer desire, arrives in public space, with both turning to performance—specifically opera's female divas—to think with women onstage. Both arrive at the conclusion that lesbian desire is particularly challenging, even dangerous, to represent. Koestenbaum argues that gay men's fanaticism for the female opera diva offers a queer identification with femininity that still allows homosexual desire to remain safely latent and unseen. A gay man can declare his love for Maria Callas, specifically her voice and the space it literally envelops one within, and a gay man's "secret," his sexuality, still remains intact.[58] Castle focuses on what she calls "Sapphic diva worship," female fans' erotic attachment to female opera stars, arguing that focusing on these female fans, rather than the gay male fan, is a dangerous enterprise that "risk[s] giving too much away." She continues, reflecting that "one of the reasons that the most vocal diva admirers of the past two hundred years have tended to be homosexual men is that it is the least embarrassing for them . . . to enthuse in public over the female singing voice: the libidinal element inspiring the enthusiasm is there . . . [but it is] most artfully disguised and displaced."[59] The lesbian's admiration of the female opera diva threatens too much identification: critical distance is absent, the assessment of excellence is suspect, and the closet is obliterated. When women name their desire for another woman, secrets threaten to bubble forth.[60]

Johnston urged women to disclose their secrets, even as she also recognized the possible dangers of coming out as a lesbian. By the time her lesbian identity was truly public in 1971, Johnston launched a crusade to renounce the idea that sexuality, especially homosexuality, should be a secret. As she put it in the second of a series of columns she wrote titled "Lois Lane Is a Lesbian," "I'm urging all Snow Whites to get up out of their caskets and mobilize and claim their own sexuality."[61] Her refusal to be secretive about her lesbianism did not mean, however, that she "came out" on heterosexual, male-centered, patriarchal terms. Instead, she imagined the lesbian as someone both onstage and off, someone who revels in being seen but who knows how to make a decidedly subtextual invitation to the right audiences: the women with whom she sought sexual and political solidarity.

Johnston would eventually describe her play with being seen but not fully legible as a particularly lesbian sensibility. Throughout the early 1970s, she wrote columns lauding lesbians ranging from writer Gertrude Stein to visual artist Agnes Martin, artists she admired for passionately displaying something that could be imagined for and by lesbians, without bothering with identifying themselves in terms easily comprehensible to men, straight people, or institutional figures of power more broadly. In a series of 1972 columns focused on Stein, Johnston pondered if what she had described as Stein's "stylistic obscurity"—a characteristic Johnston saw her writing sharing with Stein's—might be emblematic of a lesbian approach to writing.[62] And Johnston's love for Martin and her work is perhaps best encompassed in an exchange between the two that Johnston described as her having praised Martin for being a woman who had navigated the male-centered world of abstract painting, to which Martin responded, "i'm not a woman, i'm a doorknob, leading a quiet existence."[63] "Ce qui pour pour l'une est une poignée de porte, pour l'autre est un cheval."[64]

This is also not a dream ... but maybe it is.

The day after almost getting kicked out of the Dance Division's women's bathroom, I stand on the doorstep of the Lesbian Herstory Archives, looking for Jill again. Founded in 1974, the space houses all manner of lesbian ephemera: buttons and posters, letters and photos—all lovingly, if idiosyncratically, archived by volunteers. I am nervous to knock but, particularly after the events in yesterday's archive, also relieved to be at the Brooklyn brownstone that houses the Herstory Archives. While I know that lesbian spaces, notably lesbian feminist spaces, have not always been a space of radical acceptance, particularly for lesbians of color and trans people, I also know that 1970s lesbian feminism offered refuge to more masculine-presenting women who were often chastised within mainstream feminism, where their gender presentation was treated as evidence they wanted to be men or "male-identified."[65] In short, I can trust I'll be able to use the bathroom here.

What I did not expect is a woman opening the door and telling me that although it's almost 5 p.m.—the archive's official closing time—I am welcome to work "until the crew hanging out in the kitchen runs out of wine." (Lesbian time?) The "crew" turns out to be a group of Herstory Archives volunteers, and as I work in the reading room (clearly formerly a dining room), I listen to a debate unfolding in the kitchen. The wine-drinking crew/archive crew, my clock for the moment, loudly discuss who should be hired to document an upcoming event primarily focused on issues related to lesbians of color: How do the identities of the photographers documenting the event matter to the action? To how history gets documented?

Desire doesn't always get you where you wanted to go.

I keep my head down as the kitchen conversation spills into the dining room/reading room. I plan to scour the folders marked "Jill Johnston" and depart. A woman in her late twenties enters the room and begins asking people at the table what they are working on. I stammer, "Jill Johnston—she was a writer." I hope this is enough to earn a pass from further engagement. As I look down, however, I see the woman's hand stretched near my face, wrist flexed, fingers pointing upward, palm beckoning. "Let's see whose fingers are longer?" she says to me but also to everyone. Her hand is still but insistent, close enough to my body that I have to turn my whole torso to face her, to meet her palm and, finally, her gaze. Everyone else at the table eventually follows suit, judging finger lengths against our interrogator. I am certain we were all extras in a seduction scene unfolding for the benefit of someone still in the kitchen. We have also all just subtly, to one another, with our bodies, come out. Or perhaps, more precisely, we have all *come in* to lesbian identity. No one quite said it, but now there is an unspoken, yet acknowledged *we*.

The physical encounter, at once awkward, hilarious, and even a little sweet, prods me to consider how the folders I am examining are evidence of other coming in-s among multiple lesbians, despite the folders bearing only the single name "Jill Johnston." The files related to Johnston in the Lesbian Herstory Archives mainly contain copies of her columns, with many columns appearing multiple times in multiple folders. I initially assume this to be a by-product of the volunteer archiving system: with no real catalog of what each folder already contains, there is no way a new volunteer would recognize a column as a duplicate. I assume each copy that comes to the archive just gets stuck in one of the "Jill Johnston" folders.

But there is more here. As performance studies scholar Ann Cvetkovich has written of the Herstory Archives, the collection is "subject to the idiosyncrasies of the psyche and the logic of the unconscious, emotional experience and . . . memory [producing] an unusual archive . . . that . . . resists the coherence of narrative . . . fragmented and ostensibly arbitrary."[66] I suddenly notice the note attached to a pile of clippings. "These files were from my partner of 30 years . . . who died March 1999 . . . Alice was a writer and collector of all things."[67]

The note is from a woman—"Carol" reads the signature at the bottom—who donated her partner's collection of Johnston's columns collected throughout a life. Embedded amid the stack of 1970s writing, when Johnston focused almost entirely on lesbian life and feminist organizing, the note appears on the back of a postcard featuring a William Blake painting. The note, the name, and the stack of writing beneath it render even Blake a protolesbian: his pastel, somewhat amorphous image of a cave feels, in the context of the Herstory Archives reading room, more Georgia O'Keefe than British male poet. To the repertory of lesbian touches across time that Dinshaw began with "imitation and caress" this adds yet another possibility: remarkable transformations.

Other columns appear to have been clipped and sent from one woman to another. On a slightly torn copy of a May 1973 column titled "Kraut Fishing in Amerika," a handwritten note reads, "Jill Johnston on vegetarian lifestyle," with "vegetarian lifestyle" in all caps. There are also hand-drawn boxes surrounding pertinent sections. This copy of the column includes a homemade reading guide. The owner of the handwriting shifts her tone on the second Xeroxed page, writing in the margins, "Read it all, it's a gas."[68] These are not just notes taken for a reader but encouragement to another reader to jump in—to notice the politics and then stay for the pleasure.

Other Xeroxes of columns in the folders seem to have elicited such enthusiasm from readers that blank margins compelled them to address, not another reader, but Johnston herself. On a copy of one of the three 1971 "Lois Lane Is a Lesbian" columns, the most obvious announcements of Johnston's lesbian identity in the newspaper, a note in the margins reads in all caps "RIGHT ON JILL."[69] The notes throughout the folders offer proof of connection among readers—anonymous, veiled, not always fully aware of one another or in the same temporal moment—but present. I can feel them, and an encounter in an archive with another woman, another lesbian, made that connection possible. She helped me to read differently. Touch, and the relationships it signifies or invents, renders the bevy of lesbians and lesbian connections felt, if not fully seen.

Her Archive

Emphasizing lesbian adjacencies underscores how much lesbian archives are collections of relationships as much as they are collections of materials. These relationships are not just ones of the past but also those made in and through the archive. The first time I opened a box in Jill Johnston's personal archive, one of more than seventy boxes containing her journals, correspondence, and drafts of columns and essays organized and maintained by Ingrid Nyeboe, Johnston's wife, I felt as though I had already been in the archive for years. And, in some ways, it had been years. A number of women in Johnston's and Nyeboe's networks, most of them lesbians, vouched for me, which eventually led to a long series of meetings with Nyeboe, having oatmeal together in Manhattan's Far West Side when I visited New York with me always hoping that this would be the trip I would "get into" the archive. In retrospect, I was already there: these were necessary moments, almost as important as touching the archival materials themselves, a building of trust between two lesbians born of different times.

After several years (and many breakfasts), Nyeboe began bringing boxes stored upstate into Manhattan, to the studio where her wife, the painter Louise Fishman, worked.[70] I, the first person Nyeboe had allowed to examine the materials, would sit at one table reading the archival material, with Nyeboe at another doing administrative work while Fishman painted next door. Their toy poodle, Ollie, moved between the two spaces. I do not see how an archival site could be more lesbian in its orientation. Ingrid—as I now think of her—has never sought to censor or steer my writing in any way, though, in addition to being Johnston's longtime partner and certainly the most protective of her legacy, she is also trained as a performance studies and theater scholar. I feel a heavy debt to her and sometimes would turn my chair around in that room to run ideas past her. Though I suspect they will disagree with some of what I say in this book, it is for and dedicated to the lesbians who made it possible: Ingrid and Louise (and Holly Hughes and Esther Newton, the lesbians who promised Nyeboe I would do right by Jill). The scene in Fishman's studio-turned-archive reminds me that this book has responsibilities to the networks that emerged from Johnston's writing, as well as to the contexts from which Johnston's writing emerged. Her writing led many to invest in fandom as a blueprint of possibility, much like what film scholar Jackie Stacey has argued female fans do as they scrutinize film stars to identify strategies for living.[71]

Who is she?

I imagine someone whispers the question in my ear as a tall woman in a jean jacket walks through the door of an industrial space in downtown Manhattan. This is the type of space—a warehouse in the area now known as Soho—where in the early 1970s Nyeboe and Johnston first met at a covertly advertised women's dance party. Nyeboe recalls waiting to see an ad appear on the last page of the *Voice* that read "D.O.B. Dance" with a phone number below it. The acronym "D.O.B." stood for Daughters of Bilitis, a lesbian liberation group founded in 1955 in San Francisco and best known for publishing the magazine *The Ladder*. If you were in the know, you called the number, got an address, and then headed downtown. This is recognition without confirmation in late-nite journey form—just enough information to know where to look but not enough information to be sure about much else. As Nyeboe remembered:

> What you would do is you show up at this door, and you would have to circle around many times in order . . . to be sure that this was really it. . . . Even though you'd been given the address through these phone numbers, you still weren't sure. . . . You would get in, finally, and somebody at the door would check you out and you'd go up to the floor, wherever the dance was, and you would basically be in this big, big open space. There would be a bar. And just a bunch of women dancing all night long.[72]

In one of these spaces, somewhere near West Third Street and Sixth Avenue, in a room full of women dancing, ready to go all night, Johnston bummed a cigarette from Nyeboe. The two would have occasional exchanges for another decade, beginning a relationship more intensely in the late 1970s. Nyeboe was at Johnston's side for the rest of her life: her editor, archivist, and, in her final years, caretaker (see figure I.1).

Where did the person who became that Jill begin? If ever there was a queer historical subject that should be approached with Jack Halberstam's warning to scholars of queerness to "be suspicious of mastery," of imagining that questions can be truly answered, it is Johnston.[73] Telling the story of the person behind the writing is not an easy task, especially when the storyteller has written twenty-plus years of journalism and more than ten books, all with an approach to autobiographical writing once described as "poetry, prophecy, criticism, history, and self-revelation."[74] It's a lot. There is also Johnston's love of layered, complicated uncertainty. She once described herself, her aesthetics, and the world more generally by writing, "I like things that are certain about not being very sure about what they are."[75]

While this book is decidedly not a biography of Johnston, I do work to carefully situate her life in history: as a dance critic who wrote about one of the most celebrated moments in US concert dance and as a woman who lived as a lesbian before and after Stonewall. I focus primarily on Johnston's life from 1960 to 1980, when she contributed to the *Village Voice* and circulated most widely as a public intellectual, first in the dance and art worlds and then in the movements of feminism, lesbian feminism, and gay liberation. In reading these columns and the publicity Johnston garnered in large part because of their wide circulation, I am most curious about the ideas Johnston proposed: theories of how to engage with performance, what it means to be an audience, and what it means to be a lesbian in public.

Yet there was a Jill Johnston pre–*Village Voice*; she was thirty-three when she began working for the then five-year-old weekly. Her first book-length autobiography, *Mother Bound* (1983), covers this "before" period in depth. The volume (the first of four autobiographies) offers a more straightforward description of Johnston's childhood, adolescence, and life as a writer, often assessed through psychoanalytic frames. As Johnston continued to write, psychoanalysis was a passion for her and an area in which she was an autodidact. Her journals, which she wrote in every day, detail her massive investment in reading, including lists and reflections on the books she read. Psychoanalytic texts ranging from Freud and Carl Jung to more popular authors like R. D. Laing proliferate in her journals' accounts of "books read," as she titled each list.

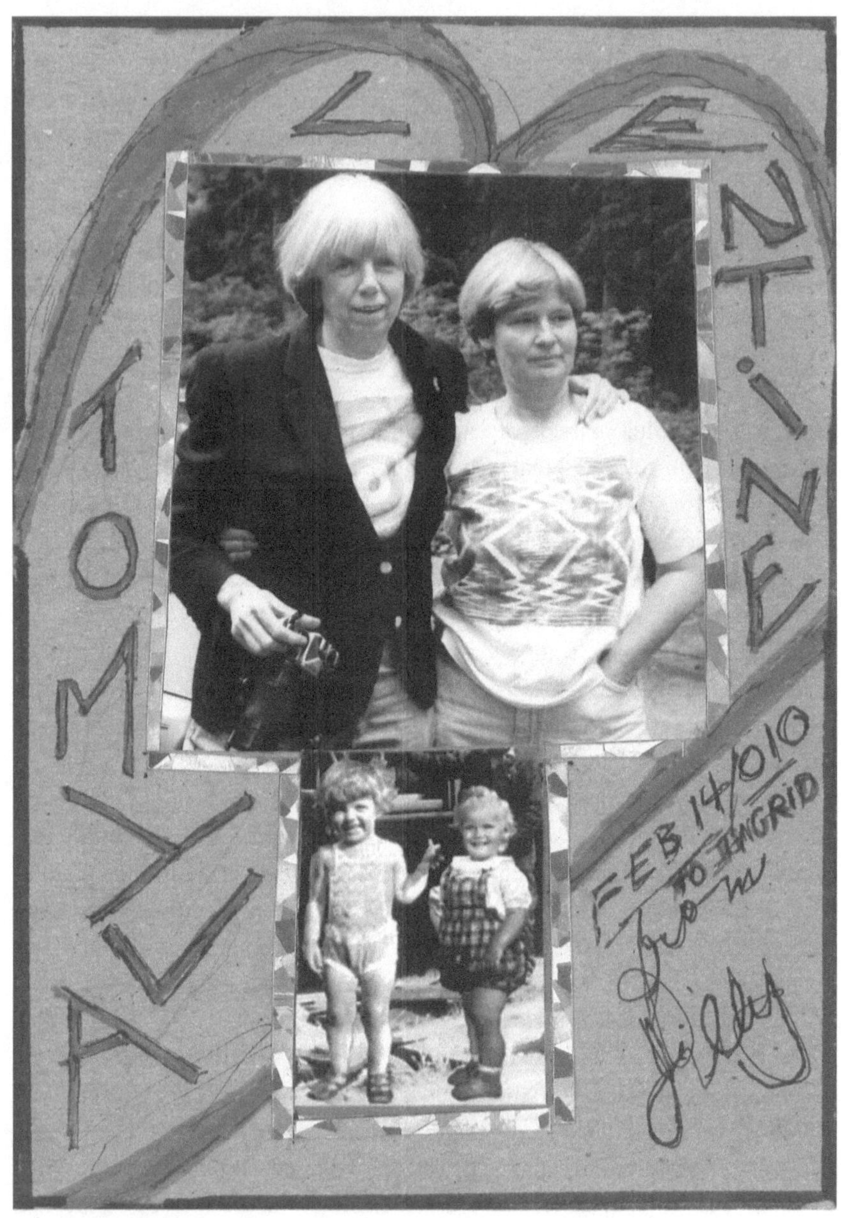

I.1 Collage made by Jill Johnston for Ingrid Nyeboe, featuring Johnston (*left*) and Nyeboe (*right*) in the 2000s and as young children. Inscribed “TO MY VALENTINE / FEB 14/010 / TO INGRID / from / Jilly.” Courtesy of the Jill Johnston Literary Archive, New York.

Before Johnston was a writer or public intellectual, she could most accurately be described as a granddaughter, a dancer, a student, and a young woman growing up amid the restrictive gender norms of the midcentury United States. Conceived in a transatlantic crossing, Jill Johnston was born to Olive Johnston on May 17, 1929, in Finchley, a suburb of London. Initially, Olive, an American, and Jill lived with a friend of Olive's in Brighton Beach, where Johnston's British father, Cyril F. Johnston, once visited, likely the only time he saw his daughter. Olive and Jill returned to the United States permanently when Jill was around two years old. She remained an ardent Anglophile her entire life, always happy to be greeted with "Welcome home" when arriving in Europe via London's Heathrow Airport.[76]

Johnston grew up largely in the care of her grandmother, Pauline, in Little Neck, a Queens suburb of New York City. Olive lived and worked in Manhattan as a resident nurse at the Waldorf Astoria Hotel, visiting Jill and Pauline on weekends. While Jill enjoyed a relatively warm relationship with her grandmother, the same could not be said of Olive and Pauline. As Jill put it in *Mother Bound*, "Having me was the one thing my mother did for which she was never criticized by her mother."[77] Olive always worked and lived at a distance from Jill and Pauline, with the time in Manhattan eventually giving way to work periods in Nova Scotia and Paris once Jill went to boarding school at St. Mary's in Peekskill, New York. Of the shift from Little Neck to the all-girls Episcopal school, Jill wrote, "The nuns of St Mary's provided the resistance I needed to express my rage at being abandoned there."[78]

Johnston went from one home full of women to another. In retrospect, she felt that in these worlds of white women and girls, she had been able to slide among various gender performances and presentations, even as she also knew that in the world beyond these female enclaves, gender norms were less flexible. (Later in life, she would also recognize that the boarding school's racial homogeneity erased other questions of difference.) Of being a child and early adolescent, she describes vacillating quite happily between "successful girl" and "adventurous boy." At St. Mary's she understood herself as among what she calls the "boys" of the school—"very dashing girls who were fine athletes." Yet confessing her attraction *to* another girl, rather than the more palatable adoration *among* girls, offered her the first taste of being what she described as "a failed girl"—a situation she could only remedy by falling for a "real boy"—a student at a nearby all-boys school.[79]

Johnston's relatively female-centric childhood and adolescence were, she thought, an outcome of her father's death before her birth. But as she would come to learn while in college at Tufts University in Boston, her father had been alive her entire life, only passing away in 1950—an event her mother revealed by sending Johnston a copy of his obituary from the *New York Times*. (The appearance of the obituary in the prominent newspaper made Olive fearful Jill would learn the truth on her own.)[80] Olive's letter landed like a bomb in Johnston's life. She called it the "outstanding event of my college years."[81] Nyeboe calls it the most important event in Johnston's entire life.[82] Later, Johnston's hatred of secrets would largely have to do with gender and sexuality, but the seed of her strong regard of secrets as dangerous began with the discoveries about her lineage. Not only had her father been alive all this time; he and Johnston's mother had never been married. Johnston was a "bastard," a status that, as Ann Cvetkovich has described in the life of lesbian activist and writer Dorothy Allison, means one is "disenfranchised by the official institutions of the state."[83] Olive had sought to shield Jill from official bastard status, but the stain of "illegitimacy" affected Johnston deeply and forever complicated her already strained relationship with her mother. Discovering she was the product of an affair left her feeling she had been "the unwitting keeper of her [mother's] secret."[84] In many ways, this tectonic shift set the stage for the rest of Johnston's life as an outsider railing against patriarchy, heteronormativity, and the secrets each of those oppressive social norms encourages so many to keep.

Learning the news of her father from her mother while in college tangentially also set the scene for other aspects of Johnston's life to fully surface: her love of dance and her desire for women. Her college dance professor, who would become her "first female lover," was the first (and for some time the only) person to whom Johnston divulged the news about her father.[85] Dance, desire for women, and a place to tell one's secrets came together in Johnston's relationship with the older woman. That professor was the person who first introduced Johnston to the New York dance scene, where she would move after doing more schooling first in Minnesota (where she had her "first male lover," also a professor) and then in North Carolina.[86]

In New York, seeking out the world her former lover and professor described, Johnston found herself "delivered over to culture, the great realm of paper and performance where our ancestors have taken up immortal residence."[87] Privately, Johnston hoped that her attraction to women would pass, as she "had not failed to observe that something must be wrong with me if I liked only my own sex."[88] That first lover/dance teacher had even suggested to Johnston that a turn toward men could be precipitated by letting her "hair grow long and by encouraging me after all to be a dancer."[89] The gender norms of modern dance, by the 1950s now firmly enmeshed in institutions of performance and pedagogy, might prove to be lesbianism's antidote.

The first years in New York were difficult. The gendered structures of dance did *not* train Johnston into normative femininity and heterosexuality. In a 1991 essay, Johnston remembers the New York dance scene of the 1950s as one where she felt pinched between the adjacencies Jagose describes lesbians as enduring, always living alongside the categories of *woman* and *gay man*. Johnston was a young woman in José Limón's school, a world shaped by Limón; his wife, Pauline; Doris Humphrey; and Charles Weidman. Dancing in Limón's studio among these four, Johnston experienced what she later called a "classic nexus in the dance field . . . the women appeared to be straight, or were assumed to be, while the two men were known to be gay and seen to be actively serviced by the women."[90] Though Johnston was, by several accounts (including her own), good at Limón's technique, she always knew she had little likelihood of success in a system where women tended to be, in her terms, "conventionally feminine" and where homoerotic desire created bonds among men to the exclusion of women (see figures. 1.2 and 1.3). As she remembers of her young self, "I'm sure I wanted to be one of [Limón's boys, but] . . . I was simply stranded there between the sexes." She couldn't quite be with the women, nor with the men. And though it would be the late 1960s before Johnston began to explicitly describe herself as a feminist, serving men was never of interest to her.

The mid-1950s proved to be a turning point but a tough one: a period Johnston would eventually categorize as a time when she "discovered problems by crashing into them."[91] A dalliance with a male dancer produced a pregnancy, and the abortion Johnston managed to obtain at home had major complications, landing her in Roosevelt Hospital (where her mother had trained to be a nurse)—an event Johnston said led to a "realignment of direction."[92] Her broken foot justified her departure from the Limón school, and the subsequent brief full-time job at the Dance Collection led to the fateful encounter with Horst described earlier in this chapter. While that was a positive development in a difficult period, another new situation, marriage, proved to be possibly the worst of her life. Johnston writes about her choice to marry a man with much the same tone she writes about becoming a "real girl" in high school: undesired but inevitable. Initially, marriage seemed it might heal the relatively still-new knowledge of her bastard status. As she put it decades later, "The utmost convention was at work in my own story: the only reason to marry was to be legitimate. [Even though nothing]

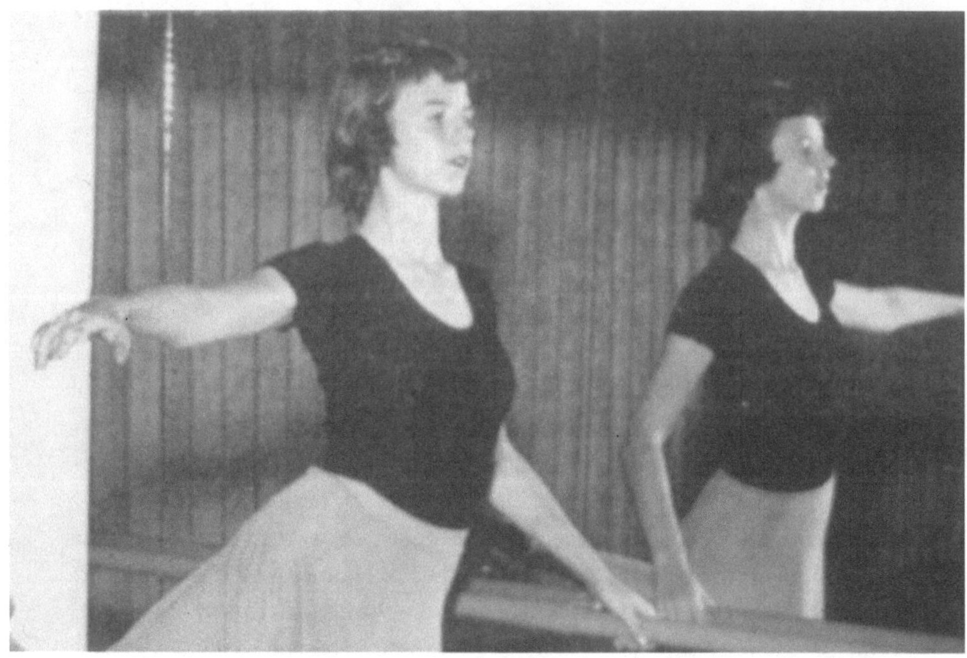

1.2 Jill Johnston studying at the José Limón school in New York City, likely in the early 1950s. Photographer unknown. Courtesy of the Phyllis Birkby Papers, Sophia Smith Collection of Women's History, Smith College, Northampton, MA.

in my mother's life or words suggested men as desirable partners' and nothing in my own life to date suggested them as that either."[93] The yet-unspoken proved true: marriage was terrible. Around 1961 Johnston managed to leave her abusive relationship, moving with her two young children from Washington Heights to East Broadway. She officially divorced in 1964, and her children were largely raised by her mother, Olive, an arrangement Johnston described as beginning because being a "lesbian mother [was] an oxymoron" and continuing once Johnston began what would be a series of periods committed in mental hospitals, where she was diagnosed as "schizophrenic."[94] Notwithstanding these complications in her children's lives, which reverberated for the rest of Johnston's life, Miles Bellamy, son of Johnston's close friend Sheindi Bellamy and art curator Richard Bellamy, remembers the East Broadway Jill Johnston of his childhood as his "hero," a woman willing to be "in your face, in the face of the establishment, [and] in the face of male-dominated society."[95] In early 1960s downtown New York, Johnston found the New York she needed, the place and people who helped her become a

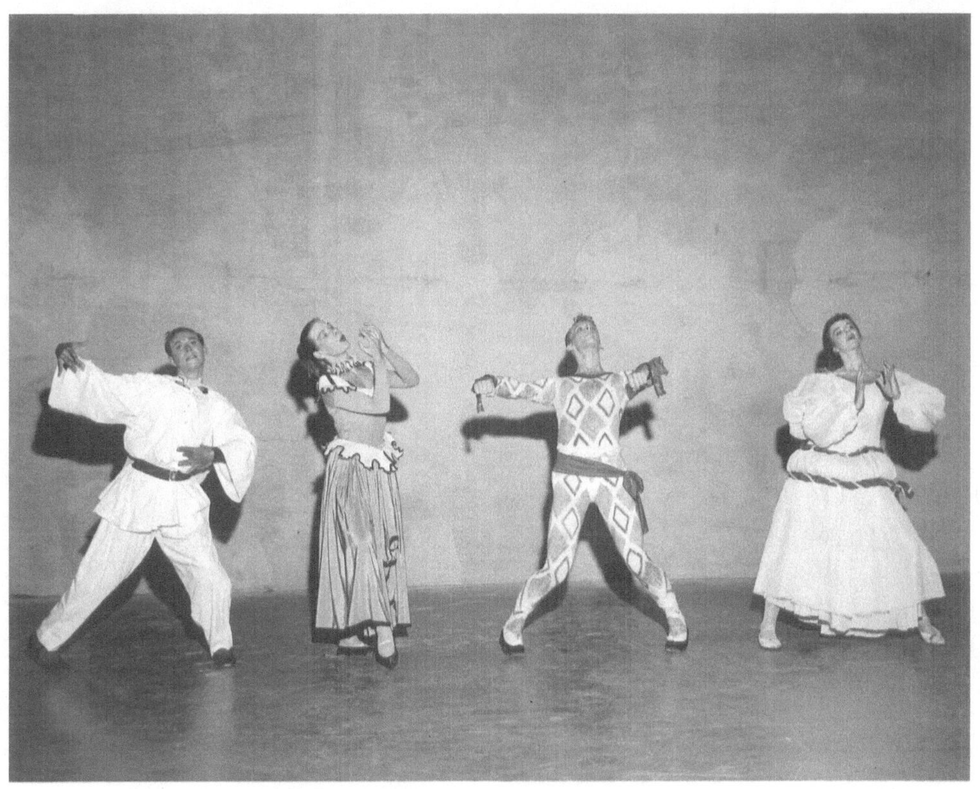

I.3 Jill Johnston performing with Joseph Gifford's company at the YM-YWHA in New York City, 1955. *From left to right:* Gifford, Lorna Burdsall, Chester Wolenski, and Johnston. Photograph by Peter Moore. © Northwestern University.

well-known arts critic. She immediately loved the messiness of her East Broadway neighborhood. Reflecting on the scene—as neighborhood and as artistic community—she wrote of loving how "intimacy was not obscured by manners, and strange behavior was condoned and indulged" (see figure I.4).[96]

She Was a Writer

Now the writing takes over—the writing that birthed the byline "jill johnston," the lowercase version of Johnston the public came to know through the newspaper. By 1960 Johnston had multiple regular publication outlets, and that would remain the case for the rest of her life. Even at events where she is perhaps best known for something else—swimming as Betty Friedan

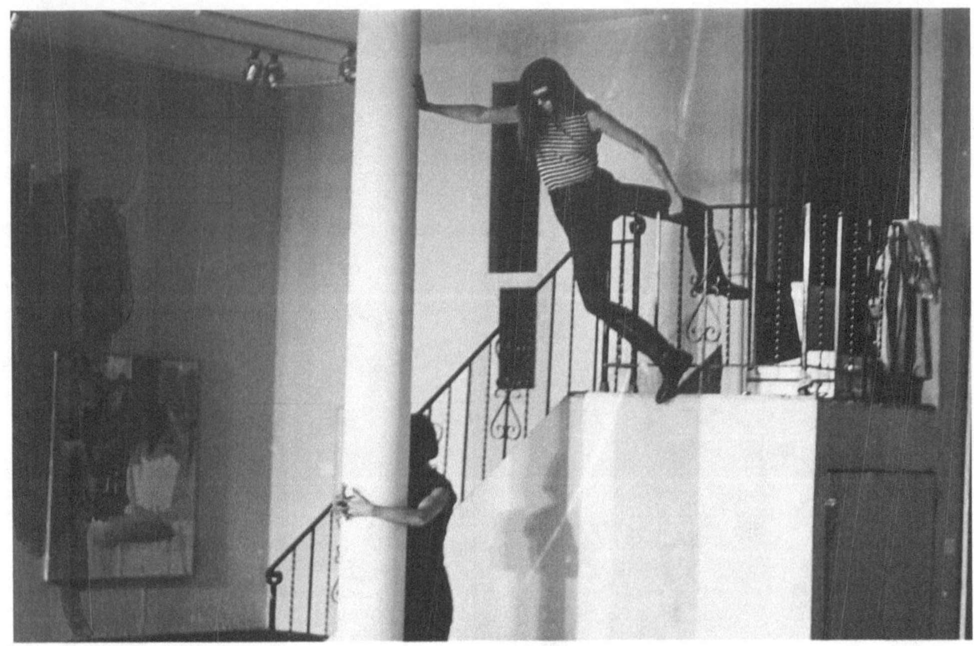

I.4 Yvonne Rainer (*left*) and Jill Johnston (*right*) performing at Washington Square Art Gallery, New York, NY, 1964. Photograph by Peter Moore. © Northwestern University.

spoke, making out with women to shut up Norman Mailer—she was always at the event as a writer and often shared a beautifully crafted piece of writing as a preamble to physical disruption.

Just as writing seemed to anchor Johnston, her writing anchors this book. In an early interview with Nyeboe, as I asked about significant events in Johnston's life, Nyeboe cut me off and said, "You can find all you need to know in her writing."[97] At the time, I worried I was asking tiresome questions, but I now know that Nyeboe was simply stating a fact. As Johnston did when writing about artists, this book places Johnston's work in wider contexts, but her writing is always at the center.

Writing, in Johnston's life and in this book, is more than ink on a page. Instead, as the preface introduced, this book recognizes writing (and reading) as embodied acts. This introduction, then, follows that body, Jill's body, and the mark(s) she left in her wake, considering what she required of her readers and how that might translate into something of a guide for those, like me, who hope for touches across time. The book unfolds across five chapters, interspersed with shorter pieces of writing I refer to as "interruptions," which appear between the chapters. This structure ensures the book is a rigorous analysis of Johnston's written and performed contributions to dance, feminist, and gay history and reflects Johnston's deployment of her lesbianism as a disruptive factor, strategic excess delivered in an alternative key. In the 1967 column "Take Me Disappearing," Johnston decrees, "The world is in a mess because of its clean boundaries. . . . A truly messy world is a consummation to be wished."[98] This book's "interruptions" are an attempt to abide by Johnston's wish—a wish aligned with my argument that the ability to recognize the lesbian who never goes so far as to confirm her identity might be one of the most powerful, most interesting aspects of writing about lesbian life. If one refuses coherence, takes on being "incoherently constituted through discourse," how does one learn to see and move differently?

In addition to the preface and introduction, *Jill Johnston in Motion* includes four body chapters, three complementary interruptions, and an epilogue. Chapter 1, "She Was a Critic," traces Johnston's emerging writing voice, focusing specifically on her approach to dance criticism from 1955 to 1965. The chapter expands the narrative of Johnston as dance writer, departing from the usual focus on her as the critic who chronicled the Judson movement and instead focusing broadly on her emphasis on leveling hierarchies onstage and off. This chapter also places Johnston adjacent to Susan Sontag and Audre Lorde, lesbian writers all invested (very differently) in the erotics of writing. Following chapter 1's explicit attention on Johnston as writer, a subsequent interruption focuses on Johnston's public performances as a dancer, with particular attention paid to a 1963 Andy Warhol film that features Johnston dancing with Judson artist Fred Herko. Chapter 2, "She Was an Audience," focuses on Johnston's transformation of the page into a performance itself, creating a sensorial experience for readers that shifts the focus toward the audience experience and expands the very idea of an audience. This chapter tracks the years from 1965 to 1969, when Johnston's writing shifted toward the experimental, due in part to her interest in Antonin Artaud's theories of spectatorship and in the enumeration of difference within audiences. These interests result in a queer performative writing strategy Johnston often used, which I have named *powerlisting* and which I argue was a particularly lesbian strategy by placing Johnston's writing of lists alongside lists written by Lorde and Black lesbian playwright Lorraine Hansberry. In chapter 2's interruption, I track Johnston's passage through a version of what Peggy Phelan has termed the iterative nature of queer death, bringing dance with her as she becomes a lesbian feminist activist via a surprising inspiration, French poet and critic Guillaume Apollinaire.

The next two chapters extend the focus on performance and embodiment with specific attention to lesbian feminism. Chapter 3, "She Was a Lesbian Feminist," situates Johnston within the historical milieu of gay liberation and women's liberation, focusing on her repeated performances of "coming out" in public spaces, including her confrontations with Friedan and Mailer and her writing in the *Village Voice* and other public venues. I approach these wide-ranging contexts using structures drawn from dance: performance, choreography, and improvisational scores. Considering Johnston's lesbian feminist writing as a score allows me to examine the ways in which she promoted new forms of lesbian alignment, some that invited connection across difference and others that overlooked important differences, particularly those between white lesbians and lesbians of color. In the interruption that follows chapter 3, I comb through the voluminous letters written by Johnston's readers, those published in the *Voice* and those sent directly to her, considering how her writing activated not only her body but also her readers' bodies. Chapter 4, "She Was a Writer," begins with a discussion of Johnston's 1996 book about artist Jasper Johns but shifts the attention from the gay male artist toward the lesbian artists frequently discussed in her columns: Stein, Martin, and Rainer. In addition to a focus on lesbian artists, this chapter also focuses most explicitly on Johnston's positions on mental health in its discussion of the bond Johnston and Martin developed partially because of their shared experiences dealing with mental health institutions and diagnoses.

The epilogue, "Last Sentences: An Epilogue," takes its cue from Johnston's ending of her columns with playful scramblings of time and place. I discuss how she made space for lesbians in social movements and why those efforts remain potent today. In this final chapter/essay, I seek to—as Johnston did in her column endings—push the ideas of *Jill Johnston in Motion* further while also remixing past and present via an autoethnographic account of walking in the 2019 Dyke March with Nyeboe on the fiftieth anniversary of Stonewall. The epilogue concludes with its own scores—prompts toward collective and solo motion inspired by Johnston's work.

At times this is a book about what it means to write about bodies, a question I think dance usefully requires of scholars. At times this is a book about attachment, even love, and what it feels like to have a history. This is also a book about what the category of lesbian allowed Jill Johnston to do and how that might make a future from the past. But, always, it is a dance with Jill.

1

She Was a Critic

I became a critic . . . just when the entire art world was entering a convulsion of dissolving boundaries.
—Jill Johnston, *Marmalade Me*

Writing criticism involves many acts of sorting. Critics decide what to see, what to skip; what to write about, what to leave unmentioned. There are also more evaluative forms of sorting: labeling art as good or bad, old or new. As Jill Johnston became one of New York City's most prolific arts writers in the 1950s and 1960s, the criteria by which critics did their sorting were in flux. With "the entire art world . . . entering a convulsion of dissolving boundaries," so was criticism.[1]

This was a time when dancers were almost as likely to perform in an art gallery as on a stage, and sculptors were as likely to consider bodies their material as they were clay. Amid such shifts, treating criticism as an act of sorting made little sense. Instead, as queer performance theorist José Muñoz has described, the task of criticism required dispensing with "previous systems of classification" and participating instead in the creation of "new circuits of belonging."[2] Muñoz celebrates Johnston as a prime example of this shift, naming her as someone who treated being a critic as a "queer practice," someone who approached criticism as "a mode of being in the world that is also inventing the world."[3] Somewhat curiously, Muñoz also describes Johnston as a "lesbian dance and art critic," despite the fact that she did not publicly identify as a lesbian in the period when she was best known as a critic.[4] Reading Johnston's early writing with Muñoz's larger point about criticism in mind, however, makes his "lesbian" label seem just right. Maybe Johnston's contributions to the "gay revolution"—the slogan on the T-shirt she wears in Fred McDarrah's famous 1971 photo of her at a Stonewall anniversary celebration (figure 1.1)—started well before Stonewall or her public announcements about her identity. Maybe Johnston's investment in gay revolution was seeded in her category-refusing arts criticism.

As a critic, Johnston looked for layers and collisions and celebrated performances that, in her words, refused to respect "clean boundaries" and thus created "truly messy world[s]."[5] This orientation to being a critic evolved across publication venues and art forms, first with her writing for the magazine *Dance Observer*; then the neighborhood rag that was becoming a nationally known alternative weekly, the *Village Voice*; and also, beginning in 1962, her work for the visual art publication *ARTnews*. (Of these publications, her association with the *Voice* lasted longest, from 1960 until 1980, with shorter stints at the other publications: 1955–60 at the *Dance Observer* and 1962–66 at *ARTnews*.) At first glance, the writing Johnston did in her first decade as a critic resembles more traditional criticism. She describes and evaluates performances and artists' development. A closer examination of this writing, however, illuminates how Johnston queers the act of criticism, how she tracks and then enacts "new circuits of belonging," following artists into a "truly messy world," a category-refusing practice she calls "a consummation devoutly to be wished."[6]

Tracking the emergence of queer possibility in Johnston's criticism reveals her commitment to tenets that would later become central to definitions of feminist criticism: that art must be understood within its contexts of creation and circulation and that audiences must be understood as heterogeneous and specific. As a feminist, lesbian, and/or queer critic should, Johnston also critiqued criticism itself, arguing that hierarchies that separated critics from artists must be leveled.

For all Johnston did to dissolve hierarchies and categories, dance history has not allowed her to remain in the "messy world" she helped create. Too often she has only been celebrated for her writing about the Judson Dance Theater, the group formed by dance and visual artists in the West Village's Judson Church from 1962 to 1964 and often credited with creating what has become known as *postmodern dance*. Johnston did chronicle how Judson, as

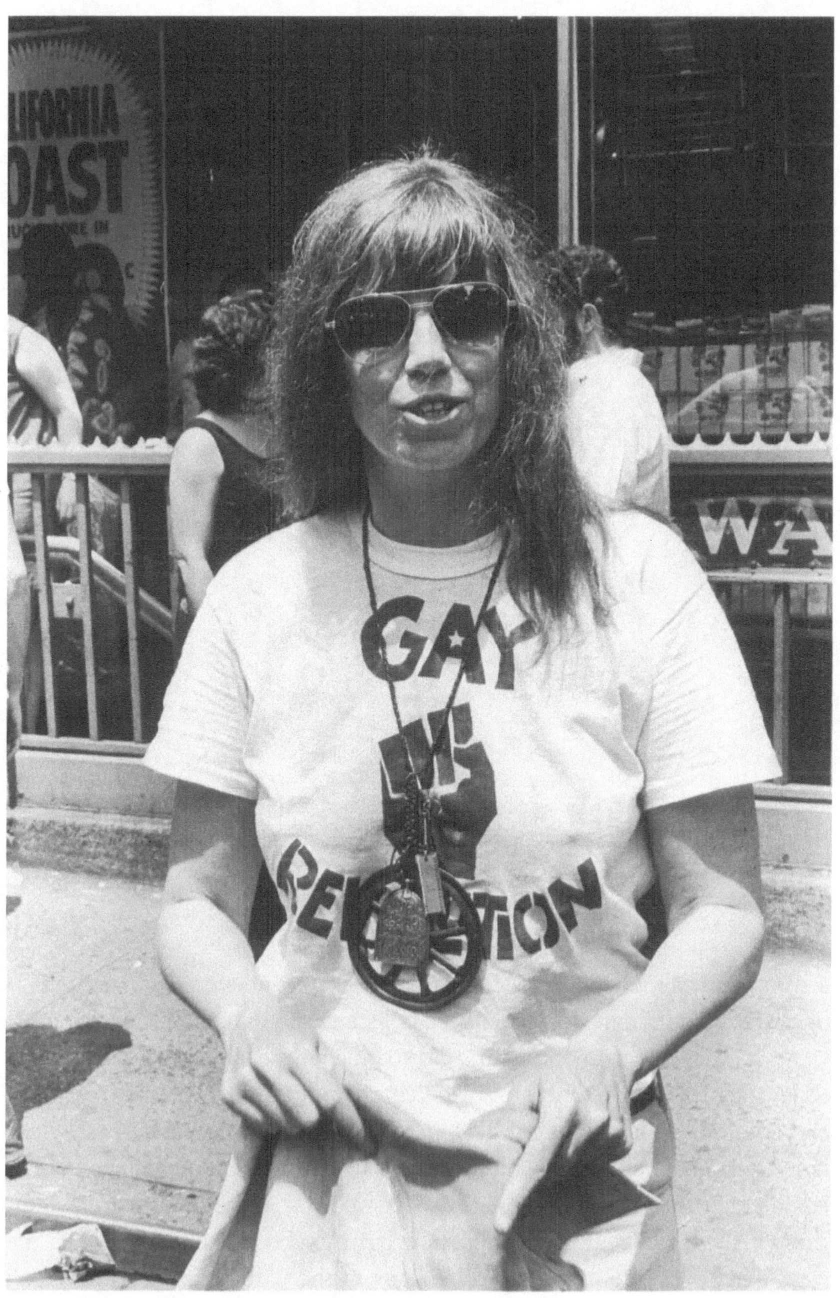

1.1 Jill Johnston, second anniversary of Stonewall Riots, New York City, 1971. Photograph © Fred W. McDarrah/MUUS Collection.

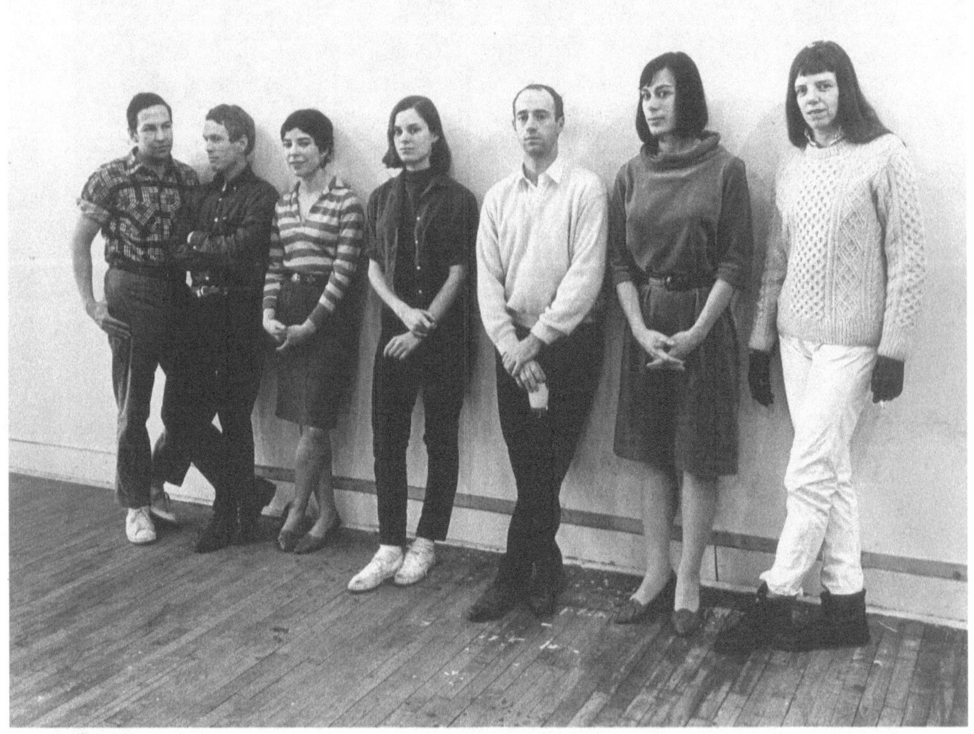

1.2 Figures of Judson. *From left to right:* Robert Rauschenberg, Alex Hay, Deborah Hay, Lucinda Childs, Robert Morris, Yvonne Rainer, and Jill Johnston. Photograph by Al Giese. © 2023 Hottelet/Giese/Licensed by Artists Rights Society (ARS), NY.

a group and as individual artists (see figure 1.2), contested major principles of earlier modern dance, especially an insistence on unity as a choreographic value, but her criticism of the time did so much more. She also wrote about a wider range of performance, for instance, championing the then-young Black choreographer Alvin Ailey for his kinesthetic effect on audiences, as well as writing about a number of white women she saw as expanding ideas of what could constitute femininity onstage. Considering Johnston's writing about these artists, as well as her important writing about Judson, expands the way Johnston's role in the dance ecology of the 1950s and 1960s has been remembered.

Examining Johnston's body of criticism through a wider frame allows another shift: a move away from recognizing her primarily for who she wrote about and toward taking more seriously how she wrote. From this vantage point, this chapter arrives at the first of this book's lesbian adjacencies, placing Johnston's writing alongside that of her contemporary, arts writer and fellow queer woman Susan Sontag. Specifically, I consider how both Sontag and Johnston imagined criticism as a potentially erotic practice, with Sontag theorizing criticism as erotic in her 1964 essay "Against Interpretation" and Johnston enacting criticism as erotic throughout the 1960s. The final portions of this chapter triangulate Sontag's and Johnston's different relationships to erotic power in criticism with the 1978 essay "The Uses of the Erotic," written by Black lesbian thinker and artist Audre Lorde (also a primary figure in chapter 2). Lesbian criticism abounds once you start looking for it—"a consummation devoutly to be wished."[7]

Call Her by Her Name: Queer Lesbian Feminist Dance Critic

Johnston's dance criticism addresses what feminist philosopher Toril Moi argues has been one of feminism's most persistent problems: how to undo patriarchal categorizations that understand women's bodies only as objects for men to gaze on for pleasure and/or as tools to be used in service of men, both of which result in women being alienated from their bodies.[8] By attending to bodies, often women's bodies, with her own body, Johnston's dance criticism provides a feminist antidote to such alienation. Instead of using her critical perch to evaluate how artists used their bodies, imposing preexisting codes onto others, Johnston relied on description and sensation to describe how artists scramble existing codes and imagine new types of physical connections.

A particularly clear example of what could be seen as Johnston's feminist approach to criticism comes in her 1963 *Village Voice* review of a group she called the "romantic dancers": Sybil Shearer, Merle Marsicano, Aileen Passloff, and Beverly Schmidt. In a swirling, looping list, Johnston describes the women's contributions through a comparison to early modern dance matriarch Isadora Duncan, writing, "If Isadora was romantic, it was because she loved men and the ocean and flowing Greek gowns and Beethoven and 'the Marseillaise,' and her own emotions, and she got up in the salons or on the stage and let everybody know she loved those things."[9] Johnston conjures desire via multiple senses and passions and manages to frame a woman expressing her desires as a feminist act. Erotic desire exists on the same level as a love of the sights and sounds of water, grandiose music, and the visual and kinesthetic excess of a gown. It's not just a matter of content but conveyance that makes the writing so powerful. Don't you just want to reach out and grab the flowing Greek gowns' silk as it passes by your eye on the page?

Johnston's writing invited constant reorientations that often accentuated women's agency. Recognizing her pre-Stonewall descriptive dance criticism as providing ways of looking that might be described as feminist, even lesbian, offers an example of what Muñoz might mean when he writes, "By my clock we were queer before we were lesbian and gay."[10] The better-known, more clearly demarcated categories of sexuality that gained traction post-Stonewall emerged from queer practices and relationships that preceded them. In the early 1960s, Johnston might have been living, as she put it, "in a state grandly oblivious to all forms of politics."[11] Yet in queering categories and describing relationships developed among and created by women with their bodies, she indeed was a "lesbian dance critic" before she was a "feminist" or a "lesbian."

"Lesbian dance critic." What does one need to do to earn the title? Lesbian and feminist theater scholar Jill Dolan describes one key task of the lesbian and/or feminist critic as refusing to understand audiences as monolithic. There is no such thing as a singular "ideal spectator," a phrase Dolan notes is often code for a very particular spectator, the "white, male taxpayer."[12] From the very first review Johnston wrote of what would become Judson Dance Theater, she explained how performance spectatorship could be both egalitarian and multiple—an act without an ideal. What Johnston most loved about Judson was her sense that it invited an open manner of witnessing that offered "something for everybody, including a nap if desired."[13] She understood that performances could hail audiences in numerous ways and that performance itself created new ways of viewing (or napping) for audiences. Lesbian dance criticism might then be said to describe the multiplicity and desire of bodies in motion and to recognize how people can experience their own bodies and desires in multiple ways in the space of performance.

Feminist scholars of literature and performance have long noted that bringing feminism to bear on criticism means never treating art as somehow floating separate from the world in which it was read, made, or viewed.[14] Johnston entered the world of criticism and immediately told her peers that they needed to catch up to their contemporary moment. She admonished midcentury dance critics to stop focusing on modern dance's past and instead see how what she called the "new dance" was evolving from its present contexts. Johnston essentially skipped the stage through which most critics begin their careers, reviewing lesser-known artists, and immediately looked elsewhere. Jill Johnston became a dance critic by first reviewing her peers, other critics.

Johnston's critiques usually went in one of two directions. One set focused on critics still privileging dance modernism's emphasis on unity over postmodernism's experiments in collage and assembly. Her second set of critiques targeted critics' tendency to evaluate art as though critics were superior to artists. As feminist thinkers would later do, Johnston argued that critics needed to be in the world of and with the artists they followed. A Fluxus artist and longtime friend of Johnston's, Geoffrey Hendricks, described her critical disposition toward artists as one of "curiosity, and a feeling of closeness and affinity to all of what was going on in the avant-garde." When it came to emerging artistic trends, Hendricks said Johnston from "a very early point [recognized] that traditional dance was something she ha[d] to leave behind to get involved with these . . . new things that she was finding exciting and wanted to chronicle."[15] These reorientations allowed Johnston to forge a mode of criticism both generous and rambunctious, a criticism that refused hierarchies of all kinds and that sought to change and grow with artists.

These sentiments found their first home in the *Dance Observer*, where (as discussed in the introduction) Johnston's writing first appeared in 1955 and where she took aim at the emphasis on unity in art championed by the magazine's editor, Louis Horst. Johnston's first pieces in Horst's publication focused on what she thought critics should do: upend their aging approaches to writing in order to be present to the changing arts world. Horst and the many critics he influenced still argued that choreographers should focus on "structural and dramatic unity," with all aspects of a production aligning around one clear idea—a position he developed and advocated for via an earlier generation of modern dance choreographers, most notably Martha Graham.[16] Looking at the New York City dance world of 1955, Johnston argued that something new was emerging, work built not from unity but from what she called "strange logics" of collage and assemblage.[17] Johnston had just joined the ranks of New York critics, but she did not hesitate to call for change. She demanded that dance critics live and write in the present.

Horst's notion of dramatic unity might have been aging, but the platforms he had built, like the *Dance Observer*, kept his position powerful. Until his death (and the magazine's end) in 1964, Horst used the three to four lengthy reviews he generally published in each month's issue to cheerlead for the importance of unity to dance making. A 1953 *Dance Observer* editorial aptly conveys the reach, weight, and solidity Horst's positions had. The piece claims there are two things in the dance world that will never change: "dancers themselves and Louis Horst."[18] Horst's omnipresent inflexibility created a problem for artists forging new directions, especially those making "new dance"—as Johnston termed the work of Merce Cunningham and, eventually, those associated with the Judson Dance Theater.

Critics' evaluation of Cunningham's work lays the problem bare. In 1954, the year before Johnston began writing, Robert Sabin reviewed an evening of work by the then one-year-old Merce Cunningham Dance Company in the *Dance Observer* and dismissed Cunningham's newest work, *Suite by Chance*, as "inert, static, and almost chaotic at times." Looking for unity, Sabin could only see what he described as the "feebleness of [Cunningham's] basic choreographic material." Sabin noted that the choreography contained "some valuable experimentation" but quickly dismissed this because Cunningham's play with how elements cohered left the critic "drained and unsatisfied."[19] The terms by which Sabin dismisses Cunningham's innovation mark him as a critic within Horst's "unity" empire, in which—as Horst biographer Janet Soares has written—all "new dance" was, at best, an "irritant."[20]

Johnston entered Horst's orbit at the *Dance Observer* by complaining about this closed perspective, so overly focused on the past. Her initial letter of complaint to Horst, which led him to invite her to write for the magazine, likely became the content of her first *Dance Observer* publication, the 1955 essay "Thoughts on the Present and Future Directions of Modern Dance." In this and two subsequent essays published in the magazine in 1957, Johnston sought to reimagine dance's critical terrain. She dismantles existing ideas about dance criticism, often through perceptively scrutinizing the terms of debates about what constitutes "good" choreography, perhaps drawing on her relatively recent training in philosophy at Columbia University,

Johnston's 1955 *Dance Observer* essay focuses on the term *progress*, which Johnston defines as "not only the discovery of new techniques and methods, but the development or exploitation of them."[21] She then assesses progress as arising from ideas of both "discovery" and "birth." Artists focusing on "discovery" work in well-known aesthetics, looking for potential in what is already known. Innovation—"birth"—is more likely to arise from artists experimenting with lesser known ideas. Seeing progress in this capacious way, allowing for categories known and unknown to shape how she approached dance, meant Johnston could value a wider range of artistic voices: new ideas weren't necessarily replacing the old—they were just new. In her next *Dance Observer* essay, "The Modern Dance—Directions and Criticisms," she returned to this foundational generosity, using the image of a "plateau" to describe how a critic needs to look out at "all sides in all directions."[22] Her critical perch is a vantage point of horizontality from which she can track range and possibility, *not* reinforce old hierarchies or create new ones.

The horizontal persists throughout Johnston's career as a useful concept for understanding her critical approach. In "Critics' Critics," a 1965 *Voice* column in which she focused on what by then she was calling "the ART of criticism," Johnston forcefully demands an end to hierarchies that elevate critics over artists. The piece opens with a stark, visual juxtaposition, calling for the "ancient practice of [the critic] pretending to be top man on a barber's pole" to be replaced with an understanding of criticism as a "land [that should] look . . . level enough to be a wide open field."[23] Her writing is strident and powerful. By the essay's end, she seems to propose that hierarchy busting has already happened: "The future is upon us and the ART of Criticism has already come into its own in those public places where the critic is lying down on a soft piece of ground to enjoy a bit of blue and yellow scenery."[24] This image of the critic, prone and pleasured—no longer in need of a plateau, let alone a tall pole to watch from—intertwines the feminist and queer impulses in Johnston's writing. In Johnston's vision of criticism, the critic experiences her body and has pleasure *with*, not over, all that she writes about.

Johnston wrote "Critics' Critics" while institutionalized in New York's infamous mental health hospital, Bellevue, where she received a diagnosis of schizophrenia—another label, this one imposed on her, that she would resist her entire life. Knowing that this was the situation in which Johnston found herself, and yet she still focused on the role of the critic, says something about how much criticism meant to her. Her persistence was also partially inspired by an urgent need to disagree with another powerful male dance critic, *New York Times* dance critic Clive Barnes, and his recent "think piece," "Critic's Credo." In the two, related pieces, Johnston and Barnes begin from a similar premise: that description is essential to dance criticism. And, in "Critics' Critics," Johnston even acknowledges that she "liked" Barnes's recent piece.[25] But the two part ways in their categorizations of the critic-artist relationship. For Barnes, critics are "parasites" who live off artists, whereas Johnston hopes to be a critic "staking out a claim to being an artist."[26] She wants to write *with* dance, forging "the ART of criticism" from others' art.

As she came to understand criticism as an art itself, Johnston represented a shift in the evolution of the dance critic in the United States. Dance historians Lynne Conner and Ann Daly, in their writings about the rise of the dance critic in American newspapers, describe most critics as initially having been "'insiders' who were writing to and for their own self-selected community."[27] This insider status often meant dance critics were simultaneously, somewhat paradoxically, advocates *and* gatekeepers. Once someone became a critic, they were both for and against dance artists but not quite within the artists' world anymore. John Martin, Barnes's predecessor at the *Times*, is a prime example. Martin wrote and spoke about dance in popular and scholarly venues, building an argument for dance as not just a supplement to theater or music but an art form in its own right.[28] His go-to case study for this argument was his favorite choreographer, Martha Graham. Martin tended to judge all dance makers against Graham's emphasis on universality and Jungian-inspired emotionality. As both advocate and critic, he was judge and jury, establishing the measures by which work should be judged and then analyzing it through terms he created.

As was the case with many of her predecessors, Johnston also came to dance criticism with insider status. She was a former dancer who socialized with many of the artists she covered. But unlike many of her predecessors, she also came to criticism intent on understanding it as an act of writing. She was less like Martin or Barnes in this regard and more like Martin's contemporary and Johnston's fellow queer dance writer Edwin Denby, whose dance criticism reads much like the poetry he also wrote. As Daly notes, Johnston crafted her writing to extend Denby's blending of writing genres, "uniquely register[ing] the untenable, unstable, unbearable condition of the critic, . . . at once invisible and . . . the center of attention."[29] Johnston often notes the critic's presence—usually via invoking her own body—and then reckons with what it means that dance has a witness. Categories ebb and flow.

Johnston stepped into the role of the critic during a larger shift in journalism, a time when many were infusing populism into the critical elite. Music historian Jack Hamilton has argued this shift is most notable in the emergence of the rock critics of the 1960s, the group of mostly male critics who helped make rock music a subject of analysis for popular and intellectual readerships (and who also produced different criteria for white and Black musicians).[30] In venues like *Rolling Stone*, founded in 1967, rock critics underscored music's role in producing counterculture and vice versa. *Rolling Stone*, like the *Voice*, was also a primary platform for one of the supposedly most populist strands in criticism of the time, the New Journalism movement. The genre, often associated with the braggadocio of writers like Tom Wolfe and Hunter S. Thompson, borrowed techniques from fiction, including dialogue and character development. New Journalists deployed a style that, not unlike Johnston's, played with the critic as both visible and not, sometimes going so far in their emphasis on the critic's presence that they begged the question of whether a piece was about the art or cultural scene on which the writer ostensibly focused or was really just about the writer himself. (And yes, the gendering here is intentional.)

New Journalism made more space for the critic-as-artist, but the form, almost exclusively associated with men, did not otherwise disrupt the hierarchy between critic and artist. Writing about Johnston in *Vogue*, critic John Gruen argued her work was "in no way" related to "new journalism," which Gruen dismissed as "overly ego-oriented reportage."[31] When faced with the categorization of herself as a New Journalist, Johnston protested, pointing to her enmeshment in the scene about which she wrote. She dismissed New Journalists, particularly Wolfe, for voyeuristic descriptions of what she lovingly referred to as New York's "freaks." To Johnston New Journalists were outsiders, insistent on their difference from those about whom they wrote. She sought to write about New York's bohemian class as she saw them: a group of "struggling poor real people who loved the carnival we were making up."[32] Her "we" is key. Johnston sought to build a world (or "carnival") with these artists, despite being an artist of a different stripe. She enacted a form of queer criticism that resembles what dance artist and writer Anna Martine Whitehead terms a "freak technique," a practice Whitehead describes as central to both queer and Black ways of being: a "turn away from all that is associated with normativity" and a turn toward "sensuality, creativity, and oppositionality," moves that pose new possibilities for connection and belonging.[33] Judson artist and choreographer Deborah Hay remembers that in the early 1960s she thought of Johnston as a "friend who was a critic. Or . . . a friend who was a peer. . . . She was in our circles. She was at our parties; she was part of that community."[34] Jill Johnston was a critic shimmying down from the top of the pole that overlooked the action, joining the "carnival" of "freaks" to be in the world with artists, and describing all the complications and complexities of bodies in motion from within the mess.

Entering Johnston's Criticism

Dance history has largely rendered Johnston not as the documentarian of a freak-authored carnival but as the documentarian of one dance genre/movement, the Judson Dance Theater. Dance historian Sally Banes has beautifully argued that Johnston and Judson were an ideal fit for one another, sharing a "directness, this immediacy in vividly presenting the kinesthetic facts of life that informs Johnston's writing as well as the dances and other events she wrote about."[35] The linking of Johnston and Judson has produced, however, one of the odder phenomena in dance historiography. Both Judson and Johnston actively questioned categories and definitions, yet Judson (and Johnston through association) have since then been revered in ways that treat each as iconic and bounded—practically the opposite of the dissolution of boundaries Johnston relished in Judson and beyond. Understanding Johnston's contributions to dance criticism requires recognizing how far she reached beyond Judson, looking for what she called "strange logics," not "fits." Reading Johnston's body of criticism written from 1955 to 1965, not just her writing focused on Judson, displays a wider field of what constituted New York dance midcentury and the decidedly queer, wide-ranging critical practice Johnston developed to describe it.

NOT JUDSON

Expanding the map of Johnston's writing terrain begins with the intermedial events that were Happenings. The interdisciplinary nature of these events and their emphasis on liveness closely parallel the liveliness of Johnston's criticism. As Fluxus artist Geoffrey Hendricks said of Happenings and Johnston, "Happenings, Fluxus, [and] Intermedia w[ere] all about breaking down boundaries and things fused into kind of one larger mix. . . . Her being there, you know, partially participant, partial writer, critic, observer—[felt] perfectly natural."[36] Happenings and Johnston were not so much a fit as they were a pairing that did not require the other to fit within preexisting categories.

Not all critics felt such a compatibility with the increasingly interdisciplinary arts scene of the time, especially Happenings. "It is difficult to review this genre," admitted *Village Voice* theater critic Jean Robinson in a 1960 review that spectacularly failed at describing a series of Happenings created by Robert Whitman, Jim Dine, and George Brecht—visual artists who had moved into the performance-oriented genre—and choreographer James Waring.[37] A week after Robinson reviewed the event by not really reviewing it, the *Voice* published Johnston's review of the same set of performances. Johnston described the evening as "really a joke, but with serious underpinning." To explain how the Reuben Gallery event was both funny and serious, she referenced the Dada movement of the early twentieth century, writing that the performance "was funny because it usually makes people laugh when they see materials brought together that are not supposed to go together in ordinary life and which are arranged in a bizarre fashion. It was serious because it came out of a thoughtful revolt against a world in chaos that was pretending order.... It said: 'Why shouldn't this go with that and be called something else.' Why not indeed?" The last two sentences describe Happenings but, even more so, Johnston's larger critical curiosity: "'Why shouldn't this go with that and be called something else.' Why not indeed?" These two questions animate all of Johnston's criticism—and later catalyzed her critiques of patriarchy and heteronormativity. Johnston ends the column with a jab at Robinson, calling him a "bad boy" who "doesn't know how to enjoy himself."[38] For Johnston, pleasure was a critical practice too.

The blurring of distinction between art and life through illogical, often mundane and humorous arrangements of seemingly unrelated tasks first captured Johnston's attention, not at Judson, but in the work of the choreographer of that 1961 Reubens event, ballet-trained dancer turned avant-garde catalyst and comic James Waring. In a 1961 *Voice* piece about a Waring concert, Johnston described the genre-bending event as a "happening with dance as the protagonist." She applauded Waring for countering modern dance's—and Louis Horst's—emphasis on unity and instead building an illogical structure through asides, tangents, and layers. Johnston loved how Waring crafted a world in which gestures "erupt like small windows on a slice of life," highlighting the "illogical (but relative) scheme of things."[39] If Graham was Horst's primary case study for valuing unity, then Waring was Johnston's initial case study for pleasurable disunity.

Johnston's interest in asking, "Why shouldn't this go with that and be called something else"? also emphasized how dance could be interspliced with other disciplines. She countered Martin's theorizing of dance as distinct from other art forms and rebraided dance back into a larger arts context. Johnston particularly emphasized the need to rethink the relations between writing and dance. As dance historian Gay Morris has noted, Martin had argued that the "task of the [dance] artist was to express irrationally what others would later rationalize in writing."[40] Martin's formulation tasked choreographers with expressing interiority and left writing to do the work of reflection and rationalization—all ego, no id. This was a binary that could never hold Johnston. She refused the idea that one's mode of communication mandated what could be done in that mode. Dancing and writing were not opposites or even entirely separate for Johnston. In her criticism, dancing reshaped, infused, and changed what was possible on the page. As she put it in a review of another of her favorite dance artists of the 1960s, Fred Herko, she celebrated the "strange logic of parts that have no business being together, but which go together anyway because anything in life can go with anything else if you know what you're doing."[41]

In her first decade of dance writing, Johnston built her own strange logics, both in terms of structure and at the level of the sentence. Interdisciplinary artist Meredith Monk remembers Johnston as unique in her "structural vision," which Monk thought emerged from Johnston having "c[o]me up through taking dance" but then also having a "panoramic . . . vision [closer to that] of painters or visual artists."[42] An increasingly interdisciplinary, intermedial arts scene and Johnston's desire to move away from the dance modernism of Horst and Martin led her to develop a poetic, yet rigorously experimental and experiential, writing praxis.

Publishing in a wide range of venues supported the critical expansions and experiments Johnston undertook. *ARTnews*, the most conventional of the three publications to which Johnston contributed in her early career, was perhaps a most unexpected site to seed experimentation. The monthly magazine relied on conventional arts journalism formats—essays, short reviews, and what would become known as *listings*, very short descriptions of shows. Known among artists as "the Watchtower" for its panoptic role in American art, *ARTnews* seems an odd fit for a hierarchy buster like Johnston. Except it was *ARTnews* that regularly sent Johnston into the rapidly changing landscape of New York's visual art scene, where interdisciplinarity proliferated. In addition to hosting Happenings, galleries exhibited artists like Claes Oldenburg and Robert Morris, sculptors who emphasized the physical experience of visual art. *ARTnews* critics had to create new strategies to describe these works, and Johnston was one of the boldest voices to meet the artists' challenge. As art historian Carrie Lambert-Beatty has noted, Johnston, more than her critical peers in visual art, seemed particularly unencumbered by disciplinary fidelity.[43]

Instead of categorizing art by genre or discipline, Johnston focused on the sensual and affective aspects of artistic encounters. She wrote most about events at the Green Gallery, which was managed by her close friend and East Broadway neighbor, curator Richard (Dick) Bellamy, and those at the Reuben Gallery, where dancer Simone Forti and sculptor Robert Morris often performed together. Covering these sites for *ARTnews* in the early 1960s, Johnston departed from the more conventional reviews she had written for the *Dance Observer* and sometimes still wrote for the *Voice*. Forti/Morris collaborations famously extended the physical imperative of abstract sculpture—that it is best viewed by walking around it—and created sculptures that compelled viewers (often by a dancer doing so first) to touch, open and close, and even climb on objects. Inspired by these experiments in sensation, play, and provocation, Johnston began writing the body of the viewer into her visual art reviews. For example, in an *ARTnews* review of a Mon Levinson sculpture show, Johnston noted that the work "require[d] the observer's movement to fulfill its potential of shimmering reflection."[44] In a more personal turn toward the role of the spectator, Johnston included her then-young daughter's comments on Oldenburg's now-famous *Store*: "This reviewer's daughter could not grasp the significance of good food lying around that was not to eat."[45] Johnston incorporated the works' requirement of physical motion and invitation of a range of perspectives into her writing.

While visual art nudged Johnston toward new approaches to art and criticism, being a regular contributor to the *Village Voice* allowed her to experiment with writing in the broadest manner and to do so in an episodic format. Recommended to the *Voice* by none other than James Waring, Johnston joined the then five-year-old paper in 1960.[46] The *Voice*'s founding editors, Dan Wolf, Ed Fancher, and Norman Mailer, had conceived the paper as a platform against hierarchies in publishing, "a living, breathing attempt to demolish the notion that one needs to be a professional to accomplish something in a field as purportedly technical as journalism."[47] Writing for the young paper was a less-than-glamorous gig with little pay, a situation exacerbated by gender hierarchies. Johnston once described her early years at the *Voice* as "writing as a girl for a man's paper for nothing."[48] But the paper encouraged, even required, that writers experiment. Johnston thus came to critical prominence among a constellation of playful, yet serious thinkers who were redefining criticism: Jonas Mekas, Andrew Sarris, and Nat Hentoff, among others.

At the time Johnston joined its ranks, the *Voice* was more experimental neighborhood rag than vaunted, nationally known alternative weekly. It primarily covered New York's West Village neighborhood, then a mostly white mix of Italian and Polish immigrants and bohemian artists, as well as urban activists who fought perceived threats to the neighborhood. The paper's coverage ranged from neighborhood residents' efforts to challenge the Tammany Hall political party machine to debates around whether the city could demolish the neighborhood's centerpiece, Washington Square Park, to make way for Robert Moses's cross-city expressway.

Village resident Jane Jacobs led the neighborhood's fights against these outside forces, particularly the proposed highway, defending the value of daily, mundane interactions on neighborhood sidewalks by arguing that they were "street ballets."[49] Jacobs's phrasing, first published in 1961, is oddly prescient of what Johnston would begin to chronicle a year later at Judson Church, a building which stands on Washington Square Park's southern border and a home since the late nineteenth century to a liberal Protestant congregation. Originally conceived as a site that would bring together New York's wealthiest, who lived north of the park, and New York's poorest, the tenement dwellers who lived south of the park, the church had always hosted social justice and arts efforts.

By the time this social experiment had become home to the artistic experiment of the mid-twentieth century, artists' focus on the mundane and egalitarian had become more predicated on sameness than the Church's origins had been. A similar homogeneity was assumed in the "street ballets" Jacobs sought to protect in the neighborhood. As Johan Anderson has written, "Jacobs may have written against the oppressiveness of top-down modernist urban planning, but the small-scale surveillance of her neighborhood ideal was fraught with its own form of authoritarianism."[50] What Jacobs promoted as a way to maintain the neighborhood's character, "eyes on the street," often translated into a suspicion of anyone imagined as an outsider, particularly the people known colloquially in the Village as "A-trainers," usually Black and/or Brown queer people who came to the downtown neighborhood for its gay bars and cruising scenes.[51] A similar form of watching likely shaped Judson audiences. As the neighborhood's streets and arts spaces grew whiter, there were few opportunities for what dance historian Susan Manning has called "cross-viewing," people of multiple races in the same theater witnessing how others respond to a performance.[52] The *Voice*'s attention to its neighborhood generally failed to critique hierarchies if they were of the neighborhood the paper emerged from and most intensely covered.

The New York hierarchy the *Voice* did help upend came in its elevation of artists working in the Village and other downtown New York neighborhoods over artists showing work in the city's more commercial, uptown art spaces. In 1956 theater enthusiast Jerry Tallmer joined the paper, quickly becoming an associate editor, theater critic, and founder of the Obie Awards, which recognize off-Broadway performance. These awards and the paper's coverage of neighborhood venues cemented the connection between the *Voice* and what's often called the "downtown" performance scene: a geographic reference that still indexes experimental performance in New York.

Johnston loved downtown as a place and an artistic flash point, particularly her East Broadway neighborhood, where she lived near several artists and curators she admired, befriended, and wrote about: Bellamy, minimalist choreographer Sally Gross, sculptor Mark di Suvero, and others—a crew she described as "failed bourgeois American[s]."[53] In the twenty-first century, the downtown neighborhoods of Manhattan have become a dense mix of commercial and residential properties. But Carolee Schneemann, another Judson artist whose work Johnston frequently reviewed, described the neighborhoods in which Johnston thrived in the 1950s and 1960s, particularly East Broadway and Soho, as spaces that "fed the bohemian artistic scene through its mysteriousness of all the empty lofts small manufacturers had fled... these adventurous, big, rough, crummy spaces where we could really spread out."[54] Schneemann's image seems apt for understanding Johnston as part of a larger midcentury downtown ethos regularly captured in the *Village Voice*: bohemian, mysterious, interested in the unknown, and taking up more and more space.

Two years into Johnston's association with the *Voice*, an accident of labor transformed the paper from a neighborhood experiment into a publication with national prominence. In late 1962, just as Johnston began covering Judson, a typographical strike took almost all of New York's newspapers out of circulation. The *Voice*—printed outside the city as a cost-saving measure—suddenly became one of few available papers in the city. The surge in readership during the strike vaulted the paper from one focused on a single neighborhood into, first, a citywide source and then a national bullhorn for experimental and leftist writing. By 1967 the *Voice* was the United States' number-one-selling weekly newspaper, and the paper's readers—new and old—came to know the (increasingly white) Village as a home for experimental art.[55] The paper's transformation is key to understanding how a dance movement, Judson, which took place in one neighborhood in New York for only a few years, came to such prominence in dance and art history.

Though they did not win the attention Judson did, Johnston actually tracked artistic developments downtown, uptown, and out-of-town. Some of her best early writing comes from her annual trips to the American Dance Festival (ADF), then in New London, Connecticut. There she continued to cover modern dance giants, like Graham, Doris Humphrey, and José Limón, as well as her beloved "rebel group," which, pre-Judson, generally meant Merce Cunningham. Back in New York, she admired newer voices, notably a young Alvin Ailey, the Black choreographer who founded his own company in 1958 and premiered his iconic *Revelations* in 1960.

Johnston loved Ailey's work, lauding him in the *Voice* well before critics in other predominantly white newspapers did. Although art and performance historians generally associate the *Voice* with white avant-garde/experimental art making, the paper did feature extensive coverage of the civil rights movement, deploying writers to the American South and reporting on appearances by Black leaders in New York.

The interest in racial change eventually spread to the paper's arts coverage as well. In the year Johnston first lauded Ailey, avant-garde Black dance artist Eleo Pomare's departure for Germany warranted newspaper coverage, Langston Hughes's New York readings made the front page in July, and Norman Mailer wrote about playwright Lorraine Hansberry.[56] Against this backdrop, Johnston recognized Ailey's importance. She opened her 1961 review of his company's performance at the West Side YMCA with an uncharacteristic (for her) command: "If you see a notice any place that says Alvin Ailey is going to do his *Revelations*, try to go and see it."[57] Her enthusiasm is interlaced with phrases and tropes, like descriptions of Black dance as natural or evidence of spiritual possession, that make clear she is a white writer with little exposure to Black thought or art. However naive her understanding of race, the attention to movement and environment in Johnston's criticism still allowed her to describe Ailey's genius, particularly his integration of Africanist elements with modern dance and ballet—even though she didn't understand the lineages from which Ailey drew. Writing about Ailey himself dancing *Revelations*' "Take Me to the Water," she describes how his charisma accumulates from his ability to make "his big torso heave and ripple like serpent magic, better say human magic." Her description of the undulations of Ailey's torso, a central characteristic of Africanist dance, leads her to the artist's skill and humanity. Johnston also recognizes that it is Ailey's coupling of dance and drum, another hallmark of Africanist dance, that makes *Revelations* so compelling. She lauds the combination of Brother John Sellers's gospel arrangement, Ailey's choreography and performance, and the role of the drum, writing, "That DRUM! The drum will never let you go."

Writing a year later about another Ailey performance, Johnston's fandom is clear: Ailey is "the man with the two most exciting dances in America at the present moment."[58] She recognizes Ailey's brilliance, partially due to his skill at reaching spectators emotionally and kinesthetically. In her 1961 Ailey review, she writes that "an audience might (should) be moved to get up or sit down or lie prone or do anything that would express its participation" and that she was frustrated no one in the YMCA audience did so—a choice she says is evidence of "society" being "so ridiculous." She writes as though she can see *Revelations*' future—a future in which audiences almost never remain seated for the work's closing choreography, a testament to Ailey's reshaping of US concert dance via Black culture. I also can't help but wonder if she—watching Ailey's company throughout the 1960s as a woman in relationships with women but not yet thinking of herself as a lesbian—might have somehow sensed the ways in which, as dance historian Thomas DeFrantz has demonstrated, Ailey performances were becoming a gathering place for homosexuals, particularly Black gay men.[59]

Her interest in Ailey did not, however, necessarily extend to his contemporaries in Black dance. In another 1962 review, Johnston describes Katherine Dunham's work as being in "an advanced stage of nymphomania."[60] Johnston, a white woman who would one day use her own body to disrupt social norms around gender and sexuality, dismisses what dance historians have described as Dunham's embrace of female sexuality and choreography of "black sexual dissidence."[61] Johnston is decidedly on the outside of Dunham's work, unable to engage in the choreographer's Black and diasporic refusals of respectability. She cannot find her way into what Black queer theorist Amber Musser has described, in her writing about Dunham's *Shango* (1945), as the ways in which Dunham's work "thrives on the tension between insider and outsider knowledge."[62] The pleasure of recognition without confirmation that Johnston experienced among other white lesbians (as further discussed in chapter 3) and occasionally with the many gay men of the dance world met its limits in Johnston's writing about work by the prominent Black woman choreographer. Johnston writes that Dunham took her display of sexuality "too far," but it was probably more a case of Johnston not being able to travel with her.[63]

Hints of Johnston's feminism to come are easier to find in her writing about white women choreographers. Through attending to details of how these women put bodies in motion in ways that ignite sensation and power, Johnston paints a complex scene of what it means to be feminine onstage. For instance, in her 1963 review of "romantic dancers," Johnston introduces Merle Marsicano, a choreographer known for her collaborations with abstract expressionists, by writing that Marsicano is "romantic the way a [Mark] Rothko painting is romantic." Through the comparison to Rothko's stark saturation, she upends definitions of *romantic*. Johnston continues, still seemingly with painting in mind, that when she watches Marsicano dance, she sees "the image [as it] spreads and suffuses like some luminous, internal light that soaks the space with gradual, subtly persistent intensity." Johnston holds an idea—in this case, the romantic—and turns it round and round, letting it accumulate dimensions as it touches other artists' works. Much like her description of Isadora Duncan cited earlier in this chapter—"she loved men and the ocean and flowing Greek gowns and Beethoven and 'the Marseillaise' and her own emotions"—Johnston sees a woman's complexity and, in response, writes of a femininity that is layered, multiple, ever-changing, and that has impact. The best example of this comes in the lengthy comparison Johnston makes between Marsicano and Graham:

> Miss Marsicano also expresses an ideal feminine image. I'm not sure what that is, but I can't imagine a man with the same quality, or I could

> but wouldn't like it. The image is certainly more mysterious than the projection of a woman like Martha Graham, because Graham always involved her idea of herself with a literary psychological content. Marsicano begins and ends with movement. What makes her so great is the magic she exudes through the total immersion of her personality in a quality that moves from the center outward and that has the clarity of silk sheen and the transparency of vapor.[64]

Again images spread: "she exudes through the total immersion of her personality in a quality that moves from the center outward." There is also a notion of the feminine as something created, not a preexisting form into which a dancer steps, the "projection of a woman" invoked by Graham.

Johnston might not have meant to analyze gender or, certainly, race in her early dance criticism, but that's where description took her. She watched performance unfold with care and playfulness and described what she saw with detail and zest, letting performances (when she could access them from her social position as a white woman) lead her to new ways of writing. The result was a documentation of how dance and, indeed, the world were changing in the 1950s and 1960s, rendered in accessible, sensual, evocative prose.

JUDSON JUGGERNAUT IN CONTEXT

Though Judson came into existence just as the *Voice* transformed from neighborhood paper to a citywide, then national, weekly, it's useful to think of Johnston at Judson as a beat reporter, someone who, over the course of years, watches and documents as a local phenomenon arises, unfolds, and, finally, disperses. The last step, dispersal, is key to reconsidering Johnston's much-valued (overvalued?) interest in Judson, a movement that fascinated her but that she never intended to make into an icon. In fact, what Johnston valued most in Judson was its resistance to institutionalization. In a 1965 column penned as a farewell to Judson, she wrote, "Judson was never a stable institution, thankfully . . . the entire arrangement was a momentary expediency and . . . modern dance *at its best* remains an individual affair and not an institutional business. The milieu created by the Judson collaborations was tight enough to afford a stimulating exchange of influence and loose enough not to constrict personal ambition."[65] Refusing the imagined stability of institutionalization allowed Judson to privilege openness and innovation, qualities Johnston celebrated in her writing. Writing about Judson's first performance in 1962, Johnston highlighted how the evening provided "something for everybody, including a nap if desired; and in fact there was so much [going on] that special moments arose as expected and at least three dances provoked a big response from everybody."[66] Judson evenings, full of dance, music, and visual art enacted across wide-ranging bills of seven to ten works, simultaneously challenged and welcomed audiences. Audiences had choices but not explicit instructions, so they had to learn new and varied ways to be a witness.

Johnston fundamentally shaped how Judson entered dance history, but her framing of Judson—much like the framing of her career vis-à-vis Judson—was not as exclusionary as remembered. Dance historian Sally Banes has argued that Judson had three aesthetic strains—"analytic, reductive" (Yvonne Rainer, Lucinda Childs, Trisha Brown); "humorous, baroque" (David Gordon, Fred Herko, Arlene Rothlein); and "multimedia" (Elaine Summers, Judith Dunn).[67] Of these strains, Banes argues that the first, the analytic strain associated with minimalism, which "proposed and tested theories of dance as art," has become the best known of Judson's activities.[68] While Johnston's frequent focus on Rainer (a topic addressed further in chapter 4) contributed to the elevation of Judson's analytic vein, Johnston wrote about much more than that in her pieces that focused on Judson.

In a two-part farewell to Judson published in late 1964 and early 1965, Johnston wrote about many of the Judson artists and clarified her admiration for the group's range. She addresses Lucinda Childs's *Carnation*, noting the work's "rigorous formality of a commanding, implacable façade."[69] Sentences later, she celebrates Fred Herko (who had recently died) for almost the opposite: his "blend of audacious vanity and cynicism."[70] In just one review, Johnston recognizes artists who represent at least two of Banes's strains: the analytic and the humorous. Like any good queer theorist, Johnston knew the dangers of memorialization, how elevating one part over the whole leaves history's mess looking too clean and uncomplicated.[71]

In fact, Johnston often focused on Judson's range—and the tensions that range created—as central to what interested her about artists, both on programs at Judson and when they appeared outside the church. Sometimes she made this point by comparing artists to one another; other times she saw aesthetic diversity within one piece or in multiple works by a single artist. An important example of this comes in the column "Fresh Winds," which focuses on an evening shared by Herko and Rainer that was, in retrospect, a direct precursor to Judson. In the March 1962 column, Johnston wrote that Herko "kept switching tactics, and if you think about it, which I am doing, it really was a mishmash of styles, events, media, and it all made excellent sense."[72] About Rainer, Johnston writes that both her *Satie for Two* and *Three Seascapes* were excellent, because Rainer approaches work "stringently," keeping the spare but intense work from becoming a "deadly bore" and instead creating an evocative familiarity for the viewer who learns how to watch through the choreographer's crafting of material, which results in something "quite special," something both amorphous yet clear. Judson artist Steve Paxton has said that was often what captured Johnston's interest, work that "conveys but doesn't specify."[73] Maybe a taste of lesbian association, recognition without confirmation, did make it into Johnston's writing about Judson.

What did not make it into Johnston's expansive approach to Judson, however, must also be noted: any acknowledgment of the group's whiteness, in demographics or choreographic mindset. In the various iterations of Robert Dunn's composition class, which sparked Judson, almost every single person—participant or observer—was white.[74] Dance historian Kate Mattingly, in her discussion of Rainer's writing about Judson, argues that much of what was labeled disruptive about Rainer in particular and Judson more generally only seemed so because Judson artists and audiences were unaware of Africanist or Indigenous artistic practices that had long imagined performance as ritual and/or interdisciplinary. Judson's use of task-based repetition and its emphasis on interdisciplinarity seemed new because both were practices "new to white concert dance."[75]

Contemporary dance artists recognized Judson's prominence and inflated role within discussions of postmodernism before most dance critics and historians did. In 1991 Puerto Rican choreographers Merián Soto and Viveca Vázquez wrote to Sally Banes, offering to help with her new project on contemporary Latino dance artists. They told Banes, whom neither knew personally, they could assist her "with any questions [she] might have . . . with regard to the Puerto Rico and New York dance scenes," an offer they made to intervene in the degree to which "much contemporary US dance criticism . . . does not take into account cultural and racial contexts of the work and is therefor [*sic*] often subtly racist, patronizing, and an instrument in maintaining the isolation of the artists within the dance scene."[76]

Homosexuality was similarly marginalized in Judson's postmodern aesthetics and, according to the artists, in their daily lives, although it was the opposite of race in terms of demographics: Johnston was one of several gay and lesbian people of varying manifestations and degrees of outness deeply enmeshed in the scene. Schneemann, Rainer, and Hay commented that the relegation of homosexuality to Judson's unspoken margins landed particularly hard on Johnston, who was out to some degree, largely due to her relationship with Childs. Hay remembers sensing that Johnston's relationship with Childs "was very important to her."[77] Schneemann felt that Johnston (and maybe Childs) felt outside of some parts of the group's social lives, describing Judson as "very hetero" and remembering that "the girls that were all straight used to talk about sex while we're getting dressed and making up and how special we were that we were so attached and eroticized. It was apart from the gay women—not hostile, just separate, just different."[78] Rainer, who would come out as a lesbian later but who partnered with men in the 1960s, including fellow Judson artist Robert Morris, remembers an intense mix of "blatant homophobia" and "blatant misogyny" and a "scene ... dominated by men, heterosexual men and homosexual men," where "someone [a woman] ... as out as Jill was bound to get into trouble with the powers that be."[79] (Johnston's breakup with Childs, precipitated by a male painter, in Rainer's words, "coming after" Childs, "devastated" Johnston.[80]) Hay also remembers age differences further compounding the sense of Johnston as different from Judson's other women. Johnston was also among the oldest of the group: five years older than Rainer, ten older than Schneemann, and twelve older than Hay.

Despite all these complications, Johnston's reviews of Judson combine a mix of humor, ease, and almost shocking clarity, forging a critical style Banes characterizes as one of "casualness and abruptness."[81] In her first Judson review, titled "Democracy," Johnston describes Herko's *Once or Twice a Week I Put on Sneakers to Go Uptown*, writing, "Herko did a barefoot Suzie-Q in a tassel-veil head-dress, moving around the big open performing area (no stage at the church) in a semi-circle, doing only the barefoot Suzie-Q with sometimes a lazy arm snaking up and collapsing down."[82] In a 1963 review of Judson, titled "From Lovely Confusion to Naked Breakfast" (a reference to Valda Setterfield's performance in David Gordon's *Random Breakfast*), Johnston blends her usual attention to physical motion with fantastic attention to time. Writing about one piece on the bill, Robert Morris's *Arizona*, she describes Morris throwing a javelin in the latter portion of the piece and captures not just the action but how it unfolds: "Morris stood with his back to the audience, javelin horizontally extended in both hands. Quiet. Shift into readiness position. More quiet. Then the throw—clean, exact, economical."[83] In these descriptions lies what might be the key to why Johnston's writing cemented Judson's long-standing notoriety. She writes in a way that allows performer, audience, and reader to be enmeshed in sensation. She does not just let us see; instead, we enter, engage, and feel.

Lesbian Adjacency I: Susan Sontag

DANCE: FOR SENSATION, NOT "AGAINST INTERPRETATION"

This is Johnston in a 1961 review of a performance by the Merce Cunningham Dance Company:

> It is not easy to see. Outside the theatre, living as we do, most of us see very little with our eyes wide open. In action the eye absorbs space forms to function; in response the eye becomes a facial decoration as sight turns inward. And our training is such that when we do look for non-functional reasons, it is usually at something huge and spectacular, like cathedrals or sunsets. And even then it is rare to see more than a general outline. Or to see more and still enter. That is the crucial transition, from seeing to entering. Not only crucial but mysterious. . . . I think most people who go to dance concerts don't see very well, not even dancers, sometimes dancers especially, and most often the critics, who must attend special classes in becoming blind.[84]

Inspired by Cunningham, Johnston elaborates on the central task she set herself and other critics in her first decade of writing: moving "from seeing to entering." She laments how easy—too easy—it is to revert to watching performance in a limited manner, reducing art from "form to function." If the critic (or seemingly any audience member) only sees, they risk stuffing an experience of "new dance" into previously known categories. Instead, Johnston posits a possibility of going beyond seeing, of moving toward understanding performance spectatorship as an encounter between viewer and art—an entering—in which perception and, in turn, the self expand.

Johnston's evocation of "entering" a work of art offers a sensual, even erotic, notion of the relationship between critic and performance, imagining what a fusing of art and viewer might entail. Ann Daly has argued that Johnston's evocative call to move from "seeing to entering" is her most substantial contribution to criticism, describing Johnston as grappling with "the origins of art, self and writing" and reckoning with how criticism is "an inscription of the self onto the world."[85] Johnston sought to "see more"—to avoid the trap of reducing possibility by way of aiming for categorization. To enter, then, is to be enfolded into an artwork, an overlapping that for Johnston was somehow mysterious, more felt than understood. To enter, as Johnston proposes it, is a humble, yet active form of witnessing, one in which the spectator can be transformed, filled with an experience of sensation and feeling cocreated by performer and viewer.

The sensorially shaped, intersubjective relationship between witness and performance that Johnston describes infuses the best of her dance criticism. It contributes to the sense of engagement, even love, with which she writes about both Cunningham and the women she calls the "romantic dancers." It contributes to the sense of presentness (and the complexity of being in the present) that she brings to writing about Happenings. Oddly, it seems perhaps the least present in some of her writing about Judson, where she often seems most removed.

Reflecting on what it was like to read Johnston's sensation-focused, affectively sparkling dance criticism in the early 1960s, Meredith Monk remembers feeling that Johnston was bringing the era's *esprit du jour* of phenomenology and sensation into performance criticism. Monk thought of Johnston as using her "laser brain that she had and that laser eye [and being] able to manifest that broad, philosophical way of thinking" relative to dance.[86] Monk noted that what Johnston did seemed a great deal like what Susan Sontag described in her 1964 essay "Against Interpretation," where the literary and performance critic—and Johnston's contemporary in writing and queerness—called for an "erotics of art."[87]

Placing Sontag's and Johnston's performance criticism alongside one another highlights how Johnston's notion of moving from "seeing to entering" is an "erotics of art." Moreover, Johnston enacts what might be termed an erotics of criticism, writing in a manner that combined language, feeling, and sensation, or as Audre Lorde put it in her essay "The Uses of the Erotic," "a question of how acutely and fully we can feel in the doing."[88] A criticism borne of "erotics of art" or "the erotic" focuses on deepening and expanding perception, not classification or evaluation.

Johnston once told a Sontag biographer, "In our world of the 60s, . . . Susan was the only other lesbian I knew of."[89] The two women had a shared identity and profession but a tenuous bond. They each knew the other had female lovers in the late 1950s and early 1960s, and both had relationships with Childs—Johnston in the 1960s and Sontag decades later. In 1959, just as Sontag returned to New York to take a job at *Commentary*, she wrote she was "becoming aware of how guilty I feel being queer."[90] Johnston could not be more the opposite, eventually becoming, as chapter 3 describes, "America's most out lesbian," coming out most publicly in a 1971 *Village Voice* column but littering her columns years before with vague references to her sexuality. Sontag kept her homosexuality as private as possible (as she did her entire life), while Johnston kept hers as public as possible, if sometimes strategically illegible.

The women's different orientations to their sexualities and publicity bore out in their criticism as well. They were contemporaries as writers in several ways, but Johnston was, much as she was with her sexuality, far more willing to experiment in public. Both Johnston and Sontag were children of the Depression. Johnston was born in 1929, four years before Sontag in 1933. They launched their critical careers in the late 1950s in New York–based publications: Johnston at the *Dance Observer* and then the *Village Voice*, Sontag at *Commentary*, a Jewish-led publication described by one of Sontag's biographers as one of two ideal 1950s publications for those "aspir[ing] to join the intelligentsia."[91] Sontag looked to criticism to help her rise; Johnston looked to criticism to help her foster the egalitarian.

Sontag landed at sites ripe for launching an intellectual career, and Johnston, particularly once she began at the *Voice* in 1960, thrived through publications bent toward experimentation. Historian Kevin McAuliffe has described the *Voice*, particularly in its early years, as offering a "home to writers who could not write any other way."[92] Johnston, as her writing in the *Dance Observer* and *ARTnews* proved, *could* write in many ways, but she *wanted* to write in the creative manner the *Voice* allowed. In contrast, Sontag separated her creativity from her criticism: "Against Interpretation" appeared on the heels of her first novel. Johnston's approach transformed her writing into something incomprehensible to many, while also offering an intensity of feeling. Sontag called for more erotic possibility, but her maintenance of critical distance sent her into greater circulation. Put another way: Sontag became famous; Johnston, in the long run, less so. Seeing held greater intellectual cachet than entering.

Johnston described Sontag as "eloquent even if conservative . . . [and] an original hero of mine."[93] In the 1970s, as Johnston flamed across the pages of the *Voice*, including pondering the sexuality of a number of well-known women (albeit all dead), Sontag worried Johnston would out her, going so far as once calling Johnston and begging her not to reveal her secret.[94] Remembering the phone call, Johnston assured Sontag's biographers she never considered outing her fellow writer, saying she understood Sontag as similar to the closeted gay men in their overlapping art circles (Jasper Johns, for instance): people who kept their sexualities secret in ways that helped maintain their privilege.[95] Distance offered Sontag a form of safety. Meanwhile, Johnston rushed in.

Sontag, however, (at least at the time) wanted more of what Johnston seemed to have: a world full of sensation. In "Against Interpretation" Sontag calls for recovering the senses, writing, "We must learn to *see* more, to *hear* more, to *feel* more."[96] She ends the essay with the sentence, "In place of a hermeneutics we need an erotics of art"—a statement that reveals what the more oft-circulated title of the essay does not: Sontag was arguing *for* something, an "erotics of art," not only "*against* interpretation" (emphasis mine). She imagined a critical "erotics of art" that would result in "a really accurate, sharp, loving description of the appearance of a work of art."[97] She wanted criticism that did not understand the erotic only as part of the sexual realm but rather that understood the erotic as spreading throughout all of the "most vital areas of our lives," as Audre Lorde more fully elaborated years later.[98] This might be lesbian feminist criticism: a criticism that situates both critic and art in the world and in one another's worlds.

What is the path (to borrow Lorde's phrase) to "uses of the erotic" in criticism? Johnston argues that the "mysterious" is the "crucial transition" from seeing to entering.[99] In something of a contrast, Sontag seeks clarity, arguing that criticism imbued with the erotics of art will still be "accurate, sharp." Johnston is not against clarity, but hers is a perceptual clarity, not a clarity that leads to comprehension. As she put it in a 1967 review, she "like[s] things that are certain about not being very sure about what they are."[100] Johnston also imagined criticism imbued with erotics to be a mutual exchange, one that might transform both viewer and viewed.

Sontag writes about performance as a relatively distanced spectator. She strives for accuracy in her rather cold recountings of performance's events and compositional structures, whether her topic is Arthur Miller's play *After the Fall* (1964) or a Happening. For the former, a realist, plot- and character-driven play, perhaps accuracy is more appropriate. Choosing accuracy over immersion is an ill fit, however, with other forms, like Happenings, which even Sontag described, in a 1962 essay, as events "designed to stir the modern audience from its cozy emotional anesthesia."[101] By trying to make sense of Happenings' multiplicity, however, Sontag risks doing what Johnston warns critics against, reducing "form to function." Sontag knew Happenings' "dramatic spine" was their "abusive involvement of the audience," but she offers little sense of what that feels like as a member of an audience. Instead, Sontag focuses her essay about Happenings on historical and theoretical contexts, beginning with the role of speech and text; moving to listing and contextualizing key players in the scene, particularly Allan Kaprow; then delineating features often found in Happenings; and, finally, discussing how they fit into a longer trajectory of art movements, including surrealism and Antonin Artaud's Theatre of Cruelty. Even in the essay's more detailed moments, when describing specific performances she attended, Sontag's distance—a look from the outside, often from above—is palpable. This is her description of a 1961 Kaprow-directed performance: "The spectators were confined inside a long box-like structure resembling a cattle car; peep-holes had been bored in the wooden walls of this enclosure through which the spectators could strain to see the events taking place outside; when the Happening was over, the walls collapsed, and the spectators were driven out by someone operating a power lawnmower."[102] This excerpt exemplifies a criticism designed to describe and assess more than to enter and experience. While the performance almost certainly evoked not just generalized abuse but quite specifically that of the Holocaust, there is little in Sontag's writing that evokes the claustrophobia or fear the moment must have caused, especially for Jewish spectators like Sontag (who elsewhere wrote extensively about the Holocaust).[103] Whether this instance of distancing was one of avoiding trauma or merely Sontag repeating her existing writing pattern is hard to know. The essay otherwise, however, is incredibly thorough—likely a perfect guide for someone new to experimental performance or someone seeking to understand Happenings in relationship to other artistic and intellectual movements. Yet it provides little visceral sense of what it would be like to experience a Happening. Paradoxically, Sontag's writing about Happenings creates exactly the "cozy emotional anesthesia" that Happenings aimed to interrupt.

At a Happening, Sontag might be considered a visitor from uptown. In contrast, Johnston is Happenings' neighbor—in fact and on the page. Reviewing the same Kaprow-directed 1961 Happening as Sontag, Johnston writes, "At last and perforce the spectators are set free, released, 'created,' purged, when the walls of their train-tomb womb can no longer contain them, as a thunderous power lawn mower appears at one end and the sides give way to the ground allowing the spectators to step out with massive relief."[104] With her list of verbs, Johnston connotes how audience members might feel a range of intense reactions, from being "free[d]" to "purged," as their containment ended as the "sides give way." There is also the verb *created*, put in quotation marks by Johnston, perhaps gesturing to how the performance itself discursively created the subjects now called "spectators." In this description there is both multiplicity and mystery. What force makes walls fall? A womb explode?

Johnston also deploys another stylistic choice much used in her writing about performance: an enjambment of individual words, "train-tomb womb," a play with layering the onomatopoeia of words and rhyming of *tomb* and *womb* to further enmesh the two metaphors the container evoked. It's writing that gets into readers' mouths and ears. To read writing like this is to swirl, to be unsure of what exactly happened, even though, as the reader spins, there are also moments where clear images pierce the dizzying array. Intersubjective erotics emerge from the senses of multiple spectators, of multiple bodies having a range of experiences. I feel her and others, and a bit of me, too. It is not the lawnmower from Kaprow's Happening, but our bodies that make the last noise.

If one wanted to experience what it means for a Happening to stir an audience member from "cozy emotional anesthesia" (to borrow Sontag's phrase), Johnston's writing would be the one to choose. Her writing complements the performance, rather than explains it, as Sontag's does. Sontag's aim, however, was different from Johnston's. Discussing "Against Interpretation" over a decade later, she described the essay as a response to the early 1960s, saying, "I don't consider that I ever was a critic. I had ideas, and I attached them to works of art that I admired. Now I attach them to other things."[105] Attachment, for Sontag, can be managed, dismantled, and refocused in another direction. Johnston enacted a messier relationship with the performances she reviewed. From early in her career, she decided that considering a viewer entirely distinct from art, or a critic entirely distinct from artists, was not a useful practice. In criticism Johnston found that there were erotic possibilities of the kind Lorde elucidates, the "shar[ing] of joy" and "mak[ing] connections across similarities and differences."[106]

WHOSE "SERIOUS"?

Johnston and Sontag provide a compelling comparison beyond a formal analysis of their writing. Writing about the two women's relationship to feminism, early Sontag biographers Carl E. Rollyson and Lisa Olson Paddock described Johnston as a "fascinating figure to match against Sontag" because "Johnston . . . was doing what Sontag could only urge others to do," and then they go further, arguing that Johnston was "not afraid to look extreme" whereas Sontag "would not risk the marginalization that radical behavior virtually guaranteed."[107] Johnston became a symbol of lesbian feminism (or, as Rollyson and Paddock put it, a "militant lesbian feminist"), and Sontag a more tentative supporter. As Angela McRobbie has argued, Sontag worked to create an "intellectual space which she . . . defined as her own . . . [and] in which gender d[id] not figure . . . [at a time] where there was no critical space for women unless they demonstrably transcended gender."[108] In many respects, in both her writing and her public persona, Sontag benefited from emerging feminist movements, but she distanced herself from feminism through a pretense of transcending gender at the level of the individual. Johnston did the opposite, eventually allowing her writing to lead her deeper into discussions of how gender mattered.

These differing positions on writing and its relationship to gender and sexuality are more than a simple binary of timidity versus tenacity. Rather, Johnston's actions, when compared with Sontag's provocations, reflect how each woman imagined herself as a public intellectual. They index these differences in their reckonings with what it meant to be *serious*, a word both women toyed with in public and in private. Sontag's idea of *serious* revolved around inhabiting roles generally held and largely defined by men. Johnston saw *serious* as a term in need of revision, queering what it meant to be a serious critic.

"A serious intellectual dance critic": that is how Jill Johnston described herself in her 1983 memoir, *Mother Bound*. But Johnston often did not fit within the images such a phrase might conjure. Playful imagining, not distanced discernment, was central to her work. Rainer remembers Johnston as a particularly playful (and physical) presence among the art and social scenes of the early 1960s, recalling getting to know Johnston not at performances but in offstage spaces: Dunn's workshop and parties, where Johnston could often be found hanging upside down from the pipes that ran along loft ceilings.[109] Such images might seem incongruous with Johnston's description of herself as a "serious intellectual dance critic," but perhaps these playful, physical romps were an apt response to the art scene Johnston covered, a world in "a convulsion of dissolving boundaries."[110] What does it mean to categorize oneself as serious when all the rules are being either discarded or rewritten?

Johnston's serious critical play, though, cannot only be attributed to the art that inspired her and that she centered in her writing. Rather, in *Mother Bound*, Johnston suggests that her work toward serious critical play also emerged from how she had learned to manage being a woman (and a girl) in public. In the book, Johnston frequently deploys the term *serious* to distance herself from ill-fitting gender norms. Writing about growing up in the mid-twentieth-century white, middle-class neighborhoods and schools of the East Coast, Johnston uses *serious* to reference her simultaneous understanding that gender norms were constructed and that failing at the expectations placed on women could have grave consequences. Of life in her all-girls boarding school, Johnston writes, "Playacting as a girl was a serious social business."[111] Gender norms were deeply connected to norms of dating and sexuality. "Playing as a girl" required "having a proper boyfriend," a goal Johnston did not have initially, preferring to be "one of the boys" and have crushes on and close intimacies with girls. After realizing it was an inevitable part of the role of girl in which others had cast her, she did eventually get a boyfriend from a nearby boys' school. Every time she stepped into the role of girl, however, even when trying to do it correctly—as she did by acquiring the boyfriend—Johnston recognized her gender performance as "playacting . . . [despite] her feelings of loss and inadequacy [being] very real." Knowing that by being "a girl" she took on a "role" in a script of normative femininity did not lessen the stakes of performing the role badly.[112]

Five years into her career as a critic, the year she began writing for the *Voice* and the year she left her marriage to a man, Johnston found her version of serious. In the downtown New York social and arts scenes of the 1960s, Johnston saw examples of "playacting" toward different outcomes, ways to be serious with more open and imaginative ends. In her arts community and neighborhood, she found "the kind of serious milieu of displaced people [who] welcomed individuality and difference; any mark of individuality was valued over the bourgeois criteria of excellence: prosperity, prominence, and correctness."[113] In this scene Johnston learned that the skills and activities of playacting toward normativity could be rerouted, not into inhabiting existing social roles, but, instead, into imagining new possibilities. This new mode of seriousness suited Johnston perfectly and benefited her writing deeply.

Sontag also deemed being serious as central to her desires from an early age, but her serious was rather different from Johnston's. If Johnston's serious was about creating new modes of being through play and frivolity, Sontag's was more about deprivation. Writing in her daily journal after a night at the Paris Opera at the age of twenty-six (one year before she returned to New York to begin writing professionally), Sontag mused, "Seriousness is really a virtue for me, one of the few which [I] accept existentially and will emotionally. I love being gay and forgetful, but this only has meaning against the background imperative of seriousness."[114] The statement comes from a ping-pong-ing discussion (it's a journal after all) of a production of *Don Giovanni*, an entry in which Sontag chastises herself for thinking "religion must be serious, or it's not really religion." She goes on, noting that play—which is clearly, for Sontag, the opposite of serious—is key to many religions. Nevertheless, she still lands in a somber notion of the serious. Play can only be possible if one also embraces its opposite. *New Yorker* writer Tobi Haslett has argued that Sontag imagined being serious as her life's work, pointing to the 1958 Paris entry and a later journal entry where Sontag describes a writer's work as being someone who will "love words, agonize over sentences, pay attention to the world and be serious."[115] Sontag persistently saw the critic as attentive, focused, and somber.

For Johnston, being normatively serious (as Sontag sought to be) was a form of mimicry destined to fail. Johnston saw those who were widely understood to be serious as seeking to meet social expectations, an effort she found deeply uncreative. Having watched her high school classmates try to "playact as a girl" and seeing something similar when she studied at the Limón school, where teachers asked her to take on "imitating" the women dancing around her and work at "dallying seriously in their field," Johnston searched for other options.[116] She wanted "to make things up on [her] own and ceas[e] leading the life of an adult protégé."[117] Playacting at normative seriousness, at social norms—especially gendered ones—had to end for Johnston to find her creative voice as the playful dance critic and writer she would become.

Johnston's work of queer self-making, of refusing to be trapped in a gendered developmental narrative, began just as she "wrapped it all up as a dancer and [became] a serious intellectual dance critic."[118] The art world of the 1960s, the "serious milieu of displaced people like myself," offered seriousness on queer terms.[119] A serious Johnston could access art without having to assume a gendered way of being she did not want. Sontag felt thwarted by the messy world that Johnston felt freed by. Later in the 1960s Sontag lamented that, because of the entertainment industry's effect on art, intellect, and politics, "seriousness itself was in the early stages of losing credibility."[120] In contrast, Johnston often dismissed those she found lacking in their sense of play, charging them with being "insufficiently lighthearted," a paradoxical phrase she borrowed from Dada pioneer and conceptual artist Marcel Duchamp.[121] Johnston's serious dance criticism *was* sufficiently lighthearted: she could bounce among the scenes she covered (including sometimes bouncing onstage herself), and, as the next chapter discusses, sometimes hilariously blur the lines between audience and performer.

Blurring

Johnston's 1964 review "Fluxus Fuxus," which more closely resembles found art than it does a performance review, was the first indication that she was evolving her writing beyond something immediately recognizable as criticism.[122] Writing later about what that review foretold, Johnston described it as "an early fluke in containing almost all methods that I later advanced self-consciously."[123] Another significant shift, though not of Johnston's choosing, occurred a year later when she was admitted to Bellevue Hospital and labeled schizophrenic.[124] That was the Bellevue stay during which Johnston's "Critics' Critics" came to be. After her release she returned to writing for the *Voice*, her column retitled "Dance Journal."[125]

Johnston's first column published under the new title was a pessimistic one. In it, she lists all the reasons she thinks dance will never be a major art form, especially when compared to the visual arts.[126] She seems to be drifting away from dance, but it is not as though the thriving visual art scene of the mid-1960s captured her either. Her last writing for *ARTnews* appeared in February 1966. In the *Village Voice*, Johnston still wrote eloquently, but her descriptions—what helped her and so many others enter work from that of Ailey to Rainer—became so detailed that she almost eliminates the possibility for the reader to imagine outward. The density forecloses the possibility of entering with all its mystery and transformative potential.

By the end of 1965, Johnston no longer thought of herself as a dance critic. But I do. In fact, I think of Johnston as a dance critic her entire life—into the next five years when she would become an avant-garde celebrity and as dance became just one among many topics in her *Voice* column. To understand Johnston's relationship to dance from 1965 forward, it's useful to track her development alongside the artists she loved, particularly Childs, her lover and one of her Judson favorites. Johnston's writing about a Childs performance, which appeared in the 1965 farewell to Judson, is worth quoting at length:

> The observers were instructed by a voice on tape to look out the sixth-floor windows while Childs descended in the elevator and crossed the street to stand or sit on a convenient car fender; in the area designated by the "voice" as the area to look at. The voice went on to describe details—signs, items in windows, etc.—within the fixed zone, and the amazing thing that happened from behind closed windows, was that the plebian tract, much like any other stretch of jammed buildings that people ordinarily have no reason to notice, became not only fascinating in its static detail, but also a frame, stage, screen, or whatever for normal activities intensified by the theatrical illusion. A woman passing by was caught in the art. She didn't know it and neither did a fire engine which emerged at the last moment. Quite a dramatic fire engine. So, salut, '64, and more rooms with a view in '65.[127]

I ponder Johnston standing at the window, listening to the recorded directions, while watching her recent ex-lover on the sidewalk. She focuses on Childs but also lets her gaze soften and widen as it expands. She notices, even feels, all that surrounds her: dancer, passersby, and fire engine. Through watching dance, she has taught herself how to focus on a single moving body and let that lead to something bigger, no spectacle needed. I imagine she feels both the intensity and pleasure of the blurring of art and life—a blurring that was so important to all the Happenings and the dancing she had witnessed over the past decade. Her mind riffs on Virginia Woolf: the cherished isolation of "a room with a view," but goes plural, "more rooms with a view." She wants more for herself—to go outside, as the dancers had done and were doing. And so she did, prepared by all that dance had taught her.

INTERRUPTION 1

Up on the Roof

Andy Warhol's film Jill and Freddy Dancing (1963) *is a black-and-white rendering of a man and woman dancing on a New York City rooftop. Years later, Jill colored in more details in a* Voice *column: her gown is blue chiffon; the roof-turned-stage is the building where painter (and Warhol's buddy) Wynn Chamberlain lived.*[1] *Freddy is Fred Herko, the choreographer and dancer whose campy wit she loved. Warhol and his camera perch above, voyeurs watching two friends cavorting on an urban roof on a summer afternoon.*

It is fitting that Warhol—a queer filmmaker interested in the mundane—was the one to capture the most footage of Jill Johnston dancing. About Warhol's two films featuring Johnston, *Jill and Freddy Dancing* (1963) and *Jill Johnston Dancing* (1964), I almost want to write that they show us how Johnston moved her body and how she danced, except that as I write that, I know it's not true. Her writing already showed us how she moved. To read her writing about performance or everyday events is to walk with, almost walk in, Johnston's body. It's no wonder that often when critics and scholars try to describe Johnston's writing, their prose leans toward the kinesthetic: performance artist Lil Picard describes the writing as a "dream dance of words," art critic and longtime Johnston admirer Jennifer Krasinski says the prose is "perambulatory," and art historian Jenny Sichel (borrowing from Joan Didion) says Johnston's prose "slouches."[2] All seek to capture the physicality of reading Johnston.

She gets into her body and yours, an overlap that is exciting but that also threatens to disappear the specificities of her body in motion. This is one reason the Warhol films are important. Most images of Johnston dancing, whether she's in a leotard at the barre or in costume amid an arms-linked ensemble, are at odds with the commanding, if playful, physical presence she became. The Warhol films present not the student dancer but her early 1960s self, a performer Deborah Hay remembers as "always involv[ing] language and confront[ation], slightly angry, but full of humor."[3]

That 1960s Jill danced as well as wrote, and often infamously so. In John Cage's *Music Walk with Dancer* (1962), Johnston dropped her copy of the score in a puddle en route to the show. Instead of asking for another copy, she made up her own score while performing, drawing heavily on the mundane tasks of motherhood, producing what performance theorist Shannon Jackson has described as a "vacuum-ridden extravaganza."[4] In Allan Kaprow's 1964 production of *Originale*, Johnston, as she put it in the *Voice* a week later, "did [her] best to disrupt the performances of the other artists involved."[5] Kaprow must have guessed this would be the outcome. In a typecasting move if there ever was one, he designated Johnston the production's "free agent."[6]

The first thing Jill does in Jill and Freddy Dancing? *She puts down her beer. Now unencumbered, standing tall atop a chair, she lifts her arms and then lets her shoulders sway. Her elbows slide, drop, then slice, tossing her hands back and forth. Her motion is precise and elegant, like the conducting of an unseen orchestra. There is a slight awkwardness too. I am reminded of Johnston's comment about a 1964 performance she did with Yvonne Rainer, before which she drank a fifth of vodka: "I could not have performed for an audience of dodo birds without alcohol," she said.*[7] *The audience, not the dancing, was the problem. The beer on that roof must have been an early afternoon one: her movements are decidedly clear and specific. Her slight awkwardness is more likely the residue of not quite wanting to be watched. Yet, still, she makes her appearance.*

Herko wants to be watched. He appears suddenly, wearing tight, white briefs and baring a slight but muscled torso. Jill continues her conducting motion, unfazed. His execution exhibits perfect balletic form. She towers above. Her motion is increasingly buoyant, making the restriction in Herko's ballet all the more visi-

ble. He circles Jill's chair, repeating a short balletic phrase (tombé, pas de bourrée, sauté)—transition steps usually deployed to connect one spectacular thing to another. He exits, and she gathers the air around her and then, with flicks of her wrists, tosses air and energy skyward. Warhol cuts away, almost as though she told him to do so. The spectacular thing—the thing to which all Herko's transitions should lead—never arrives.

Neither Johnston's dancing nor Warhol's camera fully elaborates a subject. That seems choice, not accident, from these then thirty-something queer folks. Warhol's sexuality was always decidedly queer but never quite clearly so. As Jennifer Doyle, Jonathan Flatley, and José Muñoz argue in their introduction to the volume *Pop Out: Queer Warhol* (1996), Warhol was neither "entirely 'out' nor 'in' the closet."[8] The same was true for Johnston at the time Warhol made *Jill and Freddy Dancing*. Especially in comparison to her later lesbian publicity, Johnston's lesbianism was a murky point on an otherwise full canvas. Her involvement with dancer Lucinda Childs was neither entirely hidden nor fully known. As the 1960s went on, both Johnston and Warhol more clearly marked themselves as queer, or at least avant-garde, and they were often paired together—particularly by art collector and patron John de Menil—who brought them to art-world parties to infuse the events with boundary-crossing celebrity appeal. It worked, and it didn't. Writing about a trip to Houston with Warhol for a de Menil–hosted premiere of Warhol's *Lonesome Cowboys* (1968), Johnston wrote, "Andy is really too much."[9]

But here, in the time and space of *Jill and Freddy Dancing*, there is no notoriety. What Doyle, Flatley, and Muñoz write of Warhol is likely true for Johnston too: he and she were "manag[ing] . . . identity and . . . cultural contexts . . . rooted in the fifties, before Stonewall and before identity politics."[10] Dancing's porosity—meaning offered but rarely explained—is a good, even ideal, medium for suggesting queerness without making a full reveal. Dancing the transitions without offering the expected spectacle, recognition without confirmation.

That summer of 1963, Johnston and Warhol shared another identity: both had become fans of choreographer and dancer Yvonne Rainer, particularly her recently premiered evening-length *Terrain*, Rainer's reimagining of Merce Cunningham's chance methods for arranging choreography. Johnston dedicated two entire columns to the work, calling it "a brilliant culmination of a style and method."[11] *Terrain* inspired Warhol's first experimental film, *Sleep*, a five-hour movie he composed by splicing and resplicing together twenty-two three-minute takes of his lover, John Giorno, sleeping.[12] Johnston first described the experience of watching *Terrain* as akin to the meditative quality of "stringing beads." A week later, she muses over the effect of watching slow, repetitive, everyday tasks, arguing that *Terrain*'s appeal arises from Rainer making the work's methods of construction visible, while also providing the sense that there is more to witness than simply "understanding" the method.[13] In *Terrain*, as Johnston saw it, there was nothing to decode; instead, she had an experience with the everyday aspects of how people move and connect—or don't. She comments on the work's "love duet," danced by Rainer and William Davis, writing, "The content is really something but it's always the transformation that makes you care."[14] It's a sentence worth hanging on to (and a sentence that provides a useful frame for watching Warhol's work too).

When we last saw Jill, she was tossing her arms and wrists up and into the air. Warhol's film's splice, a technique with which he must have been newly experimenting, comes just after. A hiccup, a fast-forward, or a trip, and Jill is on the ground. The chair has disappeared, as has Herko. Jill begins a cantilevered solo, taking jerky, awkward side steps to cross the roof's square expanse. She launches from the ball of one foot to the other, causing a slight pulse in her pelvis and leaving her upper body drifting just behind the lower. The tiny jerks—the shifts in weight and direction as her body tries to go in multiple directions at once—register (again) as a mix of her being awkward and in control. She raises her arms and then opens them above her head, continuing to travel forward, her gaze and chest surging upward. Her momentum never wanes, her constancy confirming that control will win. She manages her awkwardness without having to fully subsume it. Transformation is happening.

We met a woman on a pedestal (her chair), encircled by a princely man (Herko in that first balletic step), but these balletic ingredients do not add up to what they could: a chivalrous hand offered to help her step down from the chair, a focus on man and woman together. Instead, the focus remains on Johnston: she got down on her own, took up the space on her own, and refashioned balletic vocabulary on her own.

Herko returns, launching himself into a much bigger circle this time, but she never notices him. Instead, she flips her body to face the opposite direction and continues her awkward ballet: bourrées become giant gallops. Her only partner is her long hair, which whips from side to side, sometimes falling in front of her face. She doesn't need to see.

In *Jill and Freddy Dancing*, Herko gets the one transition step—the beginning one—but then he's stuck. All the other transitions belong to Jill, and of them she creates (with the blessing of Warhol's gaze) the film's transformations. What could have been a hetero, chivalry-driven balletic pas de deux goes queer. A man and woman dance together, but she takes the center as dancer, not object.

Once the highest, the tallest, now she has the most expansive solo. Her hips swish. Her elbows drip. She sways; her torso swings above stuttering feet. To Herko's laser-like diagonal progress just behind her, she offers a jerky hip thrust—a small joke, not seduction. A man and a woman dance playfully together, separately, not alone, not toward one another, not coupled. A controlled jerk of her knee propels her forward, and then the rest of her body meets, then passes, the knee's mark. Herko (again with the ballet): tombé, fifth position, tombé, fifth position—always with his chest high. These two dancers offer two visions of control and exactitude, side by side.

Together Jill and Freddy dance a possibility for a man and woman to be present together without becoming a man and a woman whose only possibility is a hetero coupling. Biology does not foretell destiny here. Their dance together and apart recalls Johnston's writing about her love of Dada, an aesthetic she once summed up by writing, "'Why shouldn't this go with that and be called something else.' Why not indeed?"[15] One rooftop, three queers, many genders (see figures 1a.1 and 1a.2).

Another splice. Freddy's gone.

This jump in the 1963 film is a painful foreshadowing of how Herko's life would end just a year later, when the man whom artist Carolee Schneemann remembers as a "magical, dancing, flying, impossible, mad boy—so sweet, so well intentioned"—either jumped or fell from a friend's fifth-floor apartment midperformance.[16] Whether it was a planned suicide, the outcome of being overwhelmed by amphetamines, or both, Warhol's film almost predicts Herko's demise, both in Herko's abrupt departure from the side-by-side dancing scene with Johnston and in the film's final close-ups, a series of flashes on Herko's face, beautiful yet melancholy.

Perhaps it is this foretelling of a queer life ended too soon that fueled a surge of interest in *Jill and Freddy Dancing* in the early 2000s, a flurry of engagement that almost always centered on Herko's role in the film, so much so that Johnston almost disappeared.[17] Art historian Paisid Aramphongphan celebrates the film's queer refusal of the "strict gender codes" of the balletic world it references, describing it as "providing space for queer voices—or queer bodies, rather—to shine."[18] Yet as he dives deeper into the film's creation and analysis, only Warhol and Herko get attention. If a woman is not paired with a man as his partner—his wife, his ballerina, his beautiful object to be lifted—can she still share the stage with him and be seen?[19] Even in queer readings (especially in queer readings?), women too easily disappear.

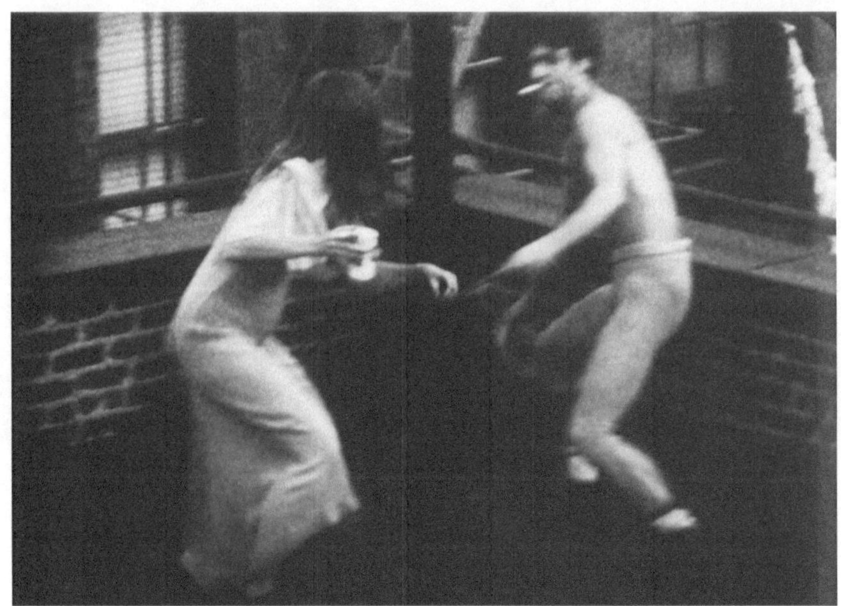

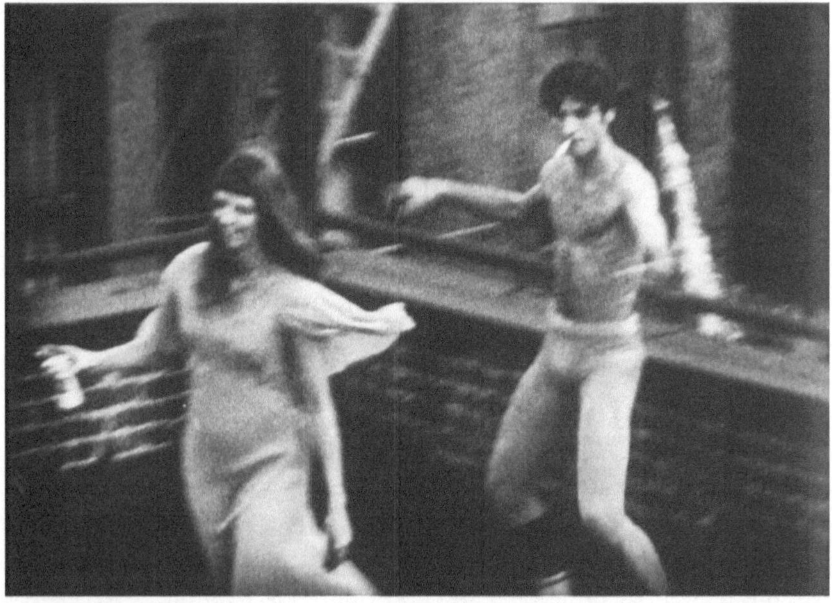

INTERI.1 AND INTERI.2 Jill Johnston and Fred Herko in Andy Warhol's 16mm film *Jill and Freddy Dancing* (1963). Film stills courtesy of the Andy Warhol Museum.

But keep watching her. Warhol's camera stays on her, with her. If you count, she gets the most screen time. If you track the transitions, they are a window into her *transformations, as well as that of the couple's possibilities.*

Johnston was a Herko fan. Writing about his *Binghamton Birdie*, which he premiered later in the summer of 1963 wearing only one roller skate, Johnston lauded his ability to bring together a "strange logic of parts that have no business being together, but which go together anyway because anything in life can go with anything else if you know what you're doing."[20]

The film jumps again. Now it is Jill's turn to demonstrate that she, too, can engage in this Dadaist/camp mélange of "strange logics." What Aramphongphan describes in Jill and Freddy Dancing *as Jill's "own looser twist" on ballet, I see as "her own looser wrist." In this, her second solo, Jill again travels through as much space as possible, making big, awkward, knee-leading steps, toward the roof's edge. She grabs a metal rod that dangles above and then, holding it as though it is an anchor, throws herself forward and sideways. She eventually launches herself into a series of turns, precipitated by the weight and momentum of her long leg, which whips behind and then around her. These tornado-like turns unfurl and repeat with such abandon that it is difficult to discern what causes their repetition: Jill's choices or Warhol's editing. Whoever the culprit, there is more and more and more and more of Jill.*

Another splice, and suddenly she has props. Frisbees? Records? Trash? For every object she throws over the roof's edge, more of the disk-like objects appear, tossed in from unseen hands. This is likely Herko at work, giving Jill new material for her increasingly ridiculous solo. It's the epitome of what she enjoys in other people's work: intriguing nonsense.

Just as both roof and screen seem close to being overwhelmed by these many disks, another jump and Jill is high again—this time atop a corner of the roof, grinning at us as she perches one foot against the ledge and steadies herself using a pole she grips and drives into the ground. A big grin spreads across her face. Now I can actually feel her: the physical pleasure amassed from completing all these ridiculous tasks spreads her lips and reveals her teeth. Grinning wit. The slight dangle in her limbs suggests a bit of exhaustion too, but it's the pleasurable kind.

As Susan Sontag would write of camp a year later, one can be "serious about the frivolous, frivolous about the serious."[21] Johnston already knew that, having learned it from her voluminous wordplay and her dancing. Herko made campy work of ballet early in *Jill and Freddy Dancing*. But Jill tells the rest of the story: men hold no special purchase on camp, the sensibility du jour. Writing about when Warhol showed the film for the first time at the Gramercy Theatre, Johnston says both she and the audience loved it. Of her comedic performance, she refuses the comparison her friend David Bourdon made of her dancing to that of swimming film star Esther Williams. Instead, she offers up Bea Lillie, a midcentury actress and comedian known for being able to make seemingly anything into double entendre, a practice Lillie often punctuated with a wink at the audience.[22] Johnston's wink comes in grin form, a suggestion that her body isn't quite telling the full story.

The next and final series of images—quick cuts among a myriad of close-ups on Jill's face—allows her joy to linger, even as close-ups of Herko close the film. The last flashes of her face: gaze focused just past the camera, mouth open, slight grin. She is lesbian camp.

2

She Was an Audience

. . . just another ordinary evening in the life of a lady gangster . . .
—Jill Johnston in the *Village Voice*, 1968

In 1965, in Buffalo, New York, Jill Johnston stood on a box. The occasion of her standing was the Buffalo Gala Festival of the Arts, for which Johnston had curated two programs. For one program she chose artists she had recently written so much about: those at the center of the Judson Dance Theater, including Yvonne Rainer, Lucinda Childs, and sculptor-turned-dancer Robert Morris. Her other curated program featured Johnston herself in what she called a "lecture-event." Such events were solo performances created and performed by Johnston that, in form and in their focus on her as critic-turned-performer, confused distinctions among performer, critic, and audience. As Johnston described them, "lecture-events" combined "action tableaux" (hence Johnston standing on that box) with recordings of herself "reading passages about art or fragments of conversation or quotes or newspaper items."[1] Her critic persona sonically encircled her performing body.

As Johnston had often admired in Judson and in Happenings, lecture-events frequently featured interactions with objects to create a "moment of transition from a static construction to the kind of construction that invites manipulation."[2] At the Buffalo event, two objects functioned in this manner: the box on which Johnston first stood and a rectangular column built for her by Morris. The latter hung from the ceiling and was designed to support Johnston's weight if she hung from it . . . but only for a few seconds. The likelihood of the column giving way was a design Morris and Johnston agreed on to highlight not just the object's invitation to manipulation but the causal chain set off by a person manipulating the object. When Johnston engaged the rectangular column, both parties, performer and object, changed.

By standing on the box as her recorded critic voice filled the air around her, Johnston created a scene that transformed the box into a soapbox, accentuating her usual roles in the theater as critic and performance expert. But then, stepping down from the box, she ceded her elevated status. She crossed the stage and leapt up to grab the column suspended above. Gravity took over. The lecture-event ended with Johnston sitting on the floor, the remains of Morris's artwork all around her. The critic, the most particular of audience members, had come to the stage, invited by art objects, and caused the whole show to fall apart.

Johnston was immediately critical of her performance. Sitting on the floor amid that pile of broken material, she felt that "from a symbolic point of view, [the moment was] perhaps interesting, but as an event [it] left something to be desired."[3] Making the symbolism's point so visible, the destructive role that critics can play, had superseded the physical action. Johnston had long been dismissive of performance she viewed as too reliant on "symbolic form," which she derided as "artful exaggeration, dilution, [and] idealization."[4] She thought that performance's most radical potential emerged in instances where an audience saw "itself nakedly reflected"—saw someone engaging with an object, an obstacle, a situation in a real way, in public, with others.[5] By Johnston's standard, her Buffalo lecture-event failed because it merely symbolized the relationship between critic and performance, rather than actually transforming it.

In her writing, in her life, and in her occasional performances, Jill Johnston was always most interested in situations in which the boundary between performer and audience transformed beyond either party's control. In these mixed-up moments, the presence of the audience truly mattered. The audience was not just present *for* the performers; the audience was central to making meaning, to making action, and to creating the possibility of a performance as a site of reorientation for all involved.

This chapter focuses on Jill Johnston's approach to being an audience member: how she theorized and reimagined what could take place in a theater, especially the active role audience members can take in the transformations and reorientations that are often the hallmark of experimental performance. For Johnston, being a spectator was a mode of physical, desirous experimentation—not a passive act of watching. When artists did not make space for such a possibility in their performances, Johnston was fully capable of taking on that challenge herself. If Johnston's first ten years of writing, the focus of chapter 1, involved her recognizing how a critic could scramble the categories by which art is assessed, then her work from 1965 to 1970 imagined the critic as part of the show, even if she was still in her seat.

I begin my investigation of Johnston's critical transformations in this period by tracking her impulse toward disruption and reimagination, which grew from her refusal of the role of expert. Johnston was always suspicious of expertise, but as she found herself elevated in the mid-1960s as *the* expert on the so-called *new dance*, she turned her suspicion into action—otherwise, she was in danger of becoming the very type of critic she had critiqued. I then turn to Johnston's interest in the possibilities that emerge when artists understand the audience as composed of people with sensing bodies, a theory Johnston explored through her frequent citations of French director, playwright, and theorist Antonin Artaud. Inspired by Artaud, Johnston turned her column into a performance site itself, extending the blurring of lines between audience and performer into the realm of reading as well. This blurring can be best seen in Johnston's writing about Charlotte Moorman—another woman in New York's avant-garde who centered her work on the disruptive effects her body could cause. Finally, I consider a particular writing strategy Johnston developed, what I call *powerlisting*, writing lists toward performative outcomes to highlight queer possibilities and communities among audiences. I offer Johnston's powerlisting practice as worthy of consideration alongside Black lesbian feminist theorist and poet Audre Lorde's use of lists as a strategy for queerly making declarations to audiences, one way both women acknowledged and celebrated the complexity of collectivity that constitutes being an audience.

Late 1960s/New Jill

Jill Johnston did not entirely desire the platforms she had gained by the latter half of the 1960s. By 1965 Judson Dance Theater, the dance movement based in downtown New York that Johnston had prominently chronicled in the *Voice*, had splintered. The artists at Judson's core were making their way into other collective and solo endeavors, leaving Johnston's writing as the most obvious representation of what had unfolded in Judson—a strange circumstance for a writer whose attraction to Judson was partially due to the group's resistance to institutionalization.[6] In August 1965, *New York Times* dance and music critic Allen Hughes published an overview of what he called "the 'avant garde' movement in dance," paying particular attention to the writers who had publicized that "movement." Johnston was one of the four writers discussed and, of the four, the only one who still wrote regularly for an (increasingly) mainstream publication.[7] Judson and Johnston were now effectively synonymous.

Johnston further cemented the connection. In the volume *The New American Arts* (1965), which charted developments in film, theater, poetry, painting, dance, and music, Johnston contributed the sole essay on dance, giving outsized space to Judson. The essay, like Johnston's dance criticism, covers an array of concert dance aesthetics in Europe and the United States: Marius Petipa's nineteenth-century ballet; early twentieth-century modern dance; a lesser-known group that Johnston labeled "lyric," namely, Merle Marsicano; and the group Johnston saw as Judson's forerunners, Merce Cunningham, Aileen Passloff, and James Waring. But then she devotes the entire latter half of the essay to Judson, despite it lasting for less than three years of the hundred-plus-year history she covers. The essay ends by suggesting Judson as both the present and the future of American dance, with Johnston stating "that the major directions in the dance of the next decade or two will be largely the result of the adventurous work of members of this group [Judson]."[8] Despite no longer actually existing, the Judson Dance Theater was New York's most prominent form of concert dance, and Johnston its voice.

Still, Johnston remained uninterested in being an expert, let alone the sole expert institutionalizing a movement she valued for resisting memorialization.[9] She had regularly announced her suspicion of experts through her critiques of art-world "panels," which she argued were sites where experts just told people what to think. "If the idea is to be instructive I don't believe in it. Nobody wants to be instructed," quipped Johnston after a panel organized by Robert Morris (maker of her 1965 box).[10]

Instead of embracing her status as expert, Johnston constantly sought to undermine rather than elevate expertise. Building on her lecture solo-events, she began creating situations where everyone—speakers and audience alike—shaped the rules of engagement. In the fall of 1968 Johnston orchestrated such an event at New York University (NYU), and then described it in a column titled "The Unhappy Spectator." For the event, she provided a performance score for both panelists and audience that offered panelists a range of possible physical actions they could do and invited audience members to tackle panel speakers whenever they felt a speaker should stop talking.[11] The resulting event included an audience member yelling "Fire," a man undressing onstage, and a Merce Cunningham dancer appearing with a pig. The panel performance ended with all the original panelists in the audience, a small child left alone in a panelist's seat onstage, and the pig loose in NYU's Loeb Student Center. Johnston described the event as a success because it "proved that everybody who came to hear a panel was good enough to be on it too."[12] Janet Solinger, a NYU special events manager, recalled that the pig (whose name was Wilhemina) attended the performance panel's after-party at Johnston's apartment.[13]

A year later, Johnston brought a similarly chaotic format to another panel she organized, also at NYU, "Disintegration of a Critic." Her status as critical expert was the night's primary and stated target. Andy Warhol moderated a panel composed of artists Charlotte Moorman and Lil Picard, arts patrons John de Menil and Walter Gutman, critics Gregory Battcock and David Bourdon, and activist Ultra Violet. The group honored Johnston but questioned—seemingly at her invitation—her contribution to criticism. Bourdon provided a glimpse of the night's odd tension in the tone of his remarks: "The reason that we do pay so much attention to her [Johnston] tonight—and every night—is that her past writings have proved to be so prophetic that we can't really ignore her."[14] Part of the joke seemed to be that Johnston wasn't even there, although she did appear toward the end. When asked where she had been, she responded, "Screwing."

The comedy and chaos of Johnston's panel performances belie the thoughtful experimentation Johnston was doing. Anyone who has ever grown bored during a panel discussion knows how the format can easily go dry, in its instruction and/or in its inattention to bodies. The public experiments Johnston curated helped her intervene in these dynamics and manifest the shifts her criticism had been taking ever since she wrote "Critics' Critics" in 1965, the essay discussed in chapter 1 in which she imagined critics working alongside artists, not looking down on them and their work from on high. But it was not only the role of the critic Johnston wanted to reimagine; she was also reimagining the role of the audience.

Johnston's experiments with audience encounters happened just as she experienced a series of dislocations and disruptions in her personal life. In 1965 friends checked her into New York's mental hospital, Bellevue, where she was given a diagnosis of "chronic undifferentiated schizophrenia."[15] She spent much of that summer and early fall in Bellevue, and then Mt. Sinai, writing "Critics' Critics" from the former. A year later, she was again committed at Bellevue and then sent to the psychiatric ward at St. Vincent's. Through all this, Johnston entertained an open, even optimistic view, often referring to this period as a time of having a "breakthrough" instead of a "break down."[16] (She was also, however, open about the depth of abuse she encountered as a ward of the mental health complex, a perspective explored in greater depth in chapter 4.)

In part because of her hospitalizations, Johnston wrote for the *Voice* substantially less in 1965 and 1966, publishing only eight and ten columns respectively in each year. (She was also let go from *ARTnews* in 1966, further reducing her writing outlets.) By 1967 she was back to her prehospitalization rate of writing, producing seventeen columns for the *Voice* over the course of the year. In this period her position with the newspaper changed in yet another way as well. Partially in reaction to Johnston writing less and partially in response to her columns growing less recognizable as dance reviews, the paper displaced her as its primary dance critic and hired Deborah Jowitt to fill the role. Running under Johnston's former column title, "Dance," Jowitt's first dance review appeared in the *Voice* on November 9, 1967. Johnston's column began running under a new title, "Dance Journal." For the next two years, 1968 and 1969, she produced thirty-plus columns per year, essays in which her deepest transformations as a writer took place. Looking back on her pre-1967 portfolio, Johnston assessed it (with the exception of a review of a Robert Whitman Happening discussed in the introduction) as "constant detritus."[17]

Johnston's writing in 1968 was nothing short of a new day for criticism—if *criticism* can even remotely capture what she began to create. As she put it, "I pushed the work, my review object, further and further out of the frame. By the summer of 1968 I was finally writing about 'everything else.'"[18] "Everything else" held a multitude of possibilities. Dance remained a force in the work, if no longer its obvious topic. Reflecting on the shift in her personal journal years later, she called her new approach "IMPROVISING writing." *Improvising* appeared not just in all caps but underlined twice.[19]

These late 1960s shifts grew from choice, circumstance, and a deep commitment to experimentation as a way to circumvent being crowned a critical expert. Instead, Johnston tried on a myriad of identities, personal and professional, many of which she documented in the memoir *Paper Daughter* (1985), which focuses on her life from 1965 to 1969. A partial list of the identities she ascribes to herself in this period is telling, in volume and content: "astronaut"; "weak mother" (in relationship to understanding the critic-artist relationship); one of "the husbands"; "artists' intellectual buddy"; "insider's outsider"; "insider's critic"; "the wrong kind of girl"; someone "wish[ing] to be a daughter of a (great) man"; "act[ing] in many ways like a man but . . . still only a girl"; French poet Guillaume Apollinaire's daughter, granddaughter, and niece; Apollinaire himself; "aspiring to be Jewish (incorporating black elements)"; "pre-patient"; "prepolitical"; "a mother's son"; "a girl"; "entertainer at large, party smasher, and queen of fools"; "candidate for that rare breed: the acceptable outsider"; "NOT a real boy"; "a real girl," made so "by falling irrevocably in love"; "privileged poor"; "writer"; "lover"; and, finally, "mascot to the rich."[20] The range in these descriptors is massive and includes so many possibilities: a spectrum of gender identities, roles in the art world, a white person longing to be a racial or ethnic other, and a dead French poet.

She was blurring everything around her, in her life, in her art, and in the collision between the two. As she had put it—joyously—in a December 1967 column, after being told she liked "non-art," "If we prefixed all our indications of things with 'non' we'd always be looking elsewhere for things. The confusion would be terrific. Probably the world is too sure about its things. I like things that are certain about not being very sure about what they are."[21] As 1967 turned to 1968, terrific confusions were becoming Jill Johnston's thing.

Reimagining Spectatorship / Watching with Artaud and Moorman

Paradox, often bolstered by evocations of the sensorial, characterized much of Jill Johnston's approach to writing as the late 1960s spun on. The line (which is worth repeating), "I like things that are certain about not being very sure about what they are," provides a useful entrée into how Johnston blurred lines between audience and performer, art and life. She was making up something new, but also was learning from the past to do so.

A prolific reader of theory and history, Johnston often found inspiration in theories of art from earlier in the twentieth century. In her first decade of writing, when she relished, as she called them, "strange logics," she often turned to the work of Dada artists to ask, "Why shouldn't this go with that and be called something else"?[22] In the latter half of the 1960s, she began creating her own strange logics, often in response to the writings of Antonin Artaud, the early twentieth-century French playwright, director, and theorist. His interest in reimagining what could be expected—and tested—with an audience fed Johnston's experiments, and she frequently cited him in her writing. In Artaud she found a source that helped her clarify what she came to see as the true work of performance: the collapse in distinctions between the experience of the performer and spectator so that both parties could have an intersubjective, sensorial experience. In "The Unhappy Spectator," her column about the first NYU panel performance (the one with the pig), she offered this thesis (sounding an awful lot like Artaud): "The revolutionary theatre of our time is an attempt to expose the farce of this separation between actor and spectator."[23] Ending the separation between the two roles would be Johnston's work from 1967 on.

ANTONIN ARTAUD

Antonin Artaud published what would become his best-known writing, *The Theatre and Its Double*, in 1938 just as Europe descended into World War II. The collection of essays combined Artaud's interests in early twentieth-century avant-garde traditions focused on "immersion and control" with those "speaking in the postwar movements' terms of agitation."[24] Artaud scholar Kimberly Jannarone has argued that the combination of immersion, control, and agitation made Artaud's ideas an unsettling, if also highly desired, frame for upending the more passive notions of the bourgeois audience member that had become the norm in late nineteenth- and early twentieth-century European theater. Artaud criticized such audiences as functioning only as a "recipient, consumer, or inductee," treating performance as "more of a commodity than an event."[25] As an antidote, he proposed his Theatre of Cruelty, conceiving of "the spectator as an organism to be worked upon" through "attack, immersion, and seizure." In Theatre of Cruelty, "the spectator is in the center and the spectacle surrounds him."[26] Johnston's column title "Take Me Disappearing"—the headline of the column that included the statement "I like things that are certain about not being very sure about what they are"—might be understood as a more laidback, perhaps more American casting of Artaud's edict.

Artaud's ideas of a live and lively spectator-performance relationship arrived in the United States in 1958, just as Johnston was developing her critical voice. Grove Press's publication of Mary Caroline Richards's translation of *The Theatre and Its Double* struck an immediate chord with American experimental theater makers, particularly Living Theatre founders Judith Malina and Julian Beck, artists considered to be major influences on Judson.[27] Reflecting on the arrival of Artaud's ideas in New York theatrical circles, Malina and Beck described "the ghost of Artaud" as their "mentor."[28] The artists' word choice to describe the influence of Artaud's newly translated book—*ghost*, not *writings*—accentuates Artaud's phenomenological focus: sensation anchored his proposal for theater's effect on spectators. He argued that if performance provided a sufficiently intense sensate experience, it would catalyze social transformation. As Jannarone has shown, American theater makers narrowed Artaud's proposal, treating his theories as instrumental tools to use in "service of liberatory social and political ideals."[29] Philosophers, particularly theorists Gilles Deleuze and Félix Guattari, understood Artaud's notion of the sensate more capaciously, borrowing his idea of what he called a "body without organs" to imagine a sensorial body capable of transcending limitations placed on a subject by social hierarchies.[30] Johnston's use of Artaud sits between the American theater makers and the philosophers—not as instrumentalized as the former but more praxis oriented than the latter.

Artaud's ideas fed Johnston's critique of art that overly relied on symbols in performance—the critique she made of her Buffalo lecture-event. Too much focus on the symbolic turned both the performers' and the audience's attention toward formal choices rather than attuning the audience toward sensing performers' presence. This was most clear in Johnston's 1962 criticism of an Allan Kaprow–directed Happening, which she categorized as a "fertility rite" and then dismissed as a work structured around obvious symbolism rather than engagement and transformation. Describing the performance, she writes about the experience of walking, mostly in the dark, through two inches of water, which could be avoided by "perching on a floating plank."[31] As the audience moved, an actor positioned among them pointed a light at "a naked girl," as well as other objects in the space. Johnston hated the performance. She called it a labyrinth of "mere symbols," which the actor with his light merely emphasized rather than engaged. Such overt dismissal was rare in Johnston's writing, especially since the *Voice* gave her "carte blanche" to ignore "whatever [she] pleased and talk only about the things [she] liked."[32] For her to write about disliking a performance meant she found its problems serious enough to warrant negative public critique. Johnston turned to Artaud to explain why the Kaprow evening so maddened her: "Why be symbolic about it? Might as well have the real thing, a naked man or two around at least. . . . For isn't this . . . what Artaud meant when he said: 'There is still one hellish, truly accursed thing in our time, it is our artistic dallying with forms, instead of being like victims burnt at the stake, signaling through the flames?'"[33] Kaprow was "dallying with forms," highlighting his choices, when he should have been "signaling through the flames," forcing the audience to have an experience, even though the promise of feeling what another felt was, ultimately, an exercise in futility.

Kaprow hated Johnston's review and said so in a letter to the editor. The letter was not published but was passed along to Johnston, who summarized it in a subsequent column. Kaprow apparently argued that Johnston had joined those "denouncing 'meaning' in art and favoring 'no-meaning,' or purely-existent-situations-for-themselves."[34] Johnston responded to Kaprow's critique by writing a poem. One stanza summarizes her position:

> Concerning Art, I like it quick with sauce, or over and well done, any
> old way actually and I don't usually care much what it's all about but
> I care very much how it's done and if I like the way it's done I'll care
> what it's all about.[35]

Johnston was dismissive of art that was too sure of what it was. Performance, much like panels, should catalyze transformation, not offer instruction. Like Artaud, she thought performance should affect an audience, though the playful tone she used to reply to Kaprow suggests she did not share Artaud's dark vision of the theater (and the world) as a site of extreme suffering.

Johnston's notion of an active audience moving through a variety of engagements they choose how to navigate aligns with Jannarone's characterization of Artaud as arguing that performance requires "immediacy"—experience, transformation, and/or agitation.[36] Of all the Artaudian ideas Johnston seized on, the most important to her was "signaling through the flames," an expression Artaud used to describe an actor causing a sensorial, kinesthetic, potentially intersubjective provocation within an audience. In fact, Johnston borrowed "signaling through the flames" so often in her writing that dance historian Sally Banes used it as the subtitle for her signature essay about Johnston.[37] Artaud scholar R. D. Crano has argued that "signaling through the flames" encompasses Artaud's call for performance to make "a direct, unmediated relationship with the spectatorial body."[38] Johnston desired to witness performance that presented people—and their bodies—in actual states of tumult, rather than performing *as though* they were in crisis.

Artaud's notion of someone striving mightily as others bear affective witness resonated deeply with Johnston. She did not only borrow "signaling through the flames" to invoke aesthetic possibility or performance strategy; she also invoked it to capture the intensity (and futility) of her early lesbian desires. To describe two of her first female love interests, a dance professor in college and then the choreographer Sally Gross—women with whom, "sexually, nothing really happened" but for whom her feelings were "great"—she said she felt she was "signal[ing her] intentions through the flames," using "all [her] energy . . . just trying to establish [her] intentions," unable to "take the initiative" any further.[39] "Signaling through the flames" provided a way to describe the feeling of trying to reach across a chasm, especially when the flames felt so intense they could consume both the actor and her witness. Johnston perhaps recognized the blurring of lines between audience and performer because she so deeply knew these moments of intense, often fraught instances of seeking connection outside the theater too.

It is this overlap in theater and life that Artaud references in the title *The Theatre and Its Double*. The *double* is life or its possible reinvention. As Jannarone writes, "Artaud posited . . . that the theater came first, and it had the ability to create a new reality."[40] Johnston forges a similar causal chain as the theater becomes the site that engulfs the critic, the ultimate spectator, in the immediacy and intensity of performance. Being singed by the flames of performance creates the possibility of forging a new body, one primed to sense the immediacy and intensity of life. By 1969, with dance concerts now more memory than topic in her criticism, Johnston wrote, "I heard someone attacked me for finding my own life enthralling. . . . I've been signaling through the flames."[41] Artaud helped Johnston move from being a critic of dance into being a critic of life.

CHARLOTTE MOORMAN

The necessity of blurring lines between audience and performer was, for Johnston, as it had been for Artaud, not merely a provocative idea but a real task, which she sought to carry out from the audience and in the newspaper. The possibility of simultaneously acting and witnessing was central to Johnston's role in the lesbian feminist movement of the 1970s, as her column became a site to both stage and witness lesbian life. This simultaneity was one Johnston first practiced in her late 1960s writing about avant-garde performance. While the intersection of dance, theater, and visual art had long been Johnston's critical home, the work of experimental music artist Charlotte Moorman (often with collaborator Nam June Paik) emerged as the site where Johnston's play with boundaries between audience and performer became particularly obvious, first in her writing and then in her manner of participating in events.

Moorman, who later appeared in the 1969 panel celebrating Johnston's "disintegration" as critic, was an apt match for Johnston. Both women excelled at disruption. Moorman "emphasized the materiality of different sound sources and musical instruments, most importantly her own body, as places of sound resonance and as spaces of audience projection... challeng[ing] traditional conceptions of feminine sound and embodied pleasure."[42] This was right up Johnston's alley. In her memoirs Johnston points to her October 1967 review of Moorman's Avant Garde Festival, a semiannual event Moorman curated and performed in, as a significant turning point in her evolution as a writer.[43] In 1968 another Moorman performance review provides a clear view of the audience member Johnston was in the late 1960s.[44] She was no passive witness—the domesticated audience member Artaud sought to unsettle—but neither did Moorman's work ask her to be.

In a November 1967 review of a mixed rep evening at the New School, Johnston wrote, "Much of theatre occurs on the stage and much of it occurs in the heads of the audience."[45] In retrospect, this sentence describes what Johnston had tried to do a week earlier in her review "Ship Ahoy!," which covered Moorman's Avant Garde Festival and included a review of the inside of an audience member's head (Johnston's) just as much as the actions within the performance. In the review, as Johnston strolls through the show's site, a ferryboat, it is clear she understands the audience member's mind to be present in her whole body. As was true for Artaud, the audience's mind is an experience of her body moving and sensing.

In the short five-paragraph review of the festival, Johnston's reader experiences spectatorship as a walk. As reader, I walk alongside her, experiencing my own Artaudian full-body spectatorship, even though I am "just" reading. Johnston begins the review inside herself, standing still and taking in the scene. Looking in one direction, she spies Moorman in preparation, wearing "a maroon velvet gown" and a facial expression that suggests she's "been up all night."[46] In another direction, she sees artist Lil Picard, also in setup mode, wearing sheets "and a string of lollipops around her neck." The overview places the reader in a scene that is imbued with a sense of an artist's humanity (Moorman's tired expression) and where the strange is utterly ordinary (Picard's lollipop necklace), and, perhaps most important, the audience/reader stands among them.

For much of the review, Johnston emphasizes her path through the ship: "ambling," then heading "outside again," and finally passing by Picard—whom she calls, with a nod of familiarity, even friendship—"Lil." She stops to watch Moorman, with whom she also flags an intimacy, referring to her as "Charlotte." Reading and walking with Johnston, she/I/you/we know these people we walk among; we are at ease in this avant-garde world. Moorman plays various electronic instruments with collaborators: Paik, who wears a red pail on his head, and another musician. As we move with Johnston, we see through her eyes. Her repeated discussions of her body in motion—the ambling, the scanning of multiple scenes—emphasize the performances' overlaps. We are with one person, seeing and sensing with her, but that does not translate into an experience of singularity or coherence. *She* and *I* become a *we*. As the review continues, Johnston seemingly eats a hot dog, drinks chocolate milk, and turns her gaze "back to the skyline." *Seemingly* is a necessary caveat, because her writing leaves open the question of whether the hot dog and chocolate milk are part of an art piece, simply her dinner, or perhaps both. Theater and its double.

The review closes with a last performance description, but it is Johnston's fellow audience members, not the performers, who determine how we watch. A sound piece by Jackson Mac Low is the last work mentioned. Johnston decides to watch from an outside deck after another audience member "propels" her outside, explaining, cheekily perhaps, "This is the only way to enjoy Jackson, through a soundproof glass." Our fellow spectator knows just as much—maybe more—about how to watch the work than does its creator.

Reflecting on shifts in her writing in the late 1960s, Johnston denotes "Ship Ahoy!" as a new phase of experimentation in her collage of art and life. Her love of assemblage in visual art and then performance had become a way of writing, even a way of living by then. The roles of audience and performer don't so much collapse as themselves become an assemblage, a new example of the "curious blends and cross-breeding" that Johnston always celebrated.[47] For her, "Ship Ahoy!" was an experiment where she "mixed up art and setting, artists and people . . . quoted remarks of friends, strung images together like beads, and placed myself in the center of the event."[48] The critic no longer stays in her seat.

Johnston's choices build on her previous play with collage, most notably her 1964 "Fluxus Fuxus" review (which also focused on a Paik performance, then as part of a Fluxus Happening). That review combined what Johnston called "found" sentences, comments she heard others say at or after events, with performance description—albeit description rendered absurdly, thus making it impossible to pull together a coherent image of the scene. "Fluxus Fuxus" begins with almost nonsense: "Fluxus flapadoodle. Fluxus concert, 1964. Donald Duck meets the Flying Tigers. Why should anyone notice the shape of a watch at the moment of looking at the time?"[49] With this riddle-esque opening, Johnston blurs spectators' view. Johnston normalizes not quite knowing what's going on, yet staying curious for some time, and Moorman provided opportunities to take that practice to its next level.

In 1968 Johnston returned to another Moorman performance, part of the Destruction Art Symposium. Reading the two columns, 1967's "Ship Ahoy!" and 1968's "Over His Dead Body," alongside one another reveals what contemporary arts writer Jennifer Krasinski has described, in notably physical, sensorial terms, as Johnston's prose growing "longer legs, becoming more agile."[50] Krasinski offers the metaphor to name how Johnston "punctured the myth of the passive audience," often through creative use of the first person. By the time Johnston writes "Over His Dead Body," she walks in a new body and fashion, experiencing performance primarily as an exchange between performer and audience. By the review's end, it is unclear who—if anyone—controls this exchange, just as it is also unclear what exactly constitutes a performance anymore. In "Over His Dead Body," Johnston describes the Moorman-curated evening as "the most unusual manifestation of a performer-audience situation I have witnessed in a decade of attending a theatre in which the performer-audience relationship has been pushed in every conceivable direction."[51] Notably, she says this about a performance in the very site, the Judson Church, where her notion of what constituted an audience had been tested and rearranged for years.

As she does in "Ship Ahoy!," in "Over His Dead Body" Johnston focuses on experiencing the performance in time, narrating the sequence of unfolding events in a manner that helps the reader sense how tension builds and erupts. She enters the yard that surrounds the church with her fellow spectators, noting that most are "milling around passing from one set-up to another." Her description is meager and blasé; the spectators initially seem boring, maybe bored. Then she cranks the energy. In response to artist Ralph Ortiz's announcement that he will begin a "chicken-killing event," the crowd's attention coheres and intensifies. Two men, John Wilcock and critic/scholar Michael Kirby, immediately cause what Johnston terms "interference." They rescue the chickens from Ortiz, an act that Johnston notes requires Ortiz to "re-program" himself. She doesn't remain interested in Ortiz—who transfers his attention to "attacking two trees"—but focuses instead on Wilcock and Kirby, ranking their "interference" as a "worthwhile event in itself." Soon after, in a different corner of the yard, another audience-performer interaction catches her attention too: one around an unnamed "soap-box orator." (Did everyone have a box to stand on in the 1960s?) Johnston describes how the group that previously was just "milling about," largely ignoring (but still encircling) the soapbox speaker, eventually absorbs him, "accept[ing] . . . without relinquishing their own purpose and somehow finally integrat[ing] him in the total situation." Same yard, same audience, but two different outcomes at the site of encounter: the first interference, the second assimilation. Neither party, performer or audience, has total control over the direction each interaction takes.

Eventually the group moves inside the church and watches a single performance: Moorman in Nam June Paik's *One for Violin* (1962). Johnston summarizes Paik's intended score, the plan of action for the performance, as "the destruction of a violin after a long preliminary passage in which the performer raises the instrument in slow motion from a position at right angles to the waist to a position over the head in readiness to smash the thing on impact with the table." Paik's score holds for less than a minute before a new audience-performance encounter emerges. But this time no one is milling about: quick shifts in action and power require Johnston's excellent dance critic movement description skills to track what unfolds. In the remainder of the review, Johnston captures how a solo becomes a duet: a back-and-forth involving Artaud's, Moorman's, and Johnston's favorite type of spectator, an unruly one.

The review suddenly resembles a play. In a series of short sentences that turn physical action dialogic, Johnston oscillates between describing Moorman and the unruly spectator/interference maker. Movement description becomes stage direction–esque. To emphasize how this performance review itself becomes a performance—its own script—I have taken the liberty of rewriting a portion of the review as a short play. Except for bracketed language, everything comes directly from Johnston's writing. Ellipses mark minimal redactions, mostly done to align verb tense.

MOORMAN + DETERMINED SPECTATOR: A SHORT PLAY

> A man from the back tried to stop her [from breaking the violin]. She dispatched him with a push and resumed the performance. [But now a] more determined spectator approache[s] the table and the war [is] on. . . .
>
> CHARLOTTE (*Angry, demand*[*ing*] *to know who he was*): Who the hell do you think you are?
>
> DETERMINED SPECTATOR: By breaking a violin . . . you're doing the same thing as killing people. . . . [*Said almost inaudibly*] something about giving it to a poor kid who could use it.
>
> CHARLOTTE (*Attempting to go on with the piece*): This is not a vaudeville routine. . . . This is not an audience-participation piece.

Moorman slaps Determined Spectator.

VOICE FROM AUDIENCE: Give her [your] coat in exchange for the violin.

Determined Spectator remove[s] coat but she [Moorman] [won't] have any of it.

JILL JOHNSTON (*Inspired, hollering*): GIVE IT TO HIM!

END SCENE.

Johnston recounts her entry into the exchange, writing that "[I] found myself hollering in the din: GIVE IT TO HIM." Her idiomatic "found myself" functions almost like passive voice ("Mistakes were made"), obscuring who exactly did what. She continues, saying her "hollering" is meant to support "him," suggesting she meant to direct Moorman, but in the context of the fuller description in the review, it's not clear she really meant to take sides. Disruption itself seems the goal. The solo becomes a duet, then a "hollering" unruly ensemble, an enactment of Johnston's invocation of what performance is: a place where "much of theatre occurs on the stage and much of it occurs in the heads of the audience."[52]

Against seemingly all odds and the wishes of a significant and growing portion of the audience, the performance continues, and Johnston's sympathies remain contested. Moorman accuses the interfering man of "being as bad as the New York police," likely a reference to the three plainclothes officers who had arrested her earlier that year midperformance as she performed topless in Paik's *Opera Sextronique*. Moorman's current unruly spectator, however, refuses the analogy: he sees himself not as an enforcer of violence, as the police had been, but as a protester thereof—a peacekeeper of sorts. Johnston recounts that he responds to Moorman by declaring, "We are sitting down and refusing to allow this violin to be broken." Another *we* has emerged—or at least the unruly spectator hopes so. He continues to stretch "himself out on his back on the table in front of her [Moorman]," placing his body between the violin and the surface on which it will be destroyed. But his hoped-for *we* does not save him from the fate from which the chickens had been spared earlier. Moorman proceeds to "bash . . . him on the head with the violin and the blood was spilled." Johnston concedes that her "description can't do justice to this extraordinary situation. The ramifications are extensive. It wasn't so much a question who was right or wrong (I thought, if pressed, both were right and both wrong), but what might have been done to avert the inevitable." Describing the event required imagining what could have happened *and* what should have happened *and* what did happen.

We now takes hold. Moorman immediately tends to the injured man, who shares his name (Saul Gottlieb). As the two begin talking, Ortiz and others, including the soapbox orator from the yard, begin a conversation focused on Vietnam, "the government," and the possibility (or not) of "de-program[ming]" people, which has turned out to be the night's theme, from the (almost) chicken killing through the show inside. Johnston's last comment on the events from the yard, the Moorman performance, and the numerous instances of interference is a note of appreciation for audience members because their presence illuminates the "irony of a symbol converted into a reality." Symbols create distance; audiences willing to interact create engagement. In these moments of proximity, all parties signal through the flames.

After the performer-audience divide has been breached, no single person has control. In this state, real things happen, real connections are made, and the unexpected unfolds. No longer are people seeking to elevate or decode symbols, but rather they experience a shared, if still contested, reality: blood was not just discussed but spilled. Once agitated, the formerly domesticated audience could do the real work of engagement and transformation. Johnston saw this happen, and her writing extended the work of the *I* becoming *we*.

1968: Here They Come

Reflecting on the 1968 Moorman performance decades later, Johnston riffed on the way the work multiplied itself, noting that while Paik's score "was called 'One for Violin[,]' [a] man in the audience wanted to make it two."[53] Splitting one into many happens frequently in Johnston's late 1960s experiments, especially in 1968—the year that saw her most striking play with prose, including sentences like these three: "A queen is a queen is a boy is a girl is a ballerina is a boy is a dyke is a fag is a butch is a boy is a girl is just a kinky son of a gun like the rest of us. Hello all you sexes. We're too good to be true."[54] This is a particularly bold example of what I term Johnston's *power-listing*, a rhetorical play with list making through which Johnston moved not just from one subject to two but from one focus to many. Through power-listing, Johnston queerly manifests a swirl of positionalities and subjectivities that do not just repopulate stages but expand the breadth of who can take up public space and how those conjured within an emerging multiplicity relate to and overlap with one another.

Johnston's lists describe heterogeneous worlds and write those worlds into coexistence. They offer a juxtaposition of opposites, using repetition to create rhythmic force and mount collisions that eventually body forth a larger idea that is *almost* contradictory but that the rush of previously presented elements offers evidence for. These long sentences often take a roll call of queer characters and greet them as individuals—at once specific and distinct, yet also a collective force. Performers, audience members, and Johnston's readers come together as an *us*. We are not the same as one another, but we are in one another's view, in one another's space. We are an *us* that often begins as direct reference to the performance's actual audience but then extends outward temporally and spatially. This is powerlisting, forceful in its queer practice of organizing and energizing from performance and page all at once.

Powerlisting emphasizes the queer possibilities of being beside another, *beside* being a preposition queer theorist Eve Sedgwick has lauded for its avoidance of "dualism" and its emphasis on how "a number of elements may lie alongside one another."[55] For anyone looking to undo fixed hierarchies—as Johnston was and as queer activism has often done—*beside* is a preferred preposition, unburdened of the "drama[s] of exposure" promoted by *beyond* or *beneath*. For Sedgwick, looking for how elements sit "alongside one another" makes visible a wider array of ways of relating. "Desiring, identifying, representing, repelling, paralleling, differentiating, rivaling, [and] leaning" are but a few options Sedgwick offers via her own long list, which itself makes her point about the beside and its resulting multiplicities.[56] Looking for all that is beside disrupts any idea that there is one superior queer story to track and instead tracks how many come together.

Johnston's powerlists put her beside one of her lesbian predecessors: Gertrude Stein, a writer famous for making rhetorical points via lists ("Rose is a rose is a rose is a rose"). Johnston's interest in Stein is a central subject in chapter 4 but is also useful here, a lesbian specter to illuminate how Johnston's powerlists work toward both spatial and temporal queer ends. Like Stein's lists, Johnston's powerlists enact what Stein called the "continuous present," creating the effect of each noun named in the list being "perceived as a now."[57] As I read Johnston's list, the queens and the boys and the girls and the ballerinas and the dykes assemble around one another and around me, scrambling space and time toward queer multiplicity.[58]

Johnston developed her powerlisting skills watching and writing about dance, since lists helped her capture how elements came together onstage. The overflowing excesses of her listing practice first appear as attempts at movement description. For instance, here is her 1967 description of Anna Halprin's first-ever New York concert: "Puts on two big painted shoes, runs around, stamps, tap dances, flops on her back, blows a whistle, chews gum and such like, and at one point a girl enters with a goat and stands with it in the middle of the stage."[59] There is clarity: I can see every one of these actions. There is rhythm: "blows a whistle, chews gum and such like" offers both force and distance. But there is also a sense of what it's like to be there in the present moment, as opposed to critical distance. In reading, we witness this girl and this goat and try to figure out why they're center stage. Reading, I am beside her, sitting down beside Johnston in the performance. The sensemaking (or inability to make sense) is up to the reader, and Johnston also communicates that she's not entirely sure of all the connections either. We are an audience together.

Johnston makes lists of many elements to refuse singular coherence. A list in her 1968 review of Steve Paxton's *Satisfyin' Lover* is a prime example:

> And here they all were in this concert in the last dance, thirty-two any old wonderful people in "Satisfyin' Lovers" [*sic*] walking one after the other across the gymnasium in their any old clothes. The fat, the skinny, the medium, the slouched and slumped, the straight and tall, the bow-legged and knock-kneed, the awkward, the elegant, the coarse, the delicate, the pregnant, the virginal, the you name it, by implication every postural possibility in the postural spectrum, that's you and me in all our ordinary everyday who cares postural splendor. Like the famous ordinary people who are certain they will see and be seen whether they fall down or keep walking in a forest with or without other famous ordinary people there is a way of looking at things which renders them performance. Let us now praise famous ordinary people.[60]

In this passage Johnston spins her readers' attention in several directions: toward how bodies are different from one another; how weight and gravity produce the idea of a person; and how all these elements—postures, weight, gravity, and rhythm—create a mass both individually varied and collective. Juxtaposition sparks almost every phrase: "the coarse, the delicate"; "the pregnant, the virginal." So many juxtapositions beside one another produce the larger effect of making contradictions true: there can be such a thing as "famous ordinary" people.

The performer/audience/reader boundary dissolves as Johnston's review continues. She not only describes what the dancers did but shows how their doing invites the audience member to look, to be an active witness—to feel through the rhythmic construction of her writing the gentle loping of the performers' walking. Readers can then opt in and imagine with the dancing and the writing, "the you name it." Thus added, we move toward and up, eventually joining the exhilaration of "praising" the generatively excessive, contradictory mass we helped create. In its stacking of clashing elements, Johnston's writing resembles the nonlinear structural potential of postmodern performance and its embrace of contradiction. The long list grows until it overflows, sorely testing the idea that witnessing performance and reading are fundamentally different activities.

Johnston's ebullience is often associated with late twentieth-century dance criticism's emphasis on description. Studying her powerlists, however, demonstrates that categorizing her writing as descriptive underestimates the boldness of her prose. Through the amassing of details these lists become performances of excess themselves. Their cadence provides a sense of affective connection, catalyzing the formation of a queer feminist politic that claims the ordinary and the excessive as twin modes of disruption and survival. The many specific elements—collected but not coherent—thwart attempts to organize them into a hierarchy. There is no one thing to become attached to: the thing is the whole, arising from an overflow of items commingling and spilling insistently forward.

Johnston's powerlists are a key strategy for how her performance reviews emphasize proximity: as with the elements in the list, her reviews' readers gather in the same time and place. Notable exceptions to this characteristic of Johnston's writing appear, however, when she tries to write explicitly about race in performance. With other topics, the reader walks through performances beside her, but when Johnston turns to race, particularly when writing about Black performers, it is hard to know where she stands or if one should stand beside her. In the same 1968 review that closes with the list of queer subjects (queens and dykes and fags and ballerinas), when writing about an interracial trio performed by members of the Harkness Youth Ballet Johnston seems to retreat, creating distance rather than proximity or sensation. Of the trio, which featured one white woman and two men, one Black and one white, Johnston writes, "The dance people are showing us how integrated they are. I don't think the Black Power people would appreciate this at all. That black boy in the trio tennis game is already looking lighter than he is. He seemed to be enjoying it too."[61] In this and other portions of her writing about Harkness, she observes at a distance rather than describing with detail, separating herself from the artists ("the dance people") and from those seemingly most able to weigh in on race ("the Black Power people"). As she focuses further on the two boys' attempts to get the girl's attention, she repeatedly foregrounds their racial difference by referring to them as "black boy," "white boy," and "white girl." *Boy* brings all its racial codes with it, diminishing the Black dancer, while it merely marks the white dancer's age. Everyone becomes more and more distant from one another, even as Johnston's queer playful tone throughout the review makes it difficult to discern when she describes a choreographic dynamic versus when she comments on the work. Nonetheless, the difference in her tone is palpable, as is the absence of sensorial proximity or any sense of beside-ness. She is a white woman, living a life alongside other white people, as so many of those in New York's downtown performance world were. She is thrown by the interracial piece, performed in the fall of 1968 just as the Black Arts Movement and Black Power were beginning to affect the New York arts world more broadly. Of the performance and its display of racial difference, Johnston writes, "It's very confusing"—one of the first (perhaps only) times in her writing where confusion is not a compliment.

Perhaps this confusion is part of what makes Johnston's attention drift from the stage to the audience that surrounds her on that early September night in Central Park, where a large group has gathered for what was (most likely) a free evening of dance. With the exception of the lengthy attention she gives to the Harkness trio, Johnston spends little of her review discussing the other artists on the evening's bill: one of the foundational voices in African American concert dance, Rod Rodgers; a former Martha Graham dancer, Richard Kuch; and a woman merging comedy and modern dance, Lotte Goslar. Instead, she focuses almost entirely on the somewhat random group of people around her. She writes, "It's chilly so I'm snuggling into my seat and trying to overhear three fags behind me talking about what they had for dessert." The use of *fags* is Johnston's first overt reference to queer identity in her then almost nine years at the *Voice*. The vernacular usage, still certainly a slur if issued by an outsider, signals Johnston's status as insider to the gay community, a status confirmed by the review's closing powerlist. "A queen is a queen is a boy is a girl is a ballerina is a boy is a dyke is a fag is a butch is a boy is a girl is just a kinky son of a gun like the rest of us. Hello all you sexes. We're too good to be true."[62]

Johnston often wove latent (and not-so-latent) queerness into her lists. Theater historian David Savran has described how another performance-related genre of lists, those included in many famous musical theater songs, often sequences elements so that there is an "oscillat[ion] between revealed and concealed, carnivalesque and closeted," producing an expression of queer desire at once protected and seductive.[63] Johnston's Central Park list, with its dykes, fags, and butches all beside one another, makes the list (and the audience it describes) both obvious and not. The absence of active verbs in the lists, another characteristic Johnston's lists share with the songs Savran analyzes, could function as it does in musical theater, obscuring associations among elements and providing further protection for queer identity.[64] But Johnston's lists feel a little different, a bit more like the evasions of meaning central to postmodern dance and its emphasis on rhythm and accumulation. There are often no verbs, but there is a sense of motion. Language, regardless of grammar category, can swing and sway. As Holly Hughes and David Román argue queer performance often is, Johnston's powerlists are pedagogical, teaching a pre-Stonewall readership how to experience queer possibility in all its "revealed and concealed" forms.[65]

Johnston lands beside Stein again, too. As rhetoric scholar Sharon Kirsch has written of Stein's writing, Johnston creates "a pedagogical imperative, inviting readers again and again into a potential process of meaning making and also, perhaps more so, toward an understanding that the engagement itself might be pleasurable regardless of its results."[66] In what Stein might call the "continuous present" of Johnston's "A queen is a queen is a boy is a girl is a ballerina is a boy is a dyke is a fag is a butch is a boy is a girl is just a kinky son of a gun," there is an open-ended accumulation, an unending string luxuriating in multiplicity and overlap. This open-ended quality invites multiplicity without worry of erasing difference—"a boy" does not replace "a queen," nor does "a ballerina" replace "a girl." Instead, the rollicking list assembles an *us* to be acknowledged and celebrated together, as the list's (and review's) conclusion says, "Hello all you sexes. We're too good to be true."[67] Together, this *us* is known and unknown, a too much that is a pleasurable thing to be.

Johnston recognizes and amplifies the individual characters that compose an audience, moving between those described and those addressed, confusing all the boundaries between. Queerness does not thrive in the singular, nor should it only reify existing power differentials. In "A queen is a queen is a boy is a girl is a ballerina is a boy is a dyke is a fag is a butch is a boy is a girl is just a kinky son of a gun," some get to go twice: queens, boys, girls. Is that fact or problem? Some people show up that you didn't expect: nice to see you, "ballerina." And "dyke"—at least here—gets placed before "fag."

Johnston's powerlisting creates a lesbian proto-queer articulation of what Sedgwick would write decades later when she described queer as a politics necessarily emerging from practice and from heterogeneity, a set of "political adventures" carried out by "a motley crew engaging in queer practices."[68]

Sedgwick writes yet more lists to capture the "open mesh of possibilities, gaps, overlaps, dissonances and resonances, lapses and excesses of meaning" that she argues constitute queerness. She then populates her queerly imagined "open mesh" with a list of queer types: "pushy femmes, radical faeries, fantasists, drags, clones, leatherfolk, ladies in tuxedos, feminist women or feminist men, masturbators, bulldaggers, divas, Snap! Queens, butch bottoms, storytellers, transsexuals, aunties, wannabes, lesbian-identified men or lesbians who sleep with men, or . . . people able to relish, learn from, or identify with such."[69] Again there is the large list, which closes—as Johnston's list does—with a note of overlap, of turning to one another without necessarily becoming one another.

When they come at the end of her columns, as they often do, Johnston's powerlists recap her return trip through an event with a celebration of different subjects, often queer, meeting and colliding but not merging. It is not just the performance, what's onstage, that overflows; it's all who watch. À la Sedgwick, Johnston keeps the queers beside one another, now on the page as they were in the audience. À la Stein, they exist all together in a single moment, and as people read the review weeks, months, or years later, the moment Johnston describes extends into the future. Writing does not fix queer subjects in a given moment but makes possible a commingling across time and space. Through powerlisting Johnston reconceptualizes the audience, interrupting the idea that a monolithic body watches a performance. She recognizes all who come together: the many queer types whose copresence is too powerful to be eradicated by a curtain call.

It is not, however, as though making lists is simply a queer rhetorical practice that can defy time. Johnston wrote her queerly performative list in 1968, as naming practices around gay activism were in flux. Historian Edward Alwood has traced an arc in twentieth-century gay political organizing from euphemism to explicitness.[70] Earlier groups usually chose names with oblique references to gay and lesbian historical figures, indicating insiders as the group's primary audience. The Mattachine Society, founded in 1950, took its name from groups of men in the French Renaissance who always wore masks in public. The Daughters of Bilitis, founded in 1955, named themselves by way of a French poet's passing reference to an imagined inhabitant of the island of Lesbos. Only those in the know (or informed by someone in the know) could discern a group's purpose. By the late 1960s, when Johnston sat in Central Park listening to fags discuss dessert and trying to make sense of a dance performance, gay and lesbian protest groups were shifting their names to be more explicit and outwardly focused. The Gay Liberation Front (GLF), the name of the most prominent activist group to emerge in the wake of Stonewall, is the best example of this shift toward the explicit. Martha Shelley, a lesbian who helped name the GLF, describes the difference between the GLF and its "forebears" as rooted in the group not "giv[ing] a rat's ass about being respectable. We didn't want to move up in a system of hierarchical cruelties; we wanted to overturn it."[71] The lesbian group of activists that began as "GLF women" also followed a similar route, accentuating their explicit, radical politics, by re-naming themselves *Radicalesbians* in early 1971.[72]

Johnston's powerlisting manages to be both euphemistic and explicit all at once. She seems more focused on what a list can gather and imagine in its naming than on creating a delineation between insider and outsider. She queers rather than demarcates boundaries. Johnston makes the *L*s and *G*s, and *B*s and *T*s, collide and rearrange. "A queen is a queen is a boy is a girl is a ballerina is a boy is a dyke is a fag is a butch is a boy is a girl is just a kinky son of a gun."

That this collision was intentional is likely. Johnston was quite self-aware about her use of lists. She knew she was up to something unlinear in the newspaper, the most linear of writing venues. In a November 1968 review that she designated an "expository piece about my criticism," Johnston describes her approach to (refusal of?) coherence, writing, "I like to work up a single thing into a mess of stuff about that single thing. I'm not crazy about trying to make a single thing out of a mess of stuff. Nor am I content to let it go at a listing of a mess of stuff which might be read as a bunch of different single things."[73] "Trying to make a single thing out of a mess of stuff" strives for too much coherence, inevitably losing the differences and disjunctures among elements—and differences and disjunctures were always what drew Johnston's attention. Her second option, the "listing of a mess of stuff which might be read as a bunch of different single things," fails to notice that a "mess of stuff" still holds internal connections within—those connections just might not be ones that are fully or widely legible. Confusion, the good kind, seems to be the pedagogical goal of Johnston's writing, so much so that by 1968 her writing begs the question, What is Jill Johnston, especially if "dance critic" is no longer a suitable answer? "A queen is a queen is a boy is a girl is a ballerina is a boy is a dyke is a fag is a butch is a boy is a girl is just a kinky son of a gun."[74] She (a dyke, a lesbian) is many things, perhaps better described via a list, a string of potential labels beside one another—more than one noun or one label could offer. She needs the multiple *is*'s, and maybe others do too. Full legibility is overrated, but being mistaken for nothing more than a messy pile is also not the goal. Johnston wants—and enacts—queerly generative, even pleasurable incoherence; time travel; and permeable boundaries. "Hello all you sexes. We're too good to be true."

Lesbian Adjacency II: Audre Lorde

Jill Johnston is one of three feminist writers of the late 1960s and early 1970s that cultural critic Emily Nussbaum has singled out for wielding movement-changing bravado in their prose. The other two Nussbaum names are Shulamith Firestone, activist and author of *The Dialectic of Sex: The Case for Feminist Revolution* (1970), and Audre Lorde, the Black feminist poet, essayist, and activist who wrote so many of the most crucial, still-cited pieces of 1970s feminism, including "The Uses of the Erotic," discussed in the previous chapter. Nussbaum specifically celebrates the two lesbians, Johnston and Lorde, for having particularly "swashbuckling" styles, a description that springs from both women's mode of addressing readers with a power that feels almost contagious.[75] Johnston and Lorde write quite differently but share a desire to affect audiences—an interest that, for Johnston, stemmed from her engagement with performance and, for Lorde, likely has roots in how many of her most famous essays began as public addresses to (often interracial) audiences.

As Johnston and Lorde sought to reach audiences—those literally in front of them or those reading their work at different times in history—both women frequently and proudly declared themselves as lesbians. Their declarations arrive not just as expressions of interiority made public but as announcements for (and sometimes on behalf of) others. As Lorde's biographer Alexis De Veaux has said of Lorde's importance to others with marginalized identities, Lorde wrote in a manner that "both constructed and opened the door."[76] For both Lorde and Johnston, coming out was not a singular announcement, "I am." Coming out was a gathering, "I am . . . with you." In declarations both clear and poetic, Lorde and Johnston asked to be recognized as lesbians and created space for others to be recognized as such. Both wielded the porosity of poetry and dance to poetically announce their identities and desires, and both used lists to ensure they rendered lesbian as a forceful, yet complex thing to be.

For all these similarities, Lorde and Johnston make an uneasy pairing, particularly given Lorde's centrality to Black feminist thought and Johnston's decidedly white perspective. Yet I hold them together much as queer theorist José Muñoz thinks about Sedgwick, a white woman, publishing the work of her former student, the Black gay male writer Gary Fisher, a pairing Muñoz calls "a rich, complicated, and sometimes troubling collaborative scene."[77] Black studies scholar Daphne Brooks has made another rich yet complicated scene in her writing about Ellen Willis and Lorraine Hansberry, another, at first glance, odd pairing of a white and a Black woman. Willis, Johnston's fellow *Voice* writer and radical feminist, and Hansberry, the famous Black lesbian playwright, met only once and had differing racial politics: race was always central to Hansberry's work, and Willis developed a racial consciousness only later in her career. Yet Brooks argues for them as women who "shared the profound values and concerns... [of] pursuing, speaking about, and protecting a woman's right to feeling and unfettered pleasure."[78] The same is true for Lorde and Johnston, only Brooks's sentence would need a slight modification. Lorde and Johnston were women who "shared the profound values and concerns... [of] pursuing, speaking about, and protecting a [lesbian's] right to feeling and unfettered pleasure."

Both Lorde and Johnston came into their lesbian identities in 1950s downtown New York, with Lorde fully immersing herself in, as she calls it in her "biomythography" *Zami* (1982), the "gay-girl" bar scene after returning to New York from a poetic, political, and sexual awakening in Mexico. Writing about herself and a then lover, Lorde remembers, "[What] we both needed was the atmosphere of other lesbians, and in 1954, gay bars were the only meeting places we knew."[79] Johnston moved to New York around this time, and she, like Lorde, worked in the New York Public Library system by day and moved through the rest of her life at least tacitly aware of her attraction to women. By 1960 Lorde and Johnston moved in parallel, if not overlapping, social circles. One link the women shared was poet Diane di Prima, a close friend of Lorde's since high school and a confidante of Johnston's friend (and Judson artist) Fred Herko.[80] Dating back to high school when a visit from choreographer and anthropologist Pearl Primus inspired Lorde to adopt a natural hairstyle, Lorde had some interest in dancing (or, at least, dancers), and she often hung out with young dancers while living in the Village. References to Primus and Martha Graham appear in Lorde's *Zami*, and De Veaux notes that Lorde frequently walked friends to their dance classes at the leftist New Dance Group.[81] It is tempting to imagine Lorde and Johnston, a soon-to-be lesbian writer powerhouse constellation, moving in and around downtown New York's studio and concert dance scenes.

Though Johnston, as opposed to Lorde, was much closer to dance as a practice, both seemed to strategically sense dance's potential for speaking identity into the world in a proud, yet shielded manner. Lorde titled the first of her poems to hint at her lesbianism "Pirouette." Published in 1964 in the anthology *New Negro Poets, U.S.A.*, edited by Langston Hughes, "Pirouette" is at once concrete in its materiality—four times invoking "your hands" as they touch another's body—and slightly mysterious, as we never learn exactly whose hands or body are described.[82] De Veaux describes Lorde's play with how much the writer allows her reader to know as indicative of "lesbian work of the period."[83] Too, "Pirouette" is in line with much midcentury lesbian writing in its melancholic tone.[84] The original version of the poem ends with the line "I cannot return." (In a later version, Lorde revised the final line to read "I am come home.")[85] In the original version, hands meet another's lips four times, yet the narrator cannot come back to the space of encounter—the next day or ever. Overreading the poem's title points to how dance becomes a place for the physical and material but also a place of motion, a turn never exactly captured the same way again. Yet whether this tension arises from the ephemerality of desire or obstacles presented by homophobia cannot be known.

Lorde's use of the poetic porosity that dance and poetry share to hint at lesbian desire makes it possible to see a similar potential in Johnston's references to dance in her most poetic columns of the late 1960s. The materiality, physicality, amorphousness, and melancholy of "Pirouette" map closely, for instance, onto Johnston's 1968 column "Danscrabble." Where "Pirouette" lands sparsely on the page, though, "Danscrabble" is dense, a cousin to Johnston's "found"-language columns, like her 1964 "Fluxus Fuxus" review. Yet, especially when reading with Lorde's poem in mind, there is a softness to be found in "Danscrabble," particularly in its attention to bodies: "You're not supposed to smile when I enter the room," and "Her veined hands ran quickly over the pearls and the feathers around the neckband," two of several physical descriptions in the column that suggest an interaction between women and include feminine pronouns but never settle on exactly whether the woman doing the writing is the one seen or seeing.[86] Also, as Lorde does in "Pirouette," Johnston invokes something not quite spoken in "Danscrabble." After the line prohibiting the smile of recognition, Johnston writes these words and ellipses: "But I thought... You thought..."[87] Much like in Lorde's poem, two people appear and try to find one another, but neither can speak all they desire, much as neither Johnston nor Lorde could for most of the 1960s. Maybe these coded, partial sharings prepared them to make pronouncements about their lesbian identity to audiences a few years later.

By the 1970s, Lorde was speaking powerfully for and to other Black women and Third World feminists, as the broader coalition of feminists of color called themselves. She elevated the minority within the white, straight, middle- and upper-class majority at events where she spoke, while also explicitly addressing white feminists. At a NYU conference on the occasion of the thirtieth anniversary of Simone de Beauvoir's book *The Second Sex*, Lorde delivered the speech that later became her perhaps most famous essay, "The Master's Tools Will Never Dismantle the Master's House."[88] At the celebration, organized and primarily attended by white straight feminists, Lorde aligned herself with the minority in the room, while also addressing the event's organizers, saying, "Those of us who stand outside the circle of this society's definition of acceptable women; those of us who have been forged in the crucibles of difference—those of us who are poor, who are lesbians, who are Black, who are older—know that *survival is not an academic skill.*"[89] It's a powerful and bifurcated moment. She tells the primarily white, straight academic crowd that the answers are not theirs to give—their appropriations of the "master's tools" will not do the work needed. But even more so, Lorde speaks to anyone in the audience who sits amid the larger group feeling that they are not among the "acceptable women," telling them that the outsider tools they have at the ready are the ones most needed. They are not alone. They are one of several manifestations of women "forged in the crucibles of difference." In her address to the minority surviving the majority, Lorde's act bears similarity to Johnston's address to queers within the presumed heteronormativity of the dance world—or in that audience at Central Park, "Hello all you sexes. [You]'re too good to be true." Both Lorde and Johnston assured marginalized people they were not alone and helped create a sense of connection among them.

Often through lists, Lorde and Johnston help women, help lesbians, help queers forge their own form of lesbian adjacency. In her "Master's Tools" essay, Lorde populates and describes the group outside the bounds of "acceptable women" with a number of signifiers, noting differences in race, age, and sexuality, among others. In a similar way, the possibilities for being a woman—butch, ballerina, girl, and dyke, among others—proliferate in Johnston's lists. There is a sequence for sure: it can't possibly be overstated how important it was that in the list Lorde used to describe herself—"I am a Black, lesbian, mother, warrior, poet"—she *always* placed Black first. In comparison, Johnston's lists tend toward excess: items repeat and get reshuffled. Understanding each woman's lists as particularly lesbian lists, though, makes them legible as not just announcements of identity, words pointing to some stable notion of lesbian, but also directions on interactions with an audience—"This is how I want you to see me." In this way, both Lorde's and Johnston's lists share something with the infamous lists Black lesbian playwright Lorraine Hansberry made of her likes and dislikes, which became public in a 2014 Brooklyn Museum show focused on Hansberry's lesbian identity. In that exhibit, Hansberry's lists, as Brooks writes, shone as "document[s of] her passion—sometimes sensual, sometimes aesthetic," ranging from musicians she loved to intimacies she wanted to share with her female lover.[90] Read as lesbian lists, Hansberry's, Lorde's, and Johnston's lists all share an attention to the complexity of the label *lesbian* and what might live within the category of lesbian desire.

Lists also, however, leave some things unsaid. Being next to Lorde's (and Hansberry's) lists renders the absence of any overt mention of race in Johnston's lists quite noticeable. Particularly in her 1968 Central Park review, it is the absence of any mention of race that expresses the intensity of whiteness in Johnston's personal racial formation, and, in the context of the review as a whole, it seems a conscious choice. She discusses the evening's interracial casting, seeing race onstage, but says nothing about race as she writes about the audience. In a list, a form always partial or in shorthand, absences can become naturalized. In actuality, Johnston's list is this: "A queen is a (maybe not white?) queen is a (white) boy is a (white) girl is a (white) ballerina is a (white?) boy is a (white) dyke is a (white?) fag is a (white?) butch is a (white) boy is a (white) girl is just a (white?) kinky son of a gun."[91] The thought experiment ruins the sentence, but it does highlight how absence is really its opposite: something so present it goes unnamed.

Adding to the List, with the Audience

Lists are never really complete. That's why we leave them out on the counter: as we realize we need more—another item, another stop on the trip—additions are possible, even necessary. From 2017 to 2023, as I have researched and written this book, when asked to speak, I often choose to talk about Johnston's powerlists. They are at their most captivating with an audience, and I love reading them out loud. Johnston writes sentences that feel good to speak, rhythmic enough to propel a speaker without needing punctuation and varied enough in sound that I can feel how each word crosses into the next. The "queen is a queen" list is my favorite to deliver. As I finish reading the passage I get to look up at a room, and let my eyes scan across all the many types of women, many genders, and queer folks who are always the crowd that shows up for a talk about dancing lesbians. I say, "Hello all you sexes. We're too good to be true," and I feel a connection with the audience that gives me great pleasure. I am acknowledged, and I acknowledge them. We are an *us*, beside one another as one another's audience and performers.

Several times, however, when I shared this work with an audience, it was a not-quite-live live event, a Zoom presentation necessitated by the global COVID-19 pandemic. Talks meant to be in-person—the new language of liveness created by the pandemic—were delivered from the closet in my home that my girlfriend and I had converted into a quasi-soundproof teaching space. Teaching on Zoom taught me that engagement is in short supply and that looking out into "the room" meant looking, not at faces, but at rows of black boxes. In 2020, as the ongoing pandemic of racism publicly paralleled that caused by COVID-19, I grew uncomfortable with the unmarked whiteness of Johnston's Central Park list, even as I still loved reading it out loud. I also felt unsure how it might or might not hail a trans or nonbinary listener. With more Zoom teaching tricks than I ever wanted to have, I decided to make the list interactive, to create a document I could share in the last part of the talk and invite others to write *into* the list, instructing the audience to "add a word or phrase to the list that you need, and then add a word or phrase to the list that someone you love would need."

I'd then sit quietly in my closet as the list morphed and grew. "Queen" became "Black queen." "Tomboy" and "demiboy" surround "dyke." There were "Jewish fags" and "Brown trans kids." And then things started happening that I hadn't expected: "kinky son of a gun" gained a compatriot, "a person who gives a shit." Names and titles appeared that I had to look up later and learn about. To continue to read these lists, I changed, at least a little bit. And I wasn't so alone anymore. A queer past had made a queer present/future, and that future did not have to be completely constrained by the limitations of the past. "Hello all you sexes. We're too good to be true." Or as one person put it one of those Google Docs, "We're too, too, too—so good—to be true." An *I*, a *we*, and an *us* emerged, and we coauthored each together.

INTERRUPTION 2

Born of Paper

When Jill Johnston passed away in 2010, major newspapers treated her career in dance criticism as something of an aside. The *Guardian* noted that she "began" her professional life as a dance critic but then focused almost exclusively on her life in the early 1970s: her standoff with Norman Mailer and the 1973 publication of *Lesbian Nation*.[1] The *Los Angeles Times* noted that she "gain[ed] prominence" as a dance critic but pointed to the 1969 "Disintegration of a Critic" panel described in chapter 2 as the end of her relationship to dance. Like the *Guardian*, the *Times* instead focused on her 1970s writing, describing it as "intensely personal and experimental," and her lesbian feminist activism as earning her the "wary" attention of straight feminist leaders.[2] The only paper to give ample consideration to Johnston's criticism was the *New York Times*, but, still, even there her dance writing was framed as developmental—how she "started out"—before turning to lesbian feminist activism.[3] The paper made it sound as though once her life in the arts ended, the real work had begun.

These newspapers, albeit unintentionally, chronicle Johnston's life as having a particularly queer narrative of multiple deaths. Feminist theorist Peggy Phelan has argued that all queers die twice: one death on coming out, a moment sometimes imagined as putting away a self from before, and then a second death that comes after a publicly queer life. Indeed, Phelan goes so far as to argue that "queers are queer because we recognize and we have survived our own deaths."[4] In a queer biography, there is the life that emerges after the first death but also what Phelan calls the "paper ghost," what lingers from the before.[5] Phelan's proposal is an apt framing of relationship between Jill Johnston as arts critic and Jill Johnston as lesbian feminist. The former self survived in the latter, despite many narratives (including some written and staged by Johnston herself) that make a cleaner cut. The second half of this book, the chapters to come, traces dance criticism as the paper ghost to Johnston's lesbian feminism.

First, however, there is another paper ghost, one Johnston chose as a guide—and to be yet another version of herself—French poet and critic Guillaume Apollinaire, who died in 1918 in Paris . . . we think. In the late 1960s and early 1970s, Johnston repeatedly flirted with the idea of herself as something between a reincarnation of and a metonym for Apollinaire. This was an internal fantasy but also one she made public with intentionally playful and sometimes confusing choices, including signing multiple columns as Apollinaire. This layering of self and other began in 1966, during Johnston's second institutionalization at Bellevue Hospital, where a copy of Apollinaire scholar Roger Shattuck's *The Banquet Years: The Arts in France, 1885–1918* (1958) was her only reading material. The book traces the period in France when the European avant-garde took root through the work of four artists: Alfred Jarry, Henri Rousseau, Erik Satie, and Apollinaire. Reading the book while institutionalized, Johnston felt a "divined" connection to Apollinaire—not a chosen connection—although, as she would write later in a memoir, she "had the good sense" to keep this to herself.[6] Over time, however, she would publicly state not only that she was Apollinaire but that he was her father and her uncle, despite his death happening ten years prior to her birth. These overlaps, which crossed time, gender, and country, first appeared in Johnston's columns in 1968. They start as small, nonsensical mentions: "Actually more like Apollinaire I appear to be carrying everything along with me jilly nilly fact legend gossip glory and gore."[7] By 1969 she was signing columns as Guillaume (though still only occasionally).

Was this delusion, queer resurrection, or, to borrow from Johnston, "fact legend gossip glory and gore"? Given the many transformations in Johnston's life in the 1960s, ranging from her first long-term relationship with a woman to her diagnosis with "chronic undifferentiated schizophrenia," plus her reimagining of her work as a critic into that of an artist, "all of the above" seems the correct answer.[8] Writing decades later, she described Apollinaire as the ideal figure for "my heavy transitional life in the sixties."[9] Midcentury psychologists might have called Apollinaire Johnston's "transitional object," something that produces security as a child transitions away from their mother. Dance criticism birthed Johnston as writer, but she had to move away from that realm to find all that was possible.[10] In shifting from critic to writer, she moved from thinking of herself in a "supportive role" to understanding herself as someone "who might be supported."[11] To make this transformation, she needed a "paper ghost," perhaps for security, but also for dreaming.

Enter Apollinaire. He was another writer who moved between the categories of artist and critic, and his biography overlaps with Johnston's. But perhaps he was more important for the dreaming he allowed Johnston to do: Apollinaire also died more than once. It seems he did actually die of the Spanish flu in 1918, but two years earlier he was thought to have died after sustaining a head injury during World War I. This double death made him a compelling paper ghost for Johnston, and his gender as a man proved helpful too. As she would put it later, Johnston felt she needed a male persona to "become oneself without offending the view [women were taught to have] that one exists only for others."[12] But there was an issue: Johnston was very clear that she did not want to be a man. With this in mind, she decided to "fancy" herself the daughter of a "(great) man," who was also a dead man.[13]

With this decision made, Johnston crafted a genealogy that made her a descendant of Apollinaire. Here's the story she developed. First, there had to be an evasion of death: Apollinaire's 1918 death had been faked, leaving him available to emerge in a number of sites within Johnston's family history. Johnston imagined not-dead Apollinaire as paramour *and* offspring to Johnston's paternal grandmother. With the both/and securely in place, this meant Johnston could be Apollinaire's granddaughter and his niece. She also imagined Apollinaire as having met her mother, Olive, and conceived her (Jill) on a transatlantic voyage between the United States and the United Kingdom.[14] With this story Johnston became Apollinaire's daughter, gaining a figure she'd never known, a biological father. Performance scholar Selby Schwartz describes queer life as requiring wielding "playfully defiant queer imaginaries . . . [sometimes] across vast dispersions of time and space [to] recast . . . histories of shame, stigma, or subjection."[15] To emerge into the full possibilities of herself as a writer and as a woman, Johnston knew she had to make her own history.

Re-creating herself as Apollinaire's descendant was queer dreaming and, to Johnston, quite "logical."[16] She described her experience of reading *The Banquet Years* as one of hearing a "curious . . . echo."[17] Indeed, Shattuck's overview of Apollinaire's life and contributions to the arts has an almost eerie resonance with Johnston's life and career. Like Johnston, Apollinaire confused social boundaries, including those that imagined public and private, artist and critic, as separate spheres. In terms of public/private, he circulated texts from the Bibliothèque Nationale previously deemed pornographic. In terms of the artist and critic, he wrote columns up to three times per week in a range of publications, including one in which he coined the term *surrealism*, which then became the term most widely used to describe his own innovative poetry among other art movements, including Dada. Especially by the 1970s, Johnston made similar celebrations of her lesbian life, including her sex life, turning private matters into celebrated public spectacles; and through her writing about Judson and other avant-garde movements of the 1960s, she came to be known as the critic who saw the massive shift happening in New York artistic circles of the time, including shifts she precipitated. Shattuck's description of Apollinaire as the "critic-impresario [who] helped detach the new century from the old and create a frame of reference in which the word 'modern' has come to mean 'since symbolism and impressionism'" could easily—with years and artistic movements swapped in—be a description of Johnston.[18]

But it's not really biography where the echoes grow loudest. Apollinaire and Johnston had deep attachments to the experimental possibilities of words and letters on the page. Apollinaire imagined writing as "a completely open system of word order, the supreme pun in which all meanings are possible," resulting in prose with "unstrained ambiguity . . . always tinctured with the comic" that catalyzed "a profound revelation of the inner mind."[19] Johnston shared Apollinaire's fascination with language, particularly puns, which became, in both authors' writing, the apex of linguistic ambiguity and the site where sonic, visual, and kinesthetic collide.

Where Johnston's and Apollinaire's writing draws closest is in their poetic, yet still ordinary renderings of urban, pedestrian life. One of Apollinaire's best-known poems, "Zone" (1913), follows the author on a twenty-four-hour walk across Paris.[20] Johnston rendered many columns in a similar vein, recounting the experiences of seeing a familiar-looking stranger through a taxicab's window, being part of a throng of New Yorkers avoiding the path of a parade, and tracking New Yorkers' responses to artist James Byars's mile-long dress that stretched across multiple Manhattan blocks: "People going about their business in passage are careful not to step on it, never mind their perplexity."[21] Writing about "Zone," critic Peter Read has described it as a modernist plea to see "everyday life [as equally] astonishing as any heroic legend," which is a perfect description of what Johnston did in her columns too.[22]

Elevating the meaning of the mundane was only one place where Apollinaire's and Johnston's writings touched. Both also shared an intense interest in how words look on the page. In the 1918 book *Calligrammes*, a collection of Apollinaire's posthumously published poetry (yet another moment of beating death), poems shoot across the page in diagonal lines or form into the shape of the Eiffel Tower, landing his reader in the center of Paris—a challenge to whether poetry is visual or textual.[23] Johnston's visual sensibility as a writer most takes hold in her opinions on paragraphs, which she detested and sometimes abused. Writing in 1972 about why she hated paragraphs, she said, "The paragraph is an archaic device predicated on the notion of separable categories of thought and information. The world from beginning to end is one paragraph and insomuch as there is no observable end or beginning neither is there a paragraph."[24] How one arranged words was important, and part of the point of writing—for both Apollinaire and Johnston—was to challenge their readers, not guide them.

For all these writerly overlaps, Johnston never writes about Apollinaire's writing. She focuses on what she learned from reading (and likely rereading) Shattuck. What seemed to capture her was Apollinaire's invention of self, especially his construction of an origin story for himself in the absence of his family providing an accurate accounting of his birth. Both Apollinaire and Johnston were *non noto*, the European term used on the birth certificates of children born to unknown fathers. Apollinaire was born Wilhelm Apollinaire de Kostrowitzky, and his father's identity was/is also unknown. Shattuck says the unknown father was Russian; others say Italian.[25] Johnston says, "Fathers can be anybody, especially if you never met them."[26] Johnston's father was known and not. She was conceived in an affair on a transatlantic voyage but to unmarried lovers, earning her the *non noto* designation, according to the bureaucracy of the time. Johnston grew up thinking her father was merely dead, not unknown, a story Johnston's mother had to confess to making up when her father actually died while Johnston was in college, an event—the truth telling, not the second death—that Johnston's wife, Ingrid Nyeboe, once described to me as the "defining moment" of Johnston's life.[27]

Of course Johnston could imagine that one can be born and die multiple times: her father *did* die (to her) twice.

In Apollinaire, Johnston found another bastard who made and remade himself. Learning about his life (and deaths), Johnston felt she had found an answer to how to be someone borne despite a patriarchal absence: "All I had to do was be like him."[28] She wanted to figure out how to be a woman who invented a "curious solution . . . to the [problem] of patriarchy," and in the twice-dead poet she found a path to respond to her father's two deaths.[29]

To be a bastard is to be both without a line and out of line. Writing about this particularly queer status, lesbian theorist Ann Cvetkovich describes "the bastard" as particularly aware they are "disenfranchised by the official institutions of the state."[30] From this perspective, it seems practical that Johnston created for herself not so much a lineage with Apollinaire but a circularity, making him simultaneously her father, uncle, grandfather, and self. In Apollinaire's first appearance in Johnston's column in 1968, she describes herself as "the feminine contraction of Guillaume"—*Jill* becomes the shortened, more familiar version of her poet/critic/tastemaker predecessor.[31] Apollinaire returns again in May 1969, again through nonreproductive means. Early in the column, Johnston rages against the *Voice*, which has—in the paper's usual, often messy approach to proofreading—deleted the last line of the previous week's column, a quotation from Apollinaire.[32] The deletion, however annoying to her, gives Johnston the opportunity to imagine her columns as never ending, one long piece stretching backward and forward in time, merely distributed across multiple newspapers. Rather than having stops and starts, she, *Jill Johnston* or *Jill*, arises from an endless succession of writing, midwifed by Apollinaire, whom she mentions by way of yet another nonhetero form of reproduction. She, or her column, has "sprung out of the head . . . of Guillaume." Three months later, she again mentions Apollinaire, closing a column by signing off "Goodbye and love for now, Guillaume."[33] The reader is left to decide if the phrase frames the column as a letter from Apollinaire to Johnston or an address from Johnston to Apollinaire, or if the two, Johnston and Apollinaire, have finally fused into one being. Though this might be more a case of *and* than *or*.

• • •

JOHNSTON TITLED HER 1985 memoir, the second of her four, *Paper Daughter*. In the book she defines a "paper daughter" as one "who exists only on paper"—a gendered version of "non noto," a woman borne of the page and of language, not of human parentage. In Apollinaire, Johnston found another person borne by way of non noto, but she also found a new way to imagine queer connectivity beyond lineage, a paper daughter and her paper ghost, both capable of springing paper daughters, maybe me, from their heads.

3

She Was a Lesbian Feminist

In 1974 feminist scholars Dianne Hunter and Rena Patterson opened their introduction to *Gullibles Travels*, a collection of Jill Johnston's writing from the early 1970s, by describing the book as "Jill Johnston celebrat[ing] herself in motion."[1] At the time of the collection's publication, longtime Johnston readers, particularly those most familiar with her as a dance critic, would likely have been surprised by what followed: a book with virtually no mention of dance. The motion Hunter and Patterson referenced is, instead, that of travel and political transformation, the central aspects of Johnston's life in the early 1970s. The woman who once tracked others' motion was now a lesbian feminist on the move, signaling through the flames of both the women's and gay liberation movements.

This was not a covert shift but one Johnston made in a very public manner through her *Voice* column as she grappled with, in her words, the emergence of her "gay head," as well as all that unfolded in the wake of "the feminists [having] found her."[2] Living as a lesbian feminist had now become the central performance in her life, and "her writing an extension of it."[3] As result, the

Voice retitled her column: "Jill Johnston" replaced "Dance Journal." This new version of her column became so popular that women lined the newspaper's steps each week, eager to access the latest installment of Johnston's musings on lesbian life. As readers and fans, these women accompanied Johnston as she sought to expand *lesbian* into a label that brought women together to critique both patriarchy and heteronormativity, as well as index a set of practices related to sex and desire—what Johnston described as moving from only recognizing "lesbian activity" toward embracing "lesbian identity."[4]

These "journeys in consciousnesses," as Johnston called her public provocations in her 1973 book, *Lesbian Nation*, did not just occur through writing; Johnston became famous because her advocacy for lesbian feminism often involved a creative braiding of the written and the physical.[5] Undoubtedly, her writing—its volume and its placement in increasingly mainstream publication venues—provided the anchor for Johnston's unlikely lesbian celebrity. From 1970 to 1975, the years on which this chapter focuses, she averaged forty-five columns per year in the *Voice*. (In the 1960s she averaged about fourteen per year.) She also published two books with major publishing houses: in 1971 E. P. Dutton issued *Marmalade Me*, her collection of (mostly) dance writing from the 1960s; and then *Lesbian Nation* came from Simon and Schuster in 1973. (A smaller press issued *Gullibles Travels* in 1974.) But her writing was only part of the story. Johnston also made many public appearances, in many platforms: on college campuses, at feminist conferences and festivals, and on radio and television, including a 1972 appearance on the nationally syndicated *Dick Cavett Show*. These were not, however, a writer's usual public speaking engagements. Johnston often began such events by reading her writing aloud but then used that as entrée to deploy her body to disrupt scenes of sexism and heteronormativity. The most infamous of her disruptions came at high profile feminist events: a topless swim she took to interrupt a speech by liberal feminist Betty Friedan at a fundraiser and a public make-out session that she had with two women as a way to sideline sexist author Norman Mailer during a panel in Manhattan. After such events Johnston further intertwined the physical and the written, documenting her experiences by describing her actions' sensorial impact in her column often using writing strategies she developed as a dance critic. The written, the live, and the embodied all overlapped, making Jill Johnston the news of lesbian feminism and the lesbian writer of the news.

These mash-ups of writing and action—often messy, even aggressive—positioned Johnston at once as hero and irritant to organized social movements of the early 1970s and have also kept her marginalized (and sometimes absent) from feminist and gay history. In an era of collectives, Johnston was never aligned—at least not for long—with any specific group. She briefly joined feminist consciousness-raising groups and meetings of the Gay Liberation Front, where she has been remembered as a disruptive, if engaging, storyteller.[6] Her relationship to the movements of the time is perhaps best summed up by her titling of a 1971 column "Movement Schmoovement," or as she wrote in a 1972 column, "I dislike meetings for purposes other than parties."[7] Yet Johnston was adamant that her "alignment was always with the women, across all lines."[8] She was a woman in motion, a choreographer of lesbians and lesbianism. Through her writing and physical disruptions, she crafted ways that women and lesbians could use their bodies to undermine those who sought to marginalize them, as well as to collaborate with those with whom they shared political commitments.

In these efforts Johnston drew from her immersion in the postmodern art scenes of the 1960s. Happenings and postmodern dance turned out to have been good training for the constant reorientations in US social movements of the late 1960s and early 1970s, the period when US radical activism experienced the "brea[k] down of the foundations of modernist political narratives," or what historian of feminist organizing Victoria Hesford has called the "postmodern present."[9] Having been a critic and a participant in postmodernism in the arts prepared Johnston for the "situated, fragmented, and provisional politics" of 1970s radical feminism and gay liberation. In art Johnston had already navigated the shift from modernist grand narratives to collage and assemblage, which paralleled—even foreshadowed—1970s activists' rejection of the "universalizing politics" central to the civil rights and leftist social movements of the 1960s.

The central attributes of postmodernism named by Hesford—"situated, fragmented, and provisional"—also shaped Johnston's evolving definitions of *lesbian*. In Johnston's column what constituted being a lesbian regularly morphed.[10] Some weeks being a lesbian meant being a product of imagined histories of women-centered myths; other weeks lesbians were strident figures who overlaid political criticism with seductive force. These collages excited readers, bringing them into lesbian community with one another and with Johnston. In this chapter lesbian adjacencies are no longer about theories (Johnston and Susan Sontag) or rhetorical strategies (Johnston and Audre Lorde); here lesbian adjacencies take more concrete form. In the "postmodern present" produced by Johnston and the expanding movements for gender and sexual liberation, lesbians kiss and touch, build homes and communities, and imagine a "lesbian nation." It's not, however, a utopia.

Lesbians of the time had to navigate the feminist movement's so-called gay/straight split and the marginalization of women in gay liberation protest. There were also painful divides among lesbians themselves, as white lesbians forged collectives that included neither women of color nor analysis of race in their world-building.[11] All of these are postmodern choreographies Jill Johnston helped author.

This chapter examines these choreographies from two perspectives. First, I consider Johnston's lesbian feminist activism as performance, asking how she intertwined writing and physical action as a way to approach the problem of being a lesbian in public, needing to attract desired attention while also thwarting unwanted gazes. Her disruptions of Friedan and Mailer are central case studies here. In the chapter's second half, I consider Johnston as choreographer, examining how her writing provided for her readers what dance improvisers call a score, a loose set of parameters that can shape or delimit action. As a postmodern lesbian feminist, Jill Johnston found ways to invite motion of many kinds, for herself and for other women, at scales large and small.

Part I: Lesbian Bodies in Public

LESBIAN IDENTITY IN THE AMERICAN PUBLIC

A history of lesbians in public could be a very short essay. There have, of course, always been women who shared intimacies with other women, had sex with other women, and shaped their lives around those commitments and desires. Yet these connections have often been relegated to the private, domestic sphere. Two examples among many are what Lillian Faderman, in her book *Odd Girls and Twilight Lovers*, terms "romantic friendships," relationships between upper-class white women in the early twentieth century or, as Lauren Gutterman details in *Her Neighbor's Wife*, intimate relationships between women who were married to men.[12] In both of these arrangements and many others, marriage—and the man a woman married—determined the boundaries of female sexuality and "restrict[ed] homosexuality's public presence."[13] Until the 1970s, like all women in the United States, lesbians also needed marriage, or, more accurately, a man, to access many of the items that facilitate public, social mobility: credit cards, mortgages, and leases.

Before the 1970s the overt gender discrimination that governed American public space often meant that merely being a woman in public could draw suspicion—let alone being a woman with another woman. For instance, most white-owned bars refused entry to "unescorted" women (meaning, again, a woman without a man), a policy that historian Finn Enke has described as intended to maintain an "appearance of a middle-class public free of prostitution and lesbianism."[14] Differing degrees of access to public space is, arguably, one of the primary distinctions between the histories of gay men and those of lesbians in the United States. In New York City, gay men, as historian George Chauncey has shown, "construct[ed] spheres of relative cultural autonomy in the interstices of a city governed by hostile powers."[15] The hostilities gay men faced in public could be very serious and harmful, ranging from casual derision and threats to overt surveillance and violence. Yet gay men, particularly white gay men, could—because they were men—be in public space throughout much of the twentieth century without necessarily drawing negative attention. Jill Johnston bristled at this double standard for gay men and lesbians, writing that "the male homosexual has always moved more freely in the extensive underground urban networks of bars and baths and highly developed cruising techniques and designated places to cruise. By comparison the lesbian meeting grounds have been nonexistent to singular."[16] No wonder there are so many jokes about lesbians always staying home; many must have felt they had no other option.

Laws policing women's movement in public began to change in the 1970s, allowing Johnston (and other lesbians) more freedom in public space. These changing options, however, also made Johnston more aware she had lived amid restrictions for the first forty-plus years of her life. Armed with an emerging feminist consciousness, she often reflected in her column on how limitations on women's participation in public society had shaped many aspects of her life. She began a July 1970 column by expressing frustration over just how long the laws prohibiting the movement of "unescorted women" had been in place and then recounting a recent conversation with fellow art critic and friend Ann Wilson about the many women each knew only as "artists' wives and widows."[17] Gender policing in the art world paralleled the gender-policed bar: male artists assumed they would be served (and were), while their female partners, many of them also artists, had to busy themselves serving others: making dinner and cleaning the house.

In these contexts Johnston noted that New York's dance community was remarkable. In dance, women had relative autonomy (or at least greater numbers) than in other spheres and thus could enjoy camaraderie among women outside of domestic spaces.[18] (Years later Johnston would wonder if the relative freedom dance afforded women had delayed her interest in feminism.[19]) The greater numbers of women in the dance world did not, however, spare female dancers from sexism. In dance, women could be together, in public, but they still had to accept opportunities that often came in prepackaged, male-sanctioned forms. Writing about her years dancing at the José Limón school, Johnston described how all women "had to be a Venus or a Helen," figures of feminine beauty and seduction from Greek mythology that Johnston neither fit nor wanted to fit.[20] But dance offered another gendered possibility: through the act of dancing itself, gender roles could be at least contested, even if not fully ignored. "Since I wasn't a Venus or a Helen," wrote Johnston, "my strategy was to be a Valkyrie [a female figure of Norse mythology] and consign the men to their graves by leaping higher and consuming more space faster." With her body she could exceed limiting stereotypes or plots.[21]

These feminist tactics learned in dance had significant overlap with tactics deployed by women's liberation activists in the late 1960s and early 1970s, groups often described as *radical feminists* to distinguish them from liberal feminists' legislatively focused efforts. Radical feminists took advantage of the ways women, especially women without men, drew attention and suspicion in public space, using their bodies to launch feminist critique. A number of radical feminist groups emphasized physical preparedness among their ranks. The New York Radical Feminists, for instance, required women to stage at least one public action before joining the group, and the women of Cell 16 trained in karate.[22] The most infamous instance of radical feminist–organized public, physical action came in a 1968 protest at the Miss America pageant. Radical feminists occupied the Atlantic City boardwalk near the pageant site and caused a scene by throwing trappings of femininity (what the women called "instruments of torture": bras, heels, false eyelashes, etc.) into a "Freedom Trash Can" and then crowning a live sheep "Miss America."[23] The highly theatrical event garnered national media attention for this relatively new strand of the women's movement, even as the event's guerrilla theater tactics caused tension among the activists. Some worried the spectacle had turned "anti-woman," attacking the pageant's contestants rather than the pageant as an institution.[24]

In 1970 radical feminists again used their bodies to stage public critique, this time explicitly focusing on an institution and its leadership. Led by Shulamith Firestone, radical feminists staged a sit-in at *Ladies' Home Journal*. The large group, between a hundred and two hundred women, occupied the editor in chief's office, demanding the women's magazine hire more women as writers and editors. After hours passed with little response from the existing staff, Firestone dialed up the theatrics, climbing atop the editor's desk and shredding copies of the magazine. "Confronted with the intensity and reality of this brand of women's thinking," the magazine consented to change, including publishing an insert titled "The New Feminism" soon after.[25] After this protest, however, organizers worried that Firestone's improvisational solo action had undermined the group's investment in collectivity. Bodies in motion created messy, if powerful, feminist disturbances.

Lesbians within radical feminism also turned to public, physical protest, but with other feminists, namely, straight white women, as their intended audience. In May 1970 lesbians, many of whom, like Johnston, came to women's liberation through the Gay Liberation Front, protested the marginalization of lesbians in women's liberation through the "Lavender Menace Zap" at the second Congress to Unite Women. The lesbian protesters interrupted the gathering by cutting the auditorium lights and pushing copies of their manifesto, "The Woman Identified Woman," into audience members' hands.[26] When the lights came back on, the audience of mostly straight feminists saw seventeen women standing onstage wearing lavender T-shirts emblazoned with "Lavender Menace," reclaiming the phrase Betty Friedan had used to dismiss lesbian perspectives in the feminist movement. The stories the women told from the stage—a sharing that lasted for hours—centered lesbians, their stories and their bodies.[27]

As radical feminism grew into a national—and nationally recognized—movement, those outside the movement often labeled all who joined the fight as lesbians. Many radical feminist activists, regardless of their sexuality, had stories similar to that of Ti-Grace Atkinson, a straight feminist leader, who noted, "The first time I was called a lesbian was on my first picket line."[28] Atkinson lamented that reactions to such labeling often got bogged down in an "are you/aren't you" response, rather than noting that *lesbian* was becoming a "code word for female resistance."[29] Atkinson would eventually argue that "feminism is the theory; lesbianism is the practice," a statement that Johnston often quoted and that inspired her addition of the phrase *The Feminist Solution* to the title of her book *Lesbian Nation*.[30]

Perhaps no radical feminist so publicly and intimately experienced how the term *lesbian* could disrupt feminist activism as did Johnston's friend and fellow writer Kate Millett, the radical feminist queer figure to whom Johnston is most often compared. Millett had both male and female partners and identified as bisexual. Yet she accepted the label *lesbian* when asked about her sexuality by another feminist at a public event in 1970. In her 1974 autobiography *Flying* (a book that shares much with Johnston's postmodern writing style), Millett remembers being filled with fear as she heard the question, "Are you a Lesbian?" from an audience member. She recounts her thoughts at the moment, writing, "That word in public, the word I waited half a lifetime to hear. Finally I am accused."[31] This was the opposite of the bold remixings of language and physicality in which radical feminists engaged. This was a word hitting, even harming, a body—a harm compounded shortly after, when *Time* magazine outed Millett after celebrating her just months earlier as the face of women's liberation.[32]

Johnston sought to redefine and reclaim the boldest possibilities of being a lesbian. Hers was an urgent task as the national media worked to cast all feminists as lesbians, creating what Victoria Hesford has termed the "feminist-as-lesbian." Hesford calls this mythic, moping stereotype a "potentially troubling cultural figure" composed by mainstream media coverage to reduce "the complexity and diversity of women's liberation" into a caricature "of white, middle-class women's supposed ordinariness [that] restates lesbianism as out of bounds, . . . anterior to 'normal' sexuality and, therefore . . . anterior to 'normal' women. As a consequence, women's liberationists are marked as anterior to normal women, with the lesbian the boundary figure through which that separation is made."[33] Tying all feminists to lesbianism and marking lesbianism as outside norms of femininity placed all feminist action outside of respectable society and turned all feminists—lesbian or not; white, Black, Brown, or Indigenous—into a monolithic, dismissible figure. Lesbians were not legally prohibited from the public sphere as had previously been the case, but, marked as public threat, they were homogenized and marginalized. This is the social moment into which Jill Johnston wrote.

But she did more than just write. Her lesbian provocateur theatrics shared much with her fellow radical feminists in their insertions and assertions of women's bodies in public space. To this, Johnston added strategies of Dada and surrealism, the artistic movements so central to the postmodern art world from whence she came. The question that structured her performance viewing in the 1960s now animated her lesbian feminism: "Why shouldn't this go with that and be called something else"?[34] Why shouldn't lesbians be in public space and be called women, leaders, and artists?

GO SWIMMING/AS UNBOUNDED AS WATER

What was Jill Johnston in the early 1970s? A dance critic? Writer? Activist? Provocateur? As was often the case with Johnston, all of the above is the most accurate answer. Or even more accurately, she was a postmodern collage of characters and mediums, invested in scrambling relationships between words and bodies to imagine lesbian possibility within women's liberation and gay liberation. By refusing to ever be just one thing, not only did she resist categorization; she also resisted confirmation. Jill Johnston was a lingering, loud presence always just beyond the grasp of those who sought to pin her down, a remixing of a lesbian past, present, and future. She was a lesbian echo.[35]

Key to her queer lesbian effervescence was Johnston's adeptness in shifting between writing and moving—yes, dancing but also, in the 1970s version of her lesbian echo, swimming and making out with other women in public. She constantly challenged a notion of writing as legible and bodies as illegible. She knew, undoubtedly because of her experience with dance and dance criticism, that writing could excite energy and that bodies could make clear demands. She deployed this knowledge to disrupt notions of what a woman could or should be, constantly shifting her mode of engagement with the public and blending the physical, the written, and the spoken into a queer expression of woman.

Johnston made queer work of coming out, too. "I'm gay." She never said it. In a July 1970 column titled "Of This Pure but Irregular Passion" (a phrase borrowed from French lesbian icon Colette's 1932 erotic quasi-autobiography), Johnston announced her lesbianism to the world. She did so, however, by requiring her readers to hear her news on her terms. Writing amid celebrations of Stonewall's first anniversary, Johnston began, "In support of the gay movement on the occasion of the gay celebration week: I guess yes I've been saying it in this column for a year and a half now, but always fragmentarily in the context of the literary exercises. So this will be straight on."[36] There is little "straight on" (or straight) in what follows. Johnston says she never meant to declare her sexuality in print, questions why anyone would find such an act of interest, muses why the column has become more about the "theater of my life" than the "theater of dance," and then, in a phrase that reads almost as addendum, mentions loving and having sex with a woman.

The mention of the woman, the loving, the sex, appears at the paragraph's end. It's not the big finish—it's an add-on, almost an aside—and not only because of its position within her sequence of sharing. As had become a hallmark of her writing about dance in the 1960s, Johnston used rhythm to choreograph her point on the page. Coming out to her readers, Johnston resists prose's usual linear pull and instead conjures space, time, and flesh. The flow of her words is of equal importance as her subject. And the flow of the column doesn't say, "I'm gay. PERIOD." There is an urgency, a push, a layering—an identity coming into view but not fully grasped or held. This is how lesbianism emerged/es in Johnston's writing, slipping into and around the edges of publicity.

The complexity of her shifting subject is the topic of the column's second paragraph. Johnston references her marriage to a man over a decade prior, describing herself first as heterosexual, then bisexual, and then drawn toward androgyny. She seems, all at once, to both claim and dispense with these identities. Labels are not simple. She notes the circumstances that made each label appropriate or compelling at specific moments in her life, and then she addresses how the press of the social makes each oppressive or unattainable. Heterosexuality comes with expectations and reproduction. Bisexuality becomes invisible as heteros get the public realm and homos the underground. Without access to trans and queer-affirming twenty-first-century terms like *gender-nonconforming* or *transgender*, she lands on *androgyny* and *transsexual* as compelling but eventually dismisses both as impossible, deciding their allure comes from their unattainability. Androgyny and gendered play may only be a thing of Greek myths or dreams. In her darting among identities, Johnston enacts what art historian David Getsy has described as simultaneously "engag[ing] with and diverg[ing] from . . . the imperative to embrace identity and to 'come out,'" a phenomenon Getsy elaborates relative to Johnston's good friend and Fluxus artist Geoffrey Hendricks's *Ring Piece* (1971). Getsy argues that Hendricks's performance offers a doubled, paradoxical motion of coming out, creating a "divergent and deferred experience" of public and private.[37] Recognition without confirmation returns as theme.

One of Johnston's girlfriends, Jane O'Wyatt, a fellow lesbian feminist activist, remembers feeling (before meeting Johnston at a Daughters of Bilitis dance) that Johnston's column "tipped her off" about her lesbianism but always seemed to stop just short of full announcement.[38] Johnston questioned the clarity she saw the gay liberation movement demanding of people in their announcements of identity, even as she also despised secrets. For Johnston, sexuality was "defined by our feelings," and she wanted to chart a path that acknowledged that "oppression is real" and that "lives are illusory."[39] Her insistence on sexuality as elusive angered members of the Gay Liberation Front: the gay male leadership said she sounded not at all like a proud, out, post-Stonewall homosexual but rather someone not "politically enlightened at all."[40] The Daughters of Bilitis publication, *The Ladder*, called her coming out in the 1970 column "a conglomeration of theoretical philosophy that will confuse anyone who is not thoroughly familiar with Lesbian literature."[41] Being a lesbian echo fit poorly with post-Stonewall demands for gay publicity.

“I’m a lesbian.” She doesn’t ever say it in that 1970 column, nor does she ever quite state it so straightforwardly even as she tries to reach a wider readership later in the 1970s. To be a lesbian never gets the on-the-nose attention other labels do. Johnston’s status as a gay woman swirls on the edges of legibility through the loops of her writing—another writing feat learned from postmodern dance, where meaning is never fully specified. Dancing bodies rarely tell their full story or name themselves, yet they are fully and robustly present. Johnston suggested being a lesbian as similar. A way to live a sexy, provocative life. To move across genders through sensation and desire. To claim the body and to claim sex as essential. In the summer of 1970, for Johnston being a lesbian in public seems less an announcement of alignment with a label, more a way of being—and, most importantly, a mode of disruption.

A spectacular example of Johnston’s generatively disruptive presence came a month after her initial coming-out column when she took a very public swim to silence liberal feminist activist and lesbophobe Betty Friedan. On August 9, 1970, as Friedan tried to speak to a group gathered at a fundraiser for the upcoming Women’s Strike for Equality, Johnston, wearing only black underwear and a denim shirt (and, eventually, only the underwear), swam four laps in the backyard pool of the Long Island mansion where the fundraiser was being held. Upstaged by the swimming Johnston, Friedan was left to make a last-ditch effort to keep the crowd’s attention by trying to lead everyone in a chorus of “Liberation Now.” It didn’t work. Friedan was no match for Johnston. In coverage of what *Time* magazine called a new “young assertive women’s liberation movement,” a photograph captures the moment a bare-chested Johnston pushes herself out of the pool, her white, naked torso large and in the foreground.[42] In the photo’s background, Friedan looks small and mute, despite standing at a microphone. According to *New York Times*’s coverage of the event, written by Charlotte Curtis, the reporter for the “socialite beat,” Johnston exited the pool and wrapped herself in a towel supplied by the mansion’s owner, visual art collector Bob Scull. Friedan was heard to “mutter” that Johnston was “one of the biggest enemies of the movement.”[43]

No one knew what to make of Johnston’s swim. Some tried to understand it through the frame of her profession, which only highlighted the confusion she produced. The *New York Times* coverage included a photograph of Johnston, her back to the camera as she dried off, with a caption that read “Jill Johnston, a writer.” *Time* identified Johnston similarly, describing her below the picture of her naked torso as only a “writer for the *Village Voice*.”[44]

The collision of writing and the body that produces the word *choreography*—which essentially means "writing dancing"—has perhaps never been rendered quite so (queerly) clearly.

Johnston amplified the queer (il)legibility of her swim, writing about the event a week later in the *Voice*. As her performance reviews often had, her August 13 column, "Bash in the Sculls," traced her path through the evening. In the column she arrives at the Sculls' home immediately critical of the gathering's superficiality, seeing "smiling women for equality" staging a tableaux of women's liberation for the press.[45] The mansion itself felt like a museum clamoring to be a stage, full of work by Johnston's collaborators and friends: "a gray minimal [Robert] Morris . . . [a] wood beam [Mark] di Suvero." To Johnston, the smiling women amid the modernist art reeked of the worst of liberal feminism, Friedan and her ilk fighting only for "a better distribution of maids."

The situation called for the kind of intervention in which Johnston specialized: "be[ing] serious in one's purposes but not necessarily solemn." An encounter with Friedan left Johnston angry and ready to act. As she often did when speaking with prominent straight feminists, she immediately began to flirt. Johnston writes that she liked Friedan "below the chin" and started their conversation "at that level," which was likely not meant as a figure of speech. Such tactics, especially as flirtation tipped toward seduction, would earn Johnston accusations of being a "lesbian chauvinist."[46] They also helped her leverage the physical as a way to interrupt political stances with which she disagreed. With destabilization now produced via flirtation, Johnston goes in for the big question, asking Friedan "if there shouldn't be a pub(l)ic conjunction between Women's Liberation and the Gay Liberation Front."[47] Friedan responds by getting "super huffy" and morphing, in Johnston's eyes, into a straight-woman monster: "Her eyes went big 'n bulgy and her lipstick leered crimson and she said crisply enunciating each word that 'it' is not an issue." Friedan then momentarily hedges, and says she is "against all oppression." Johnston won't let the pulsing *it* in Friedan's initial comment go. As Friedan walks away, Johnston yells, "You mean 'it' is embarrassing." The pronoun lingers without linguistic referent, but now, in Johnston's mouth, *it* has a referent, even a subject: Johnston, her, the lesbian. Johnston speaks, steps, and swims into the erasure that Friedan tried to make. Johnston's very body is the lesbianism Friedan refused to speak.

As Johnston strips off her "pants shoes socks hardware," she hopes to produce "an explosion" with an open-ended result. She's not giving a lecture or even merely targeting Friedan. The swim, the physical interruption itself, is her desired outcome. As she gets out of the pool, she says she repeatedly hears "WHY DID YOU DO THAT?," a question she renders in all caps in her column, underscoring how intensely people wanted her to provide an explanation. The lesbian swimmer, however, has layered motivations and desires: "Well . . . I was . . . uh . . . hot—and drunk. Were you hot and drunk? Yes. Were you protesting? Yes. Are you a woman . . . ? Yes. Were you part of a Red Stocking Plot to Sabotage this Party? Yes. Were you showing off? Yes. Are you a radical lesbian? Yes. Do you like the Sculls? Sure." Johnston's insistence on multiplicity and her rendering of the moment as a back-and-forth dialogue re-purposes tactics from her performance reviews, emphasizes performance-audience exchanges, and disrupts the boundary between the two. Except now Johnston is the one onstage, the one asking an audience to attend to her layers, even contradictions. It's an awfully queer, awfully postmodern swim.

She is not interested, however, in producing mere confusion. Johnston relishes ambiguity and discord, until the moment a man almost gets credit for her actions. Her only clear *no* to her interrogators comes in response to a question of whether "Mr. Scull [had] 'put her up to it.'" "No," she says, drawing a clear line. No meaning is to be inferred from him being the one to help her out of the pool and offer her a towel. The swim was not evidence of a lesbian–straight man conspiracy.

Whatever Johnston was doing—whatever *it* was—she wanted to be clear that her "it" was a product of her own choices and desires. She was, as she would describe all women who were "improper person[s]," "a ramblin woman a gamblin woman myself."[48] As she swam to interrupt a scene of liberal feminist respectability, she knew she had an audience, and as she wrote in the newspaper, she felt a "responsortibility."[49] She did not seek to meet expectations, however, with comprehension, clarity, or answers. Instead, she worked to remain "open to all combinations and interpretations."[50] Sometimes it's best to go swimming and see how far the ripples might reach.

The ripples of Johnston's creative coming outs, in writing and in the pool, reached her contemporary readers but have grown less clear over time. Johnston's play with identity and her refusal to come out in post-Stonewall terms has contributed to her disappearance from histories of women's liberation, even though, at the time, there were all the women showing up at the *Voice* and mainstream press coverage stating her importance to both women's liberation and gay liberation. She made it into *Time*'s coverage of women's liberation in 1970 and *Life*'s coverage of gay liberation in 1971, where she was described as "a full-time polemicist for sexual liberation."[51] Johnston is, however, remarkably absent from histories of both women's and gay liberation.

When historians do remember her, they usually lump her with others relegated to the margins: one writer among other lesbian authors who published books in the early 1970s, a lone case of an "absurdist form of lesbian feminism," or a mere precursor to the overly essentialist gender politics of late 1970s cultural feminism.[52]

Johnston's place (or lack thereof) in histories of gay and women's liberation movements could be attributed to a number of factors: having too radical politics or being too well known as an individual to fit in a historiography focused on collectivity. As John D'Emilio and Estelle Freedman have argued, the most radical potential of 1970s liberation movements never materialized.[53] Even a few years later, Johnston's politics may have seemed too radical a take on the place of queer women in society to be imagined as central or popular. She is probably easier to overlook, too, since she never aligned herself for any length of time with a particular radical feminist group—and only with the Gay Liberation Front briefly.[54]

A more likely reason, though, was that Johnston was caught between competing notions of publicity in the women's and gay liberation movements. Radical feminists "condemned vociferously as antithetical to the democratic ethos of liberation" any flirtation with celebrity, and certainly a single-authored column in a widely circulating newspaper would have been seen to be just that.[55] Meanwhile, in gay liberation, coming out, declaring one's sexuality in public, became the "definitive feature of lesbian or gay personhood."[56] Historian Martha Gever notes this left Johnston (and Kate Millett) in a double bind. To announce their sexuality, however creatively, as Johnston did in her column and in her raucous public appearances, was to be the wrong kind of woman, unable to fade into the male-centered politics of mainstream gay liberation and too singular and loud to be part of collaborative feminist collectives. Of course, Johnston's own disposition toward provocation over coalition building did not help her case. As she wrote in her "Movement Schmoovement" column, "I reaffirm that I constitute a movement totally myself complete period."[57] Years later, though, she offered a caveat in her personal journal: "I have a constitutional opposition to doing anything everybody else does. My one aberration was feminism."[58]

TAKING CENTER STAGE: TOWN HALL

On April 30, 1971, Jill Johnston combined her command of luscious language and provocative physical spectacle to reorient a public debate about feminism. Her skill in intertwining the linguistic and the embodied allowed her to thrust lesbian identity into an otherwise heteronormative, masculinist display. Johnston remade an event initially conceived as a debate of women versus men into an exploration of the *many* ways to be a woman in public.

The occasion of Johnston's lesbian spectacle was a panel, part of Shirley Broughton's ongoing series "Theater for Ideas," initially proposed under the title "Feminists v. Mailer," an assembly to discuss Norman Mailer's antifeminist screed "The Prisoner of Sex." Published in *Harper's Magazine* a month earlier, the essay responded to Kate Millett's *Sexual Politics*, a foundational book of feminist critique and one of several 1971 watershed publications in feminist thought (Firestone's *The Dialectic of Sex: The Case for a Feminist Revolution* being another). In *Sexual Politics*, Millett undertakes close readings of literature by D. H. Lawrence, Henry Miller, Jean Genet, and Mailer, tracking how each deployed sex as a form of power over women. She focuses on what she describes as Mailer's justification of men's violence against women in his novel *An American Dream* (1965), particularly through the novel's "hero," Stephen Rojack.[59] Millett concludes that "no one has done so much to explain, yet justify violence against women as had Mailer."[60] Reflecting on how the Town Hall debate with Mailer went, Johnston later wrote, "Kate prepared the indictment and the accused pleaded innocent using the evidence of the prosecution."[61] In other words, on the panel Mailer proved to be just the man Millett thought he was.

Most feminists, including Millett, Atkinson, Susan Brownmiller, and Gloria Steinem, declined to appear with Mailer, wanting to avoid giving his misogyny further publicity.[62] Johnston, however, said yes, perhaps to continue being feminism's favorite disruptor or trusting that her approach of combining language, comedy, and choreography à la surrealism could displace and reorient the debate. Chris Hegedus and D. A. Pennebaker's film of the event, *Town Bloody Hall* (1979), suggests she did both. At every turn, Johnston disrupted Mailer by making an explicitly lesbian challenge to patriarchy.

Johnston also extended her challenge to straight feminist respectability politics, represented on the panel by British feminist poet/critic/provocateur Germaine Greer, literary critic Diana Trilling, and National Organization for Women (NOW) New York chapter president Jacqueline Ceballos. All three were straight (though a few months earlier Johnston, as she described in a column, had tried hard to make that less true about Greer).[63] All members of the panel were white, a fact that escaped comment in the convening but that protesters outside the event noted, calling the event racist and classist. Tickets to attend cost $25 per person, roughly the equivalent of $175 per ticket in 2024.[64]

Watching Hegedus and Pennebaker's movie, it's clear why the two men made a film of the event: it was an affair to be seen as much as heard. Writing about the evening for the *Voice*, feminist critic and artist Rosalyn Drexler described it as a performance complete with highly symbolic costuming from the outset. Peeking under the curtain before the panelists entered, Drexler saw "three pairs of boots: black shiny belonged to Norman, long fitted—Germaine, heavy workman type—Jill and two pairs of sensibles [*sic*]—Jacqueline and Diana."[65] Subtext surfaces à la footwear description and word sequence. Johnston was an outsider in comparison to Mailer's and Greer's posh stardom. In comparison to Trilling and Ceballos, the "sensible" straight women, she was a gender bender. These distinctions only mounted after the curtain rose. Draped in fox fur, Greer, author of the recently published *Female Eunuch* (1970), plays the role of glamourous literati. Ceballos and Trilling sport conservative suits, with Trilling's pearl necklace almost glowing. Johnston wears jeans and her signature denim jacket.

The panel's conception and structure, however, threatened to erase all differences among the women and instead elevated Mailer as the evening's patriarch. As moderator, he took outsized status, dumping all the women into the pejorative category "lady critics," the term he used to introduce the panelists, a condescension Susan Sontag pointed out from the audience during the panel's Q&A postscript. The format further curtailed the women's power. Each had ten minutes to speak, with Mailer making frequent interruptions, narrating, and often vociferously disagreeing with each woman as she took her turn at the mic. Mailer seemed to understand his turn as moderator as never ending.

Johnston anticipated Mailer's mansplaining and thus prepared a strategy for outdoing him, drawing on her theatrical knowledge at its most surreal. Options she considered included "wir[ing] the hall and convert[ing] Norman's voice into instant static every time he spoke or to try and rise on a swing or a platform by pulley of helium balloon and demolish the stage with water bags and paper airplanes and jelly beans and confetti and rice patties."[66] The first idea, using static to interrupt Mailer, sounds much like the play with language and liveness Johnston had often commended in performances by Robert Morris and Yvonne Rainer. The latter, creating spectacles overflowing with objects both ridiculous and mundane, could be a scene from an Allan Kaprow– or Robert Whitman–directed Happening. Johnston worried, though; she knew that treating the evening as theatrical would not, in and of itself, sideline Mailer. He had "theatrical experience" too.[67] A plan that involved thinking about staging and embodiment was a tool, not a strategy inherently imbued with radical potential.

Since four of the five panelists were well-known authors (Ceballos was primarily an organizer), deft deployment of language could be expected. Johnston quickly demonstrated she could use language to center the room on women's experiences, even as she scrambled what might be meant by *woman*. She spun her signature associative style: lilting and poetic ("The lover should resemble the beloved and be the same, and the greater is the likeness brighter will the ruptured flame"), provocative ("I am a woman and therefore a lesbian"), and pointedly funny ("He said, 'I want your body,' and she said, 'You can have it when I'm through with it'").[68] Charged by Johnston's heat and wit, the room grew raucous. In the film, laughter and gasps can be heard as soon as Johnston delivers her opening line: "All women are lesbians except those who don't know it—naturally they are but don't know it—yet." The line landed a bit like a joke, announced Johnston's intention to redefine assumptions about what *woman* meant, and, in its provocative tone, paralleled the statement made a few months earlier by the Radicalesbians: "What is a lesbian? A lesbian is the rage of all women condensed to the point of explosion."[69]

It wasn't just what Johnston said that helped her capture the room's attention. It was how she took time. She takes her allotted ten minutes, and then five more, hitting the fifteen-minute mark with no pause or final period in sight. Mailer interrupts and accuses her of being "unfair" to the other panelists. The problem is not how much time *he's* taking as moderator but how long *she* speaks. The audience joins the standoff. A mix of shouted encouragement and boos—perhaps to Johnston, perhaps to Mailer—rise as a chorus. The film captures one person yelling, "Go ahead, Jill!" Johnston has upset the rules of the space by defying Mailer's rules, and now others rush in.

Johnston's theatrical experience as an audience member has paid off, so she stokes the flames of audience uproar further. She opens her arms, welcoming one woman from the audience into a (relatively obviously planned) embrace (see figure 3.1). The two hug and grope at one other's backsides. Johnston squeezes and lifts her partner in a way that feels warm and known, even as the duet as a whole is as awkward as it is erotic. Without warning, another woman walks onstage and asks—in something of a stage voice—"Hey, what about me?" In response, she gets tackled, falling to the floor with Johnston, the third woman on top. Eventually the trio stumbles back to their feet, and Johnston casually returns to the mic, her two kissing partners flanking

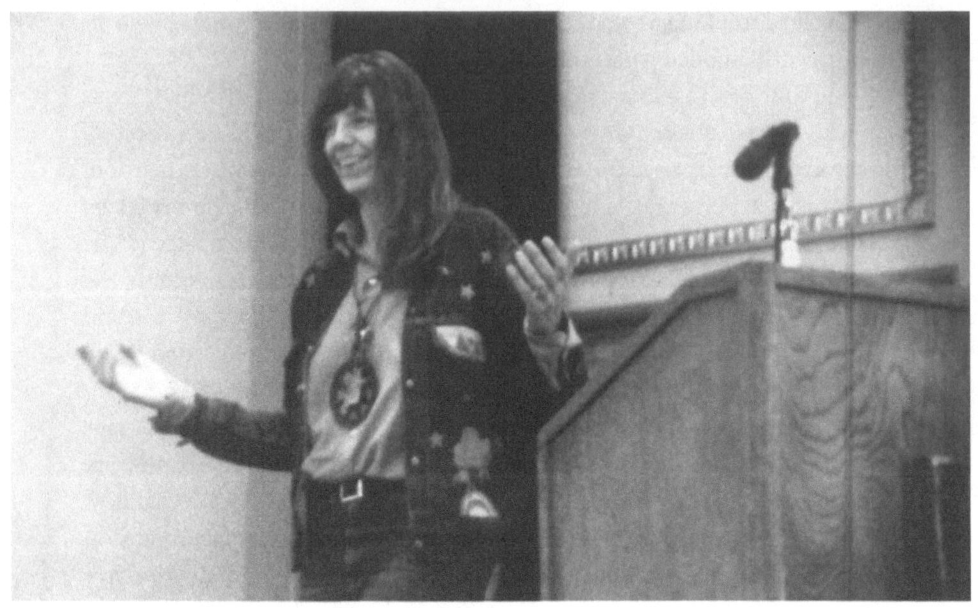

3.1 Jill Johnston invites women onstage to interrupt Norman Mailer at the Town Hall event of April 30, 1971, in New York City. From *Town Bloody Hall*, Chris Hegedus and D. A. Pennebaker, directors. Courtesy of Pennebaker Hegedus Films. Please visit PHFilms.com.

her. The brief but memorable tussle easily meets the two-pronged criteria that dance theorist Petra Kuppers has argued constitutes a lesbian dance: the explicit performance of female desire *and* a refusal to be merely an other to heterosexuality.[70] By embracing, Johnston and friends do not merely mark themselves as different from the other panelists, all of whom (particularly Greer) flirt with Mailer. These women are taking over. As the trio stands at the mic, Pennebaker and Hegedus keep their camera on the three lesbians and only the three lesbians. Mailer can be heard, yelling, "C'mon, Jill. Be a lady," but he's the one on the outside now.

Johnston laughs. She's been doing this the whole time, regularly cracking herself up as she speaks. Her laughter is big and wide open, causing her whole body to shake as she rears back from the microphone (see figure 3.2). She's laughing so hard she can't speak. Either from discomfort or in agreement with her over how ridiculous Mailer is being, her fellow panelists laugh too. Johnston is, as performance theorist Sara Warner has called her, a "joker citizen," critiquing both sexism and feminist respectability politics by way of humor.[71] Building on Warner's assessment, I would add that Johnston's

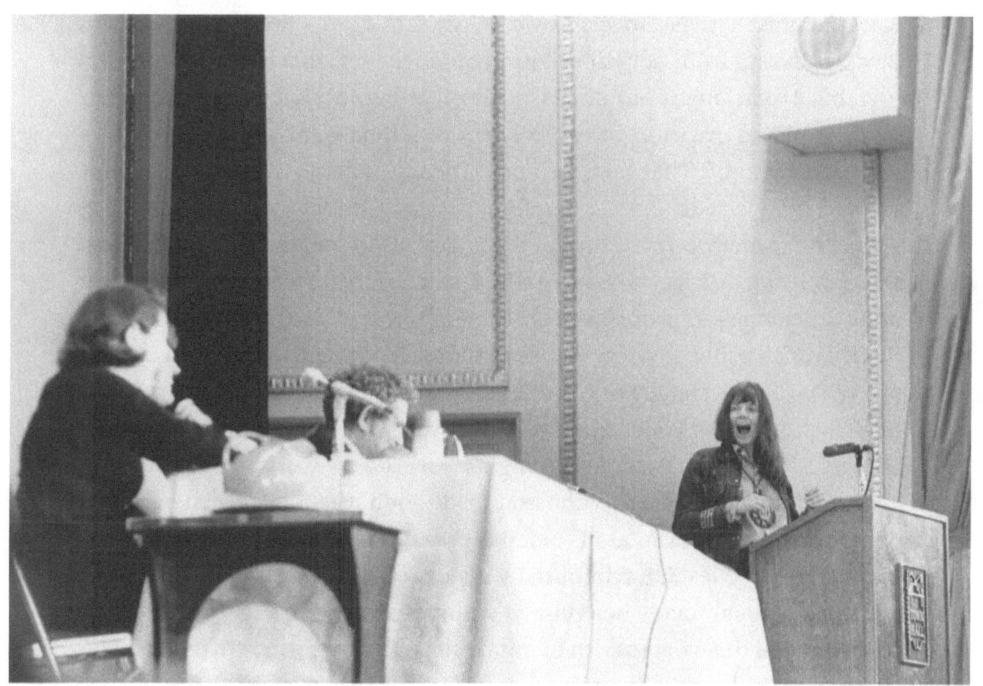

3.2 Jill Johnston turning to the panel at the Town Hall event of April 30, 1971; Norman Mailer (*center*). From *Town Bloody Hall*, Chris Hegedus and D. A. Pennebaker, directors. Courtesy of Pennebaker Hegedus Films. Please visit PHFilms.com.

jester-esque disruption issues as much from her body—the kissing and the laughing—as it does from her words. She takes up more and more space, disregarding the event's preordained rules and distancing herself from the other women on the panel, the "sensibles" (Trilling and Ceballos) and the seductive (Greer).

Taking space with her body and humor is a key and effective strategy for Johnston, yet is decidedly partially licensed by her whiteness. Radical feminists, many of whom were white, could afford to be ridiculous in public. For instance, the women who participated in the 1968 Miss America protests could disrupt a public space by crowning a sheep with little worry about punitive consequences. Those arrested were immediately bailed out and never charged.[72] Similarly, Johnston could take her disruptions to extremes with little fear of anything worse than public derision. The size, almost glee, of her laughter suggests she knows this, a security afforded by whiteness that looks very different from, for example, the laughter of her contemporary,

Black feminist activist Angela Davis. In the film *Black Power Mixtape* (2011), Davis, speaking from her jail cell in 1972, laughs big, much like Johnston in 1971, but Davis laughs out of exasperation at her interviewer's white ignorance displayed in a thoughtless line of questioning—and she does so from a room in a prison.[73] That said, it's not as though activists of color completely avoided humor. Black lawyer and feminist activist Florynce "Flo" Kennedy always wore a cowboy hat and pink sunglasses in public appearances, and she planned the Great Harvard Pee-In, leading Harvard women to pour their urine on campus to protest the absence of women's bathrooms. She was a Black woman using physical humor to make a point and make change.[74] But unlike Davis or Kennedy or other Black, Latinx, Asian American, or Native feminists, Johnston could laugh with little worry. She had greater latitude to see just how far she could push things.

At the Town Hall event, Johnston made good use of her racial privilege, decentering Mailer even as his defensive tactics turned blatantly homophobic. Though her lesbian trio initially dislodged his centrality by taking the audience's visual focus, he still had a microphone. From his seat, he calls Johnston and the women with her at the lectern "three dirty overalls," adding that it's "a shame" the audience paid $25 to see them when they could see "cock and cunt" down the street for $4. With his "dirty overalls" comment and attempts to de-eroticize and marginalize the three lesbians, he conjures Hesford's "feminist-as-lesbian" figure. Uninterested in men, these three are neither real entertainment nor real women (and maybe, for Mailer, the two categories are one). He then tries to camouflage his sexism and homophobia in a performance of liberal democracy, calling for a vote on whether Johnston should be allowed to keep speaking. It's a total charade: he sets the terms for the vote, and he'll do the counting. Not surprisingly, Mailer announces Johnston has lost the vote and gets up to take the lectern back from her. Johnston is right: Mailer is uninterested in proving Millett's assessment of him wrong. He only wants to hoard power.

But Johnston and her two dance partners have the last word (move?). They immediately begin another full-on make-out session. As Mailer gets up and then comes closer, Johnston leans her make-out partner against the lectern, so he can only reach the microphone by craning his neck and torso. His voice is amplified, but Johnston has literally taken space from him. She has displaced him from center stage, made him contort himself around the women, and overpowered his talktalktalk with her body. Johnston's choreography does not invite Mailer to be titillated. Instead, the women literally force him to the edge, away from center stage and the microphone. He is visibly uncomfortable, not pleasured in any way. Through physical choices, Johnston and her two kissing partners mark Mailer's sexism as ridiculous *and* supersede it. Multiple women—not just Johnston as lone lesbian superhero—outdo him, displaying a flexible, egalitarian relationship. As the trio kisses, falls, and tumbles, there is no sense of leader and follower—or at least not a sense of those roles as stable. To be valued in the kissing trio is to be responsive, not to be in control.

Finally, now having wrested center stage from Mailer, Johnston can leave. Seemingly on her own time, she takes one of the women's hands and strolls offstage. She never returns. For the rest of the evening, Mailer repeatedly shouts, "I would ask Jill Johnston this, if she were here!" She is still there, though; Mailer's own invocations of her prove this. She leaves a mark that remains even after she departs. Her mark is one of lesbian present absence, a powerful example of what Annamarie Jagose describes as lesbians' ability to be "less an absence than a presence that can't be seen."[75] With other women, Johnston creates a resonant lesbian echo, a powerful lingering of women's bodies, women touching, women laughing, and women being seen on their own terms. All this adds up to awfully good choreography.

Part II: Lesbian Choreographer on the Page

Jill Johnston knew where she had learned to be a choreographer of lesbian feminism. In a September 1970 column, she celebrated women in the concert dance world for "reinvent[ing]" the theatrical frame by using "the body . . . as a medium for . . . invention," rather than treating the body, especially the female body, only "as the object itself."[76] The choreographers she names—"Martha Graham, Doris Humphrey, Hanya Holm, Mary Wigman, Yvonne Rainer, Meredith Monk, and Twyla Tharp"—had fashioned frames that gave women new options for how to use their bodies in public, feminist interventions to which Johnston had had, quite literally, a front-row seat. Even as Johnston no longer wrote about dance, these choreographers' lessons shaped her writing, helped her imagine structures for and with others, and reinvented the ways women saw themselves and invited others to see them.

In Johnston's writing, lesbian identity became a social, rather than individual, project. She helped write into being imaginative frameworks to help lesbians move together. Recognizing Johnston as choreographer, a creative force for others, rather than a solo author focused only on her individual (albeit increasingly well-known) life situates her within what historian Lauren

Gutterman has described as a key shift in the 1970s, a move away from *lesbian* as adjective and toward *lesbian* as collective noun.[77] With her emphasis on invention and physical action, Johnston might have even rendered *lesbian* a verb—and inspired her readers to treat it as such.

Considering choreography as frame for reexamining Johnston and lesbian feminism also helps recognize the term *lesbian* as, like all categories of gender and sexuality, socially produced. Dance theorist Susan Foster has argued that using choreography as frame (or metaphor) emphasizes gender as emerging from "interconnectedness," "relationality," and the nonverbal/nontextual.[78] Foster offers "choreographing gender" as an amendment to queer theorist Judith Butler's widely cited notion of gender as "performed" through a "stylized repetition of acts," a formation that can too easily be (mis)understood as gender performance emerging entirely from an individual.[79] Too, since Butler's theory of gender performativity has been frequently imagined as a script, a metaphor that brings with it a script's emphasis on written and spoken language, Foster's proposal of gender as choreographed more readily brings attention to "discussions of materiality and body" and "the unspoken, . . . the bodily gestures and movements that, along with speech, construct gendered identity."[80] Butler's theory is often imagined via the virtuosic solo drag performer. In contrast, Foster's proposal invites images of groups moving together—onstage and in the audience. Johnston had spent her life studying these kinds of group interactions: how an ensemble interpreted choreographic direction and how an audience interacted with performance. In the early 1970s, she brought that knowledge to her vision of lesbian relationality.

Johnston launched her most vigorous argument for lesbian identity as a choreography of gendered motion across a triptych of March 1971 columns titled "Lois Lane Is a Lesbian," a series she wrote after being personally attacked by *Voice* film critic Andrew Sarris. In a column he cheekily titled "Heteros Have Problems Too," Sarris deemed Johnston's writing self-righteous, self-serving, and "increasingly profitable, both culturally and financially," charging her with using her column as a "homosexual confessional."[81] In a second installment, published a week later in the *Voice*, Sarris went further, describing his concern as not just about Johnston but about his perception that she was encouraging women to create "groups herding together in terms of a sexual predilection."[82] With Johnston's writing as catalyst, he feared one lesbian could become many.

Sarris caused the very thing he feared. Until his attack, Johnston mainly discussed her sexuality in subtle terms, including in the year prior's "Irregular Passion" column discussed earlier in this chapter, leaving the terms of debate somewhat opaque to those not already part of lesbian organizing. Angered by Sarris, however, Johnston came out more forcefully than ever before and blatantly encouraged others to join her.

Across her three "Lois Lane" columns, Johnston explains what a massive wave of women coming out as lesbians could ignite: greater pleasure and community for women and the end to patriarchal and heteronormative structures that constrain them. Her writing blasts patriarchy and its primary beneficiaries (men), outlines what she sees as society's greatest threat (keeping secrets), and shares the pleasures and travails of her sexual life with other women. Drafts of "Lois Lane" in Johnston's personal archive, as well as her then-girlfriend's memories of her writing process, suggest Johnston drafted the first "Lois Lane" in one sitting.[83] The writing is driven, even as it retains the poetic and sensuous looping rhythms already foundational to her prose. But the new intensity is unmistakable. Johnston now writes to "educate all the members of ourselves to certain needs which have gone unheeded or unrecognized or worse damned and vilified and thrust underground."[84] She has a specific goal and an audience to reach.

And they heard her. As *Voice* reader Susan Sands put it in a letter to the editor after the first two "Lois Lanes," "After almost two years of trying to read Jill Johnston and thinking her writing was nice while wondering what she was talking about, I was suddenly deeply impressed and moved by the lucidity of 'Lois Lane is a Lesbian.'"[85] Those who might have enjoyed Johnston's columns previously but did not have the cultural access—didn't yet know the codes—to recognize earlier calls to lesbian action finally had their answer. The "Lois Lane" columns were not so much a coming out as they were a bursting through.

Writing so boldly about lesbian life, Johnston disturbed a status quo and offered a blueprint for radical lesbian identity. She told stories of women eschewing passivity and taking active steps to name and act on their sexual and social desires. In the second "Lois Lane," she "urge[d] all Snow Whites to get up out of their caskets and mobilize and claim their own sexuality."[86] The "sexual mobilization of women," Johnston predicted, would lead to "a real sexual revolution," defined by her as "violently dislocat[ing] the social family organization, which would drastically affect the economic-political structures."[87] She linked the supposedly private (family and marriage) with the supposedly public ("economic-political structures"). If women claimed their sexuality and asserted desire for and with other women, not only would lesbianism finally garner public space, but boundaries between public and private would crumble. In June 1971 Johnston called for all women to begin "withdrawing [their] services" from patriarchal and heteronormative institutions and "to wrap them unto herself."[88] Her *them* was conspicuously singular *and* plural. Collectively, as "herself," women could catalyze "the disruption and ultimate collapse of all modern archaic forms of bondage and warfare."[89]

By describing the thrills and fears of coming out, Johnston made a bigger and bigger stage for herself, other women, and lesbians. By the summer of 1971, a few months after the March publication of the "Lois Lane" columns, Johnston's April appearance at Town Hall, and the publication of her first book, *Marmalade Me*, Johnston had a formidable public platform. Sarris was right to be worried: she was now calling on all lesbians—a group she defined as women working with (dancing with?) other women against and outside the entanglement of patriarchy and heteronormativity.

A LESBIAN FEMINIST SCORE

In December 1972 Jill Johnston, the woman who once wrote, "I dislike meetings for purposes other than parties," helped organize a gathering at Columbia University. The event's title, "A Feminist Lesbian Dialogue: Is the Sexual Political?" was apparently a question Johnston deemed worth setting aside her aversion to organizing for (or perhaps she was responsible for the conference's concluding event, a dance party).[90] According to a conference postscript written by lesbian novelist Bertha Harris and published in the *Voice* under the headline "Lesbian/Feminist Parley: Closing the Label Gap," the symposium assembled an audience of straight women and those now calling themselves either "feminist lesbians" or "lesbian feminists."[91] (Both groups were distinct from "dyke separatists," who boycotted the event, sending instead a statement protesting the absence of both childcare and Spanish-language event flyers.)

Kate Millett addressed those in attendance, straight and gay alike, beseeching all to cease wielding lesbianism as a "wedge issue." Johnston gave the conference's final talk, extending a line of thinking she had begun in the *Voice* two weeks prior, when she proclaimed, "The term lesbian now has more of a political connotation than a sexual one."[92] Johnston's keynote, titled "The Comingest Womanifesto," appeared in print in the *Voice* a week later and, eventually, in the book *Amazon Expedition: A Lesbian Feminist Anthology* (1973). The manifesto's use of punctuation—or, really, lack thereof—is notable. There is only one period in the lengthy piece, and it comes at the end of the final sentence. The writing is a rush and a tumble.

Four main points surface in "The Comingest Womanifesto," and all point to lesbian feminism as new, emergent, and borne of the early 1970s parallel movements in feminism and gay liberation. Johnston first echoes Millett: women need one another's support, not one another's condescension. She notes that most women are still "so scared," a vulnerability that results in seemingly endless splintering among feminists, with each resulting "we" "go[ing] around saying what hot shit we are."[93] Johnston proposes a complex collectivity as a solution, a coalition that allows for all women to bring their pasts, presents, and futures. Johnston, now famous as a lesbian, provides a personal example: "i am all the women i ever was," including "the last time i slept with a man."[94] She then returns to the question of fear, including the fear of "the feminist/lesbian position." She reminds the group that the reticence among feminists to embrace lesbians and lesbianism is not a problem somehow inherent to women, but a product of social structures that demonize homosexuality, marking it as "criminal or sick or sinful." When Johnston spoke that December day, it would still be a year until homosexuality would be removed from the *Diagnostic and Statistical Manual of Mental Disorders* (DSM), where it was listed as a psychological disorder. Johnston knew personally just how much harm could be done through that pathologization; she had been held in New York psychiatric wards where her "masculine identification"—doctors' framing of her lesbianism and gender presentation—had been described as her primary issue.[95] At Columbia, Johnston asked her audience to resist succumbing to these very real social forces and fears and, instead, to collectively recognize lesbians as essential to feminism. Lesbians, she says, must be "in the center as the moving force of our collective [feminist] conscience."[96]

Johnston's vulnerability and insistence on coalition run counter to how scholars have usually remembered early 1970s lesbian feminism.[97] Sociologist Arlene Stein has noted that scholarship tends to "homogenize the legacy of lesbian feminism" in two almost opposing ways.[98] One story of lesbian feminism combines the lesbian feminism of the early 1970s, the womyn's land movement of the mid-1970s, and cultural feminism of the later 1970s, conflating the three phases to charge lesbian feminists with imagining *lesbian* as a stable category whose boundaries must be policed in order to ensure all those within share a "common history."[99] The other assessment of lesbian feminism, a critique deeply informed by queer theory and its acceptance of gender categories as "unsettled and ambiguous," casts lesbian feminists of the 1970s as the "repressive mother . . . impos[ing] uniformity on the diversity of desires, identities, and practices" within the categories of both lesbian and woman. Stein elaborates these two positions as evidence of how lesbian feminism has come to be a "symbolic battleground" rather than a movement situated in specific historical contexts—another feminist movement subject to a phenomenon feminist performance critic Jill Dolan has described as the "harden[ing of] the feminisms into prescriptive and judgmental rather than critically generative categories."[100] This calcification of lesbian feminism risks being yet another version of the lesbian figure existing outside of place and time, the "elsewhere" Annamarie Jagose has argued lesbians are often exiled to. Can lesbian feminism be understood as an internally varied social movement with the "situated, fragmented, and provisional politics" Victoria Hesford has argued formed most 1970s US social movements?[101]

Jill Johnston, as an arts critic who loathed hierarchy and its effect on categorization, would probably relish being an ideal case study for recognizing lesbian feminism as debated and contested in its time of emergence. Johnston's columns, her 1973 book *Lesbian Nation*, and her public appearances demonstrate just how much lesbian feminism was an unfolding, sometimes contradictory, sometimes utopic, and sometimes limited movement. Johnston's position on even how to define *lesbian*, let alone *lesbian feminist*, shifted regularly and publicly. At times in the early 1970s—for instance, when in 1971 Johnston describes being a lesbian as a "state of mind"—she sounds like a 1990s queer theorist with a newspaper column, asserting *lesbian* as capacious and open beyond one's sexual practices.[102] In other moments, when she turns to psychoanalysis, Greek mythology, or mythic histories, imagining Amazon warriors as lesbianism's origin story, she sounds more like a cultural feminist from later in the 1970s, understanding women as connected by an essentialized sameness.[103] Beyond a slight tendency toward the latter position as the 1970s wore on, Johnston's position on lesbian feminism has no singular trajectory, a fact emphasized by the multiple formats in which she wrote. One week's column ricochets in a different direction than the last, and though presented as a single author's book, *Lesbian Nation* is a varied collection of voices and perspectives assembled from slightly revised versions of *Voice* columns, press coverage of Johnston's writing and public appearances, excerpts from her personal journals, and correspondence with readers.

The variations in Johnston's lesbian feminism might be usefully considered much in the way Blase Provitola has written about Johnston's French lesbian contemporary, theorist Monique Wittig. Provitola argues Wittig produced a body of writing impossible "to reduce . . . to a single meaning," so broad that her work has been deployed in the twenty-first century by both trans feminists and antitrans feminists.[104] This range, Provitola argues, is not indicative of Wittig's individual position but is rather "symptomatic" of tensions in thinking about gender and sexuality among feminist and queer activists and theorists, or what others have described as an ambivalence in feminism, especially white feminism.[105]

Speaking in a 2006 interview, when asked if lesbian feminism was "inevitable," Johnston cautioned contemporary activists against remembering the movement (and its tactics) without sufficient attention to its historical context. She frames lesbian feminism as a political necessity borne of a particular moment, "a revolutionary time" that made separatism an "inevitable" response.[106] She goes on, framing separatism as necessary, yet developmental, explaining, "An oppressed group of people first must gather together to define themselves and seek mutual support. A 'vision of a world of women living independently of men' was not a realistic, indeterminately future one. It was rather a stage in the process." Thirty-plus years after "The Comingest Womanifesto," Johnston saw the lesbian feminism of the early 1970s as a powerful but provisional moment in a larger fight.

Situating lesbian feminism in its historical moment also means recognizing why Johnston told those gathered at Columbia that lesbians were a necessary "center [in] the moving force of our collective [feminist] conscience." Lesbian feminists acted on their frustration that the women's movement seemingly focused only on "rights that men are going to let women have."[107] Many lesbian feminists were women who had survived being the first out lesbians in the women's movement, where they had faced being excluded from the category "woman," and/or were women who had survived sexism within the male-centered gay liberation movement. Straight women in the women's liberation movement often treated lesbians, in historian Alice Echols's words, as "male-identified 'bogeywomen' out to sexually exploit other women."[108] And as activist Ellen Shumsky has described relative to the beginnings of the group that became the Radicalesbians, being a woman in the Gay Liberation Front meant attending meetings that were "overwhelmingly attended by males" socializing in ways that replicated how gay men gathered in public. Shumsky notes that the first lesbian-organized Gay Liberation Front event was an all-women's dance that "encouraged group dancing and space for conversation."[109]

For these lesbians, Jill Johnston, a woman describing herself as a lesbian feminist in the boldest, most public ways possible—and having fun doing so—must have seemed like a beacon. No wonder so many women across the United States avidly read her column and deluged her with fan mail, as the next of this book's interruptions addresses. Interest in Johnston only grew when she came out as a lesbian feminist on the nationally syndicated *Dick Cavett Show* in 1972 (twenty-two years *before* Ellen DeGeneres came out on television). Cavett introduced Johnston as "one of the most outspoken of the women's liberationists" and someone who "calls herself a lesbian feminist," a statement he immediately followed with the question, "Would you rather I hadn't said that?"[110] Johnston enthusiastically accepted the label and then—despite many interruptions from Cavett—provided an overview of what lesbian feminist meant to her: "ending harassment for gay people... [and] straight culture's insistence on secrecy... [and supporting] the total revolutionary sexuality for everybody."[111] Johnston's lesbian feminism had multiple, overlapping goals.

The fan mail Johnston received after her television appearance suggests women were immediately grateful. Approaching Johnston's lesbian feminist politics feels more fraught fifty years later, since, in the intervening years, both lesbian feminists and their critics have reduced the early days of lesbian feminism to fit the terms of Stein's "symbolic battleground." I have spent years considering how best to approach Johnston's lesbian feminist writing. How can I acknowledge its generative complexity, while also acknowledging important critiques, especially those related to racism and trans feminism? I choose to do what Shumsky reports the Radicalesbians did in 1970: consider dancing as a way to begin a new and needed conversation.

One of dance's more flexible and generative methods, the improvisational score, provides a way forward. There may be as many definitions of *score* as there are improvisers. At its most essential, however, *score* refers to a set of parameters that shape an individual's or group's motion. As a critic writing about experimental performance in New York in the 1950s and 1960s, Johnston was very familiar with the idea of scores and how they catalyzed performers' actions—sometimes productively, sometimes not. Reflecting on what made improvisational work so interesting in 1960s Judson Church events, Johnston concluded that the best calibration of score to eventual action was one where the score provided "a viable contract between guidelines supplied by the choreographer and performers alert and imaginative enough to be existing under any circumstances."[112] In Johnston's description, the score is "supplied" by the choreographer but functions as connective tissue among choreographer, performers, and audience. In the same column, Johnston writes that for a score to be a "viable contract," it must not be "loosened" too far but also should not cause "greater restrictions." The former threatens to leave all parties disconnected from one another. The latter isn't really a cocreated work as scores should be, since, if it is too restrictive, the "choreographer is in complete control." One score is too soft, another too rigid, but there is a wide spectrum in which a score can be just right.

A score is also a useful concept for considering Johnston's influence on lesbian feminism as choreographic because scores are sites where language—sometimes spoken, sometimes written—meets physical, social action. The group iLAND (interdisciplinary Laboratory Art Nature Dance), founded by choreographer and queer lesbian activist Jennifer Monson, defines a score as "hold[ing] an account of an event in the world—a mark . . . a movement or impression that notates a moment of observation and records it for future use."[113] Johnston's writing about lesbian feminism (and sometimes my writing about her writing) feels like such a mark, made in a present moment but produced from a negotiation of ideas and action past and present. The mark, the writing, the score is not merely a record of action but also a conduit. Seen as score, Johnston's writing proposes a "contract" among multiple groups—a proposal of how to practice creating a world where women have wide, expansive power and autonomy, not just the "rights men will let them have."

How did women approach Johnston's lesbian feminist scores? Monson's iLAND offers three useful ideas about scores' functionality that are pertinent here: scores as a mode of circulating an idea that does not require its author be present; scores as a way to remind people of "systems and structures for generating research, performances and events"; and scores as parameters that are "repeatable but not necessarily structured to produce a predictable result."[114] This last definition is perhaps the most nuanced relative to Johnston's writing about lesbian feminism, as it invites attention to how she and other lesbian feminists calibrated the distinction between what is "repeatable" and what is "predictable," setting out to create a new social formation in terms of gender and sexuality but in a way that, too often, reproduced sameness due to racial exclusions. Yet all three functions of scores proposed by iLAND are important for understanding Johnston and her writing as a choreography of lesbian feminism.

SCORE AS CONDUIT

Just as Johnston turned her column almost exclusively toward a discussion of lesbian feminism, the *Village Voice* hit a new peak circulation, reaching about 150,000 readers per week.[115] Having publication platforms with wide reach, rising interest in lesbian feminism within radical feminism, and the invocation of the powerful, if contested concept of "nation" in *Lesbian Nation*'s title propelled Johnston's writing into perhaps surprisingly broad circulation. *Lesbian Nation*'s mainstream publisher, Simon and Schuster, further bolstered the circulation of Johnston's writing with a national and international release in 1973.

Lesbian Nation arrived amid something of a surge in books written by, for, and about lesbians. A year prior, community-based San Francisco press Glide published Daughters of Bilitis founders Del Martin and Phyllis Lyon's *Lesbian/Woman*, and New York's Stein and Day published Gay Liberation Front leaders Sidney Abbott and Barbara Love's *Sappho Was a Right-On Woman.* Simon and Schuster's commitment to *Lesbian Nation*, however, took the lesbian author trend to an entirely new level—of publicity and of irony, since, as Johnston put it, "the man" paid her to write the book.[116]

"The man" and a whole host of interested women helped the book get noticed. Numerous newspapers reviewed or otherwise marked *Lesbian Nation*'s publication. Discussions of the book made their way into papers from the East Coast to the West—New York, Philadelphia, Detroit, and San Francisco—and into smaller, regional newspapers, for instance, the *Oshkosh Northwestern* in Wisconsin. While critical reception was mixed, particularly from straight feminists who accused Johnston of exacerbating splits in the movement, the book spawned new lesbian collectives and communities across the United States and from Toronto to Amsterdam, with many of those groups naming themselves variations on "lesbian nation."[117]

The increased circulation of Johnston's writing transformed her from a New York name to a national presence. She became a sought-after speaker for women's organizations and on college campuses. The regular engagements helped Johnston financially, but being invited to appear as a famous lesbian feminist was never an easy (or entirely safe) label to bear, a difficulty Johnston described in a series of 1973 *Voice* columns about a tour of Midwestern colleges. At the institutions she visited, she was—as an out lesbian—primarily a pariah; one school alerted everyone in the dorm where she was to sleep to lock their doors the night she visited.[118] She began the tour hoping to inspire women but instead "left [feeling] a wave of disappointment."[119] At almost every stop, women openly castigated her for not being the person they imagined from her writing, while others found being with an actual lesbian, not just her writing, too much. At one party she danced briefly with a woman who then had a meltdown, worried that dancing with Johnston had turned her gay.[120] Johnston's disinterest in academia turned into suspicion. By the spring of 1973, she dismissed college campuses as places where—as she writes of Sarah Lawrence College—women can "feel radical" while "lolling around on a beautiful estate."[121]

The women who attended Johnston's talks were hailed, not just by the promise of lesbian feminism, but the frame of "nation," so foregrounded by the book's title. The title, however, was a decision made at Simon and Schuster, likely by Johnston's editor, Danny Moses, an advocate for leftist books and their proposals for social revolution. Moses was best known for his work on Jerry Rubin's *DO IT! Scenarios of the Revolution* (1970), one of several books written in the late 1960s and 1970s by counterculture figures who proposed ways to revise and expand what it meant to belong to a nation. O'Wyatt, Johnston's girlfriend at the time of *Lesbian Nation*'s publication, remembers the book's title as intended to reference *Woodstock Nation* (1970), activist Abbie Hoffman's account of his utopian vision of people coming together around rock music and politics.[122] Scholar Liz Millward has hypothesized that the 1967 book *Black Power*, written by Black nationalist activists Stokely Carmichael and Charles Hamilton, inspired Moses's choice of title for *Lesbian Nation*, given both titles' reliance on "two highly freighted words in a potent combination."[123] (Or maybe Moses had just heard Gay Liberation Front activist Martha Shelley's radio show *Lesbian Nation*, which first aired in 1972 on WBAI-FM.)[124] Whatever the exact influence on Moses's choice of title, it was certainly a choice that capitalized on "the promise of nationalism . . . in the air, whether at the level of official statehood or in the dreams of the revolutionary vanguard."[125]

Lesbian Nation put the ideas of nation, of belonging, and of being a lesbian into one orbit. In the book Johnston defines "lesbian identity" as "women who desired other women find[ing] a 'nation' of their own . . . forg[ing] a sense of belonging."[126] Conceived and popularized after World War II by psychologist Abraham Maslow, "belonging" proposed an American ideal of togetherness, usually with connotations of a white, middle-class, heterosexual nuclear family. In the 1960s and 1970s, however, as Stephen Vider has described in his study of postwar queer homemaking, first feminists and then gay liberationists challenged and expanded this script. They recognized that assimilation to dominant norms was not a required precursor to experiencing national belonging.[127] Johnston merged feminist and gay visions of belonging, imagining women recognizing one another, belonging to each other, and building their own communities. As she writes in one of *Lesbian Nation*'s more poetic passages, "How do you start saying you're a dyke even to another dyke when there wasn't a dyke in the land who thought she should be a dyke or even that she was a dyke"?[128] Knowing yourself requires seeing someone like you and having a name to share. Johnston argued that mutual recognition could lead to "mutual understanding" among lesbians, a first step toward a “collective means of changing society.”[129] This is among the reasons Ti-Grace Atkinson described *Lesbian Nation* at its moment of publication as no less than “the first comprehensive projection of female nationalism as an ideology.”[130]

As was the case with many countercultural visions of national revolution, Johnston’s vision of a lesbian nation and, as she also called it, “dyke nationalism,” generally hailed only one kind of person.[131] Though Johnston sometimes argued otherwise, the white, cis lesbian was generally the primary protagonist of her lesbian feminist proposals. In a 1972 column, she compared her vision of dyke nationalism with Black nationalism, describing both political proposals as refusing to accept that only one norm should define what constitutes national belonging.[132] Yet, as Millward notes, Johnston was mostly “writing about Black nationalism from a distance,” borrowing concepts of self-determination only as a rhetorical device that would largely serve white women.[133] Almost a decade later, the lesbian feminist–run Persephone Press would publish a very different vision of woman-led collectivity, *This Bridge Called My Back: Writings by Radical Women of Color*. The collection, edited by Cherríe Moraga and Gloria Anzaldúa, truly understood *lesbian* as a multiracial term. The volume, which exclusively featured women-of-color authors, included Black lesbian poet, critic, and activist Cheryl Clarke’s essay “Lesbianism: An Act of Resistance,” a blueprint for lesbian feminism that partially overlapped with white lesbian feminism but also demonstrated how different lesbian feminism would look if imagined as a score proposed by a woman of color. Like Johnston, Clarke argued against the “corrupted, predatory relationship between men and women.”[134] But patriarchy, which Clarke defined as a system of oppression formed through an interlocking web of racism, colonialism, and sexism, could only be destroyed when white women fully reckoned with how they have “certain privileges in racist patriarchy.”[135] Any revolutionary movement in a US context, Clarke argued, must focus on the “foundation” of America: “the master-slave relationship between white and black people in the United States.”[136] A score that could circulate in a way that catalyzed a truly revolutionary lesbian nation would require not just the potential of the idea of nation but also a harsh recognition of its limits.

SCORE AS REVISION, REORIENTATION

As Johnston’s writing circulated, women took it up in myriad ways. They inhabited Johnston’s writing much as dancers do scores, returning to the same or a similar prompt but taking it in new directions with each iteration. The circumstances of casting, site, and timing, among other factors, contribute to how the known and unknown intertwine as scores become "systems and structures for generating research, performances and events."[137] Johnston's proposals came to be scores for homemaking and community making, invitations to experiment with other women.

Despite her disinterest in organizing, Johnston attempted to enact a score of lesbian feminist homemaking. In 1972 she purchased and then shared a home in rural western Massachusetts with a small group of New York–based lesbians. Outside of the city and away from men, the women gathered and used feminist practices and structures, like consciousness-raising groups, to experience lesbian community; build feminist, lesbian consciousness; and cocreate lesbian feminist scholarship and art. Compared to the ways Johnston's writing circulated as a lesbian feminist score nationally and internationally, this was a score on a more intimate scale—a glimpse into Johnston's practice with others.

By living together in a home owned by a woman, Johnston and her friends already enacted something of a lesbian feminist score. For a woman in 1972, purchasing a home was itself a feminist act and one that required collaboration. Prior to the passage of the Equal Credit Opportunity Act in 1974, women had no protection from discrimination when applying for credit, which meant few women could get a credit card or a mortgage. Only women with access to their own money—or married to a man—could try for either. With the advance from Simon and Schuster for *Lesbian Nation*, Johnston became a woman with her own money. With the advance and help from friend and activist Phyllis Birkby, who had worked as an architect at a mainly male firm, O'Wyatt remembers that Johnston was approved for a mortgage on a farmhouse in Huntington, Massachusetts. O'Wyatt, Birkby, Harris, anthropologist and professor Esther Newton, and painter Louise Fishman then contributed rent, regularly coming up from New York on the weekends for, as Newton describes it in her memoir, "Johnston's ill-defined lesbian feminist project."[138] The score was loose, sometimes fraught, but also compelling.

Birkby, who was a filmmaker as well as an architect, documented life in Johnston's home, eventually making a series of short silent films that chronicle the women's lesbian feminist experiment. Most of these, now collected with Birkby's papers at Smith College, focus on the mundane and intimate ways the women, particularly Johnston, moved with and around one another. The films seem to be an extension of Birkby's activism, which entailed her traveling across the United States and asking women to imagine their "fantasy" environments—to draw and explain what spaces they wished they lived or worked within. Writing about Birkby in his work on queer homemaking, Vider posits Birkby as having helped women move their dreams into "pragmatic" possibilities, whereas he argues Johnston's *Lesbian Nation* was "gay fantasy, an imagined community" more "playful" than "pragmatic."[139] Vider isn't wrong: Johnston's larger set of proposed scores were playful, but Birkby's films show that play can also be pragmatic. Johnston's merging of play and pragmatism might even be what transformed the house into a score of lesbian feminist, woman-centered domesticity.

The films offer yet another manifestation of lesbian identity as recognition without confirmation. Birkby's images feature women goofing around in the living room, conversations that might be consciousness-raising groups, and lots and lots of shots of women tossing balls around outdoors. Much as lesbian archivist Sharon Thompson has written of lesbian home videos, Birkby's films could easily be mistaken for images of women just hanging out. When faced with scenes that could be described as "a gaggle of young women playing volleyball," Thompson wryly notes why video evidence of lesbian life often does not make it into official archives: "Good luck finding someone at an estate auction able and willing to tell the inside story."[140] Birkby's films hint at the "inside story" but cloak it in ambiguity. Bodies meet and slip alongside one another, revising scripts of domestic possibility via lesbian feminist practice but doing so without announcement. She documents a lesbian practice of recognition without confirmation as a way of living and of having pleasure—not only a survival strategy necessitated by misogyny or heterosexism.

To witness Johnston in Birkby's films is to witness a lesbian at ease, joyful and sexy. In one shot from an early 1970s film titled *Dykes at Jill's Weekend, Upstate N.Y.*, the camera lands on Johnston looking down and across her nose, one side of her mouth upturned in an almost smile.[141] She subtly brushes her fingers across her wide leather belt—just to the side of the buckle. There are resonances with the pose she strikes on the front of her book covers (discussed in the preface). If desired, one can understand the gestures and postures Birkby captures as lesbian—the swagger, the belt buckle's size, the way Johnston runs her fingers across the metal—all have undertones of sexiness and of a woman being unafraid to take up space.

Birkby so aptly crafts images of recognition without confirmation in her rendering of the lesbian feminist home that it's hard to discern what to ascribe to her filmmaking and what to ascribe to the women she films. For instance, Birkby frequently takes advantage of light flooding through the home's sliding glass doors to make it almost seem like the light produces the lesbians, while also facilitating their disappearance. Like Johnston's merging of the playful and the pragmatic, these scenes seem both magical and mundane. Brightness bursts, then recedes. As the light dissipates, the camera reveals women playing ball outside or chatting in a living room, maybe in a consciousness-raising group. There is a sense they were already there, even have always been there. But you have to look differently, follow Birkby's gaze and camera choices, to see the women emerge and coexist.

In the last moments of *Dykes at Jill's*, Birkby cuts quickly from woman to woman, producing a sense of women multiplying: one dyke, two dykes, three dykes, more. They almost touch across the frames. Jill sits in a chair, leaning. Her chin rests on her hand; her head's tilt and a slight smile mark her as knowing joker. She wears a long-sleeved denim shirt, unbuttoned just enough to reveal a white T-shirt with big blue letters that spell "GAY." It's the same shirt she wears in the photo *Voice* photographer Fred McDarrah took of her at the 1971 Stonewall anniversary. The rest of the shirt—the raised clenched fist and the stenciled word "REVOLUTION"—is not visible but could be filled in by those in the know, those who can guess what lies beneath the rest of the buttons. The shirt is bold, but Jill is relaxed, easy, and loose in her proclamations. Birkby's camera scans the group, but always returns to Johnston. The practices of this home are coauthored, but Johnston's the choreographer. The camera focuses on her eyes and then pulls away as her mouth opens in a giant laugh. The framing feels loving, just shy of a caress. Birkby revises how Andy Warhol lingered in his *Jill and Freddy Dancing* film a decade prior when the final close-up belonged to Fred Herko. No longer is it a man's face that matters most. Now Johnston is centered, among women, seeing and seen. She is lesbian in all positions: wanting, wanted, and at rest. Light fills the frame, and then overwhelms it. All the women become silhouetted outlines, a reminder that these are roles Johnston and her home allowed them to step into, a cast of women practicing together new ways of being.

REPEATABLE, REPRODUCING

The scenes Birkby captures of Johnston's lesbian feminist homemaking experiment precede—and differ from—the mid-1970s turn in lesbian feminism toward creating "womyn's lands," as well as long-term separatist communities.[142] These later enactments of lesbian feminism were ones where women actively sought to sever most or all ties with men, whereas most of the women in Johnston's home sought respite more than separation. Johnston and her coconspirators moved in and out of proximity to men and the institutions they ran. Johnston's home, however, did resemble the later lesbian feminist homemaking efforts in its whiteness. All the women who lived in the home were white, although that was not a homogeneous category, especially for those, like Fishman, who were deeply attached to their Jewish identities. Ultimately, as was the case with many lesbian feminist communities, there were no women who were not white and likely no women who, in the language of the twenty-first century, would have described themselves as trans or nonbinary—at least not at the time.

The relative homogeneity of the group who lived with Johnston is not surprising given the realities of the largely white world these women still moved in, as well as Johnston's writing about race and trans issues in her columns. As discussed in chapter 2 relative to Johnston's writing about interracial casting, she wrote about race in a way that underscored her distance from most nonwhite people. For instance, in the third "Lois Lane" column, Johnston makes the ignorant comment that "a black person these days has a certain advantage in being clearly black."[143] Frustrated by her lesbianism being unseen, Johnston romanticizes constant visibility, leaving unconsidered the problems and dangers of "clearly" being anything but white.

Johnston's ignorance is symptomatic of white lesbian feminism's inattention to the unearned benefits white lesbian feminists enjoyed. Katherine Schweighofer, a historian of separatist communities, has argued that white lesbian feminists fixated on separating from society rather than working with others, assuming they alone had "the authority to decide one's relation to an established power dynamic."[144] Schweighofer also notes that this arrogance extended to how lesbian feminists, especially those coming from urban areas, thought about land. They imagined rural spaces as uninhabited, rarely acknowledging earlier inhabitants, including displaced Native peoples.[145] Lesbian feminist scores, as enacted by white women, emphasized collectivity but still focused on ownership. In the terms Johnston wrote about relative to performance scores, these were scores held too tight by their choreographers/authors. In iLAND's terms, these were scores too focused on reproducing sameness, rather than being repeatable to a range of ends.

Such critiques are not ones visible only in hindsight. The Combahee River Collective, a group of Black "feminists and Lesbians," famously critiqued white lesbian feminists in their 1977 manifesto, tying white lesbian separatists' desire to withdraw from men to their racial privilege. The Collective names that white women did not need to "have solidarity . . . with white men, unless it is their negative solidarity around the fact of race," whereas Black women needed "solidarity with progressive Black men [in order to] struggle together with [them] against racism, while... also struggle[ing] with Black men about sexism."[146] Black lesbians, and other lesbians of color, danced a more complicated score.

When Johnston discusses race in her lesbian feminist writing, she often treats what she calls the "lesbian situation" and the "black situation" as completely distinct.[147] That Johnston and many other white lesbian feminists were rendering lesbian as almost always white was not lost on Johnston's Black readers. Black feminist theater critic Margo Jefferson, once a fan of Johnston's, eventually grew frustrated by her inattention to nonwhite lesbians.[148] In a 1974 letter Jefferson sent to Johnston (which Johnston kept), Jefferson writes, "If I weren't a black woman I wouldn't know, from your... column... that there were any [black women].... Black women and feminists do exist. And we no more appreciate being ignored by white feminists than by the garden varieties of unconcerned men."[149] Jefferson's naming of Johnston's exclusions resonates with criticisms of white lesbians in a 1981 conversation, published in *This Bridge Called My Back*, among Combahee members and lesbians Barbara Smith and Beverly Smith and volume editors Cherríe Moraga and Gloria Anzaldúa. Barbara Smith, seemingly speaking for the group, says that it was not that "white lesbian separatists [were] more racist than any other white women in the women's movement" but that white lesbian separatists put forward a "dangerous and erroneous conception" when they argued that "other oppressions, in addition to sexism, are attributed to men only."[150] As Cheryl Clarke names in "Lesbianism: An Act of Resistance," there can be no discussion of collectivity among women in the United States without reckoning with white privilege and the history of enslavement that produces that privilege.

Johnston's score for lesbian feminism also potentially excludes trans women, although the terms of this exclusion are more ambiguous. In the first "Lois Lane" column, Johnston worries that people assigned female at birth who choose gender-affirming surgery do not know they were "born... perfectly beautiful."[151] Seeking surgery as part of gender transition is, to Johnston, a "monstrosity," evidence a person finds their body lacking or wrong—the opposite of the thrill she experiences through coming out as a lesbian. Johnston's language is transphobic and harmful, especially in light of twenty-first-century prohibitions on trans people having the very access to public space that Johnston helped fight for lesbians to have.

As other lesbian separatists did, Johnston sometimes argued that "biology is definitely destiny," equating physical anatomy with gender and leaving transwomen outside her reimagined category of woman.[152] This is another example of a too-tight score that results in the continued oppression of transwomen, a "restricted understanding of what might be indicated by *woman*."[153] Kyla Wazana Tompkins has decried Johnston's "investment in womanhood as a stable category," though a close reading of Johnston's oeuvre does not fully bear this out.[154] In *Lesbian Nation*'s introduction, Johnston describes "biological destiny" and what she calls "social reality" as entangled in a complex relationship that confuses "cause and effect."[155] Johnston goes on to argue that "if the phrase biology is destiny has any meaning for a woman right now it has to be the urgent project of woman reclaiming her self, her own biology in her own image."[156] Johnston likely draws the language of reclamation from a gay liberation project of coming out, repurposing it to see being a woman as a point of pride, not a flaw.

Trans readers held differing opinions about Johnston's 1970s writing. One letter writer, who, in a 1972 letter published in the *Voice*, describes themselves as a "transvestite," calls Johnston's writing "transvestite-hating."[157] They accuse Johnston of only being "in favor of liberation for the people she likes (radical lesbian) [*sic*], [while] those unacceptable under the rigid terms of her politics can be damned."[158] The same writer, however, sent a letter directly to Johnston a month later and displayed a more misogynist side. In that letter they protest Johnston's claim that feminism inspired gay liberation, writing that "radical lesbians" had no part in gay rights and were "still doing their nails."[159] Another trans reader saw the entanglement of feminism and gay rights in Johnston's writing differently. This person, who does not name their gender but shares they feel shame for wanting to wear dresses, likely indicating they were assigned male at birth, thanks Johnston. Her attacks on "sex roles" have helped expand gender possibilities and provided language to explain why wearing a dress is acceptable regardless of one's sex or gender.[160] This reader sees in Johnston's lesbian feminist score not "rigid terms" but possibility. As a score, Johnston's writing perhaps should be approached not as a monolithic political statement to be strictly adhered to, and more like what trans activist and writer Kate Bornstein has said of her identity (and fashion): "collage . . . a little bit from here, a little bit from there."[161] In its time of formation in the early 1970s, the lesbian feminism Jill Johnston proposed was a complex score that circulated broadly, exciting some to imagine new possibilities, while also sometimes reproducing preexisting exclusions.

Conclusion: Score as Orientation(s)

Writing in 2017, feminist queer-of-color theorist Sara Ahmed, perhaps surprisingly, argues for a return to lesbian feminism, arguing it could "bring feminism back to life" by "mak[ing] sense of the sexism that becomes all the more striking when women exit from the requirements of compulsory heterosexuality."[162] Ahmed conjures lesbian feminism as a forgotten moment in feminist history that had offered an alternative way. She veers toward what Jagose warns is a utopic notion of lesbianism—lesbian feminism as an elsewhere to which one could escape. But Ahmed also understands lesbian feminism as a score of sorts, arguing that queer life requires an alternative set of orientation points that help queer women "find their way."[163]

In her writing and in her public speaking, Johnston was just that: a lesbian feminist queer orientation point. She was sometimes hard to follow, especially as she reimagined relationships between words and bodies, but her creation of confusion was intentional. She loved a good postmodern mess and its invitations toward uncertainty. She was not an orientation *point* so much as she was orientation *points*, a collage of radical feminism, gay liberation, and lessons from performance at its most surreal. Maybe that's why, in 1972, Johnston wrote, "I'm not a star. I'm an asteroid."[164] Like any interesting score, a lesbian feminist score should not overly restrict its dancers, but should allow them to move as a loose ensemble, finding new paths among constant, coauthored proliferations of possibility.

INTERRUPTION 3

We Can Hear You

Reading with the Body

Johnston is more than just an underground culture hero or Amazon cheerleader. She's a bloody genius.
—Letter to the editor, *Village Voice*, 1972

Jill Johnston had numerous devoted readers. But calling Johnston's fans *readers* is slightly misleading. These were not people merely sitting down to read her column when they received the *Voice* each week. Letters to the editor published in the paper, as well as fan mail sent directly to Johnston, paint vivid pictures of what it looked like to be a Johnston reader. Her readers were noisy, and they were physical. When the *Voice* arrived in her Lexington, Kentucky, mailbox each week, a reader named Bonnie told Johnston she "pounced [on it] with a 'Yawp!'"[1] Another wrote, "When your columns are good I want to eat them."[2] Others described coming undone. Margaret from Hollywood, California, put it most succinctly: "YOUR WRITING KNOCKS ME OUT. Simply. knocks. me. out."[3] This was full-bodied reading, a transformative moment of person-to-text encounter that was a physical event.[4]

Johnston taught her readers to read with their bodies. Her skill in describing motion, a holdover from her practice as a critic, allowed her to foreground how people used their bodies in a variety of social situations. In her writing about coming out, she had an even more heightened emphasis on the physical, especially when she focused on time and the way the sensation of time—its passing, speeding up or slowing down—lives in one's body and keeps one aware of the present moment. Johnston proves theorist Fredric Jameson's comment true: in "the temporal present . . . you have nothing left but your own body."[5] She also demonstrates how the iterative nature of coming out bears particular relationship to "the temporal present," since, in societies that assume heterosexuality as norm, the labor of coming out is never quite complete. In Johnston's 1971 coming-out triptych, the series she titled "Lois Lane Is a Lesbian," Johnston uses this kinesthetic approach to writing about time to disrupt the reader-text boundary, allowing her reader to ride the starts, stops, and anxieties of coming out with her.

In the first "Lois Lane," Johnston traces her path through a night in New Orleans, emphasizing her experience of time and rhythm through postmidnight time stamps (12:10, 12:15, 12:20, 12:25).[6] These time stamps are regular in their intervals, all five minutes apart, but they grow closer and closer to one another on the page as the writing unfolds. Several sentences separate the first time stamp from the second, but the distance between subsequent time stamps shrinks as Johnston describes fending off a "hippie guy's" advances and eventually realizes she has to "signal through the flames [to him] the message that we both liked the same sex." As the risky business of coming out as a lesbian becomes unavoidable, the clustered time stamps heighten the sensation of danger. Once Johnston shares her secret—THE secret—time loosens. She leaves the man "gaping and fuming" on the side of the road, and the next time stamp, 5 a.m., is two sentences and almost five hours later, by which time she is "on the road" not "looking back." Readers and Johnston exhale and then join her forward motion. She can now make a collective announcement: "We are bored with the news from the heterosexual fronts. We want to hear from the lesbians and homosexuals now."[7] This "now," the one *Village Voice* readers shape with Johnston, is a feeling in the body—the feeling of leaving a man confused on the side of the road while riding out of New Orleans in the back of a VW van with Jill Johnston at the wheel.

The third "Lois Lane" also focuses on an experience of time via Johnston's body. In this instance she is unable to gain control of the "now"; announcing her sexuality in the moment she describes will cause more harm than good. In this column, the finale of the "Lois Lanes," Johnston, in intentionally excruciating detail, recounts attending a dinner party with a closeted lover and suffering through their hosts' homophobia. The two women endure "the dreadful moment when she [one of the hosts] referred to a male friend . . . in tones of slow heavy import, describing him as an 'in-cur-a-ble hom-o-sex-u-al.'"[8]

As the host speaks, Johnston emphasizes how the homophobic comments infect her body and the air around her: "The place got hung purply apoplex there for a few seconds during which I flashed a number of thoughts and decisions while the Mr. who had been reclining on the couch ogling the roommate [Johnston's lover] got ready to clinch the opener and close the case for straight America with a ponderous guttural back-up 'We-l-l, *honey*, we don't rea-ll-y *know*.'" Time slows and slurs, and the lesbians must figure out, too fast and too slow and in silence, how to respond. Johnston's hyphens and italics, which extend words and emphasize tone, bring a reader into the weight and tension she felt in those very full "few seconds."

But Johnston's devoted readers know this isn't the end of the story. As she continues in the third "Lois Lane," Johnston says that night in San Francisco "lit the fuse" that catalyzed the "detonation" in New Orleans, the scene with which the first "Lois Lane" begins.[9] In her writing in the third "Lois Lane," Johnston yells everything she could not say to the hosts that night in San Francisco, refusing what lesbian theorist Monique Wittig calls "the straight mind," "the discourses of heterosexuality [that] oppress us in the sense that they prevent us from speaking unless we speak in their terms," a phrasing that emphasizes heteronormativity as an almost intersubjective, kinesthetic experience.[10] The couple's comments make Johnston feel disconnected and isolated, "stranded between the necessity of responding to an intolerable assault and my responsibility to a lover whom I couldn't betray."[11] In the moment, she cannot be the woman, the out lesbian, she wants to be. But then and there, she commits to transformation "into an armored tank smoking at the joints and hanging over a precipice," quite the image of what a lesbian in public might be if unleashed from the pressures and harms of homophobic time. Through writing, Johnston overcomes, in spectacular, fire-breathing manner, the silencing force of the "straight mind" and lets her readers experience what it means to be in a "now" shaped by a lesbian, with her body, for others' bodies.

Letter to the Editor/Letter to the Lesbian

Encountering a lesbian who could, through prose, transform herself into an "armored tank" ignited readers' ferocity, and they rushed to say so. The *Voice* treated its readers as important interlocutors, dedicating two to three pages per issue to readers' letters and making them into the paper's "extended family."[12] Some letter writers became such regular contributors that the paper hired them. That's how Robert Christgau became the paper's rock music critic, prompting editor Dan Wolf to make his own play with time, telling Christgau, "We're going to miss you" when Christgau joined the paper's staff.[13]

The *Voice*'s letter board exploded after the first "Lois Lane." Letters were mostly laudatory and mostly from women. Sue Brueggeman of Manhattan loved Johnston's presentation of herself as a woman doing "as she pleases," an act Brueggeman called "an enormous step in the direction of shattering the image of women as . . . tamers of men, second-class citizens who must always ask themselves 'what will it look like if I do such-and-such.'"[14] Another reader, Barbara, captured Johnston's spirit (and, as many readers did, took a stab at copying her style): "What you have in this Johnston chick is fire, baby."[15] Johnston was not just signaling through the flames; she was the flame itself, and readers could feel the heat.

Despite letters' celebratory tone, the *Voice* framed many condescendingly. Editors headlined a reader's letter that commended Johnston's centering of women's desire in the first "Lois Lane" with "Booby Trip."[16] The sexism only grew worse from there. The paper printed letters that called Johnston names like "stupid bitch" and threatened violence against her.[17] Johnston's fans protested such hate and aggression with their own letters, including one that framed attacks on Johnston within the *Voice*'s longer history of misogyny, concluding with the sentence: "The *Voice*'s editorial anti-women's movement policies are showing."[18] They had been showing for a while. Every letter on the page, including those written directly to the *Voice*'s female writers, began "Dear Sir." One Johnston fan pointed out the "sexist usage" and directly requested their letter about Johnston not run in the ubiquitous format that assumed a letter to the editor was an address only to men.[19]

It's not as though fans' enthusiasm left them incapable of criticism. The letters to the editor often featured extended debates about Johnston, with her creative use of punctuation a frequent flash point. One reader had seen Johnston speak in person, prompting him to plead in a letter to the editor, "I love to hear Jill Johnston *speak*—won't you please ask her to write in sentences? *Why* won't she punctuate? . . . Her articles are *impossible* to read."[20] In contrast, a male reader from Saginaw, Michigan, wrote that Johnston had taught him to read differently. At first, he "questioned the mental practicality of chopping up thoughts by mentally placing those written barriers into my reading comprehension" but then came to see Johnston's stylistic choices as ones intended to produce writing with an "absence of obstructions" that made reading more about "thoughts" than "written sentences."[21] Johnston brought readers close and pushed them into new experiences of time and flow.

Letters published in the *Voice* were just one slice of readers' engagements with Johnston. In the early 1970s, they sent hundreds of letters directly to her. These letters—at least those she kept in her personal archive—tended to be more positive than those in the *Voice*. Many offered gratitude, thanking her for slamming tales of lesbian life into a widely circulating, public platform. Letters published in the newspaper came primarily from the New York metropolitan area, but letters sent directly to Johnston carried postmarks from at least thirty-four US states and six other countries. As a reader named Suntan—from Florida (where else could Suntan possibly live?)—wrote, "It must be complicated to remember that real live people even in an improbably [*sic*] place like Florida really read those words."[22] Suntan goes on to say—sounding much like Bonnie in Kentucky—that she looks forward to Mondays because that's the day the *Voice* arrives by mail in Sarasota. As Johnston's personal letterhead read in the early 1970s (another gem from her archive), she was "Jill Johnston lesbian at large."[23]

What They Wrote/What They Felt

Reading all these letters—those public and private—it is clear Johnston's pronouncements about lesbian identity named something many felt in their bodies but few had language for. Women saw in Johnston someone they recognized and someone who recognized them. When the *Voice* published a less-than-positive review of *Lesbian Nation*, letters full of descriptions of women already living outside the bounds of normative femininity poured in.[24] Among the most striking is a letter from an army corporal and self-described lesbian, Elizabeth Campbell, who was stationed at McConnell Air Force Base in Wichita, Kansas. In a letter published in the *Voice*, she describes herself, writing, "I personally have been involved in the women's lib movement for some time and it has been of great help to me, a big-breasted, tall, cigar-smoking 20-year-old."[25] Because Campbell follows Johnston's example of describing her body, we can imagine how she might sit in a chair, looking over her cigar at her likely mostly male colleagues. Alongside Johnston, Campbell can be fully seen, can take up space—and a particular space, an air force base (both a likely and unlikely place for a lesbian to be).[26] Much as Johnston once helped readers see experimental performance, the women who responded to her through their letters helped readers see scenes of lesbian life.

Other letters celebrated more private victories. Women thanked Johnston for helping them come out, first to themselves and now to her. As Linda in Rochester, a "mostly closeted" woman, writes, "If I hadn't bought a copy of the *Village Voice* I never would have known there existed a Jill Johnston in this world. At long last—someone I can relate to."[27] Joy, a "shy lesbian" from San Francisco, closes her letter to Johnston the same way, writing that she "wish[es] to thank you [Johnston] for existing and for being who you are and for letting the world know you and for opening some minds and for being someone to relate to."[28] So many women describe reading Johnston in terms that resemble the scene from Alison Bechdel's book-turned-musical *Fun Home* (2006; musical, 2013) when a young Alison sees a butch lesbian for the first time, noticing the butch's "ring of keys," and then sings in a tender alto register:

> I thought it was supposed to be wrong
> but you seem OK with being strong...
> It's probably conceited to say
> but I think we're alike in a certain way.[29]

Women wanted to see Johnston, get into the room with her, and observe how she moved. They were often willing to go to great lengths to do so. In a July 1972 letter, a woman from Lancaster, Pennsylvania, inquires about Johnston's upcoming speaking appearances. She displays the intensity of her desire to see Johnston by writing that she will get herself to gigs not just in Pennsylvania or nearby New York but also any in "Ohio, Delaware, New Jersey, Connecticut, Rhode Island, West Virginia, Maryland, or Washington, DC."[30] Such desire could be explained by a crush or draw to celebrity, but the frequency with which letter writers note that they need to see Johnston in person because they need to see how she moves seems borne of a particularly lesbian practice. As Cynthia from Philadelphia explains in a letter to Johnston, reading physical gesture is a lesbian imperative honed across a lifetime of trying to determine whether a woman is a lesbian (or not). She writes, "You can always tell by the fingernails—that is, if theyre [*sic*] short. [And there's also] the way they light your cigarette—that is, if they hang onto your hand and such / you can always tell by the eyes—that is, if they light up while theyre [*sic*] lighting your cigarette and hanging onto your hand with their very own hand with their very own close-cropped nails."[31] Practiced in tracking these subtle gestural clues to a woman's sexuality, lesbians reading Johnston got to have their notions of lesbian physicality realized and expanded in blissfully spectacular forms. One woman describes, in a necessarily run-on sentence, the vision she has of Johnston while reading the 1971 column "The Wedding."[32] She gets to have "the image of a lady driving on a california highway, pulling to a stop and masturbating it's the most extraordinary thing i had ever read."[33]

That same letter begins with a two-word sentence, "Gay me," an exclamation from a woman transformed through reading Johnston. I imagine one woman turning to another (if she has another to turn to) and saying, "If you're not a lesbian when you start reading this, you will be by the end." Transformations proliferate in letters addressed to Johnston. Reading her essay about the Town Hall event makes Georgia in San Antonio into "a whole new chick."[34] After Johnston speaks in Portland, Oregon, Kathy writes, "Many lesbians [are] walking tall around here now."[35] Carol from Brooklyn says reading Johnston helped her come out, an experience she describes as one of "grow[ing] new brains."[36] These women speak of their transformations as physical, with many sensing their new bodies as overlapping with Johnston's. Florence from Queens finds herself "talking to you [Johnston] in my head all the time."[37] In an unsigned letter, another woman tells Johnston, "You ha[ve] done it again—reached inside yourself and me at the same time."[38] These women experience what Elizabeth Freeman calls the experience of a body that is "intelligible only through its encounter with other bodies."[39]

Perhaps not surprisingly, the physicality and intermingling of self and other that readers experience often manifests in seduction scenes. Requests for photos that can be put near a bed are not uncommon.[40] Others offer to take her photograph, to have an excuse to look at Johnston over time.[41] Others suggest dancing or swimming with her. One of the more amusing letters comes from Deborah in New Jersey, who writes, "I read somewhere, that you jumped in a pool topless at a Lib Party. I can hold my breath 30 seconds under water. Topless, i can hold about 60 seconds. Topless with you about 101 minutes. Topless with you topless I'd probably drown."[42] Others seem as much turned on by words themselves as Johnston herself. An unsigned letter from a Brooklyn woman writes that "sometimes at night—your words come faintly, engraving hollow lines—upon the thinness of my wall."[43]

Bedrooms are not the only domestic space Johnston's writing penetrates. Reading Johnston helped many women feel less lonely at home more generally. Jean in Queens says she reads Johnston regularly, astonished to find "somebody in print saying the things I say to my lamp."[44] B. from Bay Shore is grateful to read Johnston "out here on Long Island," where she has been "housewifing it with the crickets and the seagulls," with Johnston being "the first I ever heard talking my head language."[45] Perhaps my favorite of these lesbian epistles from domestic spaces is a simple thank-you note penned in the wake of the "Lois Lane" columns and written on yellow gingham stationery by a woman who signs off only as "M."[46] The cheery little rectangular note conjures a suburban, maybe rural, home where a woman sits down to write to Johnston at the kitchen table while her husband is at work.

Other women write to Johnston about how her writing helps them start new lives. Longtime reader Joan says she has tried to write to Johnston many times but always tore up the letters. But now that she is a "FREE WOMAN," "living in a small apartment after leaving my husband and luxurious suburban home, etc. etc.," she has finally found it possible to write. The last bit, the repeated *etc.*, points to a scene so well known it doesn't need to be fully elaborated. But her last question to Johnston, "Do you REALLY believe 'All women are lesbians except those who don't know it'????"—referencing Johnston's opening statement at the Town Hall panel—demonstrates it's not just about leaving the well-known but might just be about imagining something new with a little help, a prod from Jill Johnston.[47]

Women report to Johnston that she challenges them, often by recounting how they experience reading her writing over time. Mona from Ozone Park, Queens, a regular reader of the column, admits she's often "puzzled" by the writing and is "still trying to further understand your articles." Yet rather than that being off-putting, the fact Johnston "boggle[s] my mind" makes her commit to continuing. "I still read on," Mona tells her.[48] S.E. from San Francisco (one of several letter writers whose responses to Johnston appear both on the *Voice*'s letters-to-the-editor page and in Johnston's personal archives) speaks of a similar commitment to reading Johnston. S.E. has a ritualized approach: "[in the] mornings when finished [with] the coffee and want ads, I re-read 'Dance Journal' and analyze it . . . fondly . . . conspiratorially. I examine each paragraph for that occasional striking, lyrical sentence."[49] There's something in S.E.'s adverbs, *fondly*, *conspiratorially*, that points to her studied but also languid approach to reading, analytic but also sensual. There's similar subtext in a letter from a woman in Northampton, Massachusetts, who tells Johnston she enjoys reading the column out loud each week on local radio station WAMH.[50]

The sensuality with which readers approach Johnston's writing allows women to feel they are *with* Johnston, an adjacency that creates a possibility for survival. While most letters, especially those published in the newspaper, treat Johnston's style as difficult or incomprehensible, there is a set of readers for whom reading Johnston produces clarity—usually a clarity predicated on feeling themselves as unclear. As Jean of Staten Island puts it, "One day, when i was really down, [I] read 'dance journal' for the first time. it helped clear up some of the confusion in my head as nothing else could have."[51] Others (as evidenced in the story at the beginning from Bonnie in Kentucky) treat the paper itself as a stand-in for Johnston, as does Mona, a college student in Connecticut, who writes that she often finds herself "snatch[ing] the *Village* [*Voice*] in [her] arms in a few minutes of ecstasy."[52] This is more than mere excitement. With Johnston (albeit the written version in her arms), Mona can survive life in her college, where she fears other women whisper behind her back, "She likes girls you know."[53] Of course, writer Jill could be improved on. Mona says that the real Jill is welcome to come to her upcoming graduation and give her a kiss.

The kiss didn't seem to materialize, but letters in Johnston's archive provide evidence that she wanted to connect with these women and regularly corresponded with some fans. I have no access to what she wrote to these women, but many wrote to her repeatedly, referencing gratitude for support and suggestions on how to venture into lesbian life. Young people—whether chronologically young or young in their "gay age"—found her advice helpful. She seemed willing to answer questions as straightforward (and yet not) as "HOW DO YOU GET STARTED?" as posed by Donna.[54] (And yes, Donna wrote it in all caps.) Others—backing Donna up on how hard it can be to come out—worried with Jill. A regular correspondent, Shannon, who struggled with being married to a man and being an out lesbian, eventually confessed to Johnston, "Frankly, I'm scared."[55] To still others, Johnston suggested ways to meet local lesbians. She helped Pat in San Diego find lesbian gatherings, introducing her to Lin Barron and musician Pauline Oliveros (the subjects of "The Wedding" column).[56] Sandy received similar suggestions about how to find lesbians in metro Atlanta.[57]

Johnston, however, did not respond to most letters. Fans lamented the lack of response but comforted themselves with the knowledge that another column would come in a week's time. They knew they could read her again next week and could do so with fervor. For one writer, the column was "an indispensable weekly energy supplement"; for another it was a way to "enjoy my Wednesday lunch hours."[58] I imagine this woman eating a turkey sandwich while on lunch, on break from a job where no one knows her secret, relishing the column as a coveted, weekly, yet covert gift of connection. Occasionally *Voice* editors did get the headlines they wrote for letters to the editor right. Above a 1974 letter about Johnston's writing from a Joan Gregg, the editors chose the headline "Voice in the Wilderness."[59]

4

She Was a Writer

A *New York Times* review of Jill Johnston's 1996 book, *Jasper Johns: Privileged Information*, begins with the question, "What has Jasper Johns done to deserve Jill Johnston?"[1] Reviewer and art critic Grace Glueck asks the question almost out of shock; it seems she can barely believe the degree and range of detail Johnston included in the book. Yet this level of detail was common in Johnston's arts criticism in the late 1970s and 1980s, a period when Johnston openly chafed at arts critics who focused solely on formal analysis. Johnston argued that a singular focus on form resulted in "isolating art" away from the lives of both artists and audiences.[2] Reading Johnston on Johns, it's clear that the criticism Johnston desired was not merely a matter of placing art in appropriate contexts, as a historian might do. Instead she desired—and in the book on Johns presented—arts criticism forged from a dense merging of art and life. Her 1996 book is a veritable flood of information meant to drench the reader in details of form, context, and biography.

Johnston demanded this approach to arts criticism in Johns's case for a particular reason: to illuminate how his homosexuality had shaped his art making, even as he often used his artwork to obscure his sexuality.[3] To make her point, she circles and encircles Johns's works almost one by one, describing formal aspects and gazes invited (or not), and then locates the work in the contexts of its inspiration, content, and chronology. For instance, for Johns's painting *Diver* (1962/63), she describes the work's subdued palette of blue, green, and brown brushstrokes as suggestive of water and falling; considers how the formal choices draw on conventions of naturalism, surrealism, and abstraction; and then discusses how the painting abstractly depicts the suicide of closeted gay novelist Hart Crane, a life story that Johnston analyzes for its overlaps and disjunctures with Johns's own struggles with the closet. Taking in this level of formal, biographical, and analytic detail, all rendered in Johnston's signature prose—although now a more academic version than she used in the *Village Voice*—makes reading the book an experience at once dense and dizzying.

How art might be a complex exterior announcement of an artist's interior landscape fascinated Johnston. *Art in America*, the visual art magazine that published the bulk of her arts criticism in the 1980s and 1990s, described her approach to Johns as one of "tracking the shadow."[4] The description produces images of Johnston as a peculiar detective, ever vigilant for clues that help her find the edges of what is not quite visible. She still wrote criticism based in close observations of art, but did so with the goal of drawing something like a silhouette of the artist. Reviewing Johnston on Johns, Glueck refers to Johnston's approach as "psychobiography," a term from psychology (a field in which Johnston was something of an autodidact) that generally refers to a scholarly work that attempts to propose a "*dynamic* explanation" for a person's actions based on their biography.[5]

As of the 1980s, Johnston had moved beyond the blurring of her art and life that was a hallmark of her earlier writing and was folding the lives of artists into her writing about their art. Johnston had always followed artists as much as she followed art, and she was particularly drawn to artists who tested the boundaries between art and life. Artists interested in—as artist Roger Cook has written of painter Agnes Martin—orienting themselves to their artistic practice as not just a way to create art but, even more so, a way to create "life as a 'work of art'" were the artists who caught and kept Johnston's attention.[6]

The artists for whom art making was also life making were the artists who truly deserved Jill Johnston. Jasper Johns is perhaps not among this group, by his own choice. He attempted to block Johnston's approach to writing about his life and art, refusing to give permission to use any images of his artwork in her book. There were, however, artists who relished the intensity of Johnston's scrutiny. These were the artists who became central to Johnston's relational approach to arts criticism: Agnes Martin, writer Gertrude Stein, and choreographer and filmmaker Yvonne Rainer. In her writing for the *Voice* and beyond, Johnston returned to each numerous times.

Perhaps not surprisingly, Stein, Martin, and Rainer are also artists Johnston would likely locate as key artistic landmarks in her capacious definition of *lesbian*. In column after column, Johnston discussed Stein, Rainer, and Martin, imagining how each woman's relationship to art was a practice of creating "life as a 'work of art'" and how her relationship to each of them, in writing and in life, was also something of a creative practice. Reading Johnston's writing about each of these artists provides examples of what might constitute a lesbian approach to arts criticism: writing in which lesbians can and do recognize one another's complexities in public.

Lesbian-to-lesbian adjacencies are somewhat rare—or at least rarely documented. As Annamarie Jagose argues, in art and beyond, lesbians usually appear only alongside straight women and/or gay men. Johnston's writing about Stein, Rainer, and Martin undoes this pattern of displacement. As Johnston writes about these three artists, lesbians move into adjacent relationships with one another. Examining them together, her writing about the three women creates a collage of sensuality and erotics borne of women looking at one another and sensing one another. Johnston's writing about Martin, Rainer, and Stein manifests what feminist theater critic Jill Dolan has described as feminist criticism's potential "to consider what theater and performance might *mean*, what it might *do*, how it might be *used* in a world that requires ever more and better conversations about how we can imagine *who we are* and *who we might be*."[7] Johnston's criticism intertwines life and art to imagine what it can feel like to be a lesbian with other lesbians.

Reading Johnston on Stein, Rainer, and Martin does not reveal some conclusive definition of what *lesbian* means (although it does suggest that *lesbian* remained stubbornly attached to whiteness in the worlds in which Johnston moved). There is no "aha" moment of defining *lesbian* in Johnston's art criticism, even in moments where she overtly discusses these artists' genders and sexualities—which she sometimes does but often does not. The iterative nature of her approach to criticism does not clarify but rather proliferates what *lesbian* might mean. Martin, Stein, and Rainer—and even Johnston, to some degree—are cantankerous fits with the categories of both lesbian and woman. Stein did not describe herself as a lesbian, and scholars only began noting her sexuality in the 1970s.[8] Rainer came out later in life, but, for most of the period in which Johnston wrote about her, she was in relationships with men. Agnes Martin, who did have relationships with women, infamously refused most—practically all—labels. Johnston recounts visiting Martin in New Mexico in 1973, and the elder painter asking the younger writer why she was so interested in her. After Johnston shared that she was awed by Martin's skillful navigation, as a woman, of the male-dominated world of painting, Martin replied, "i'm not a woman, i'm a doorknob, leading a quiet existence."[9]

Recognizing these artists as fitting only within the most capacious notions of *lesbian* and/or *woman* leads to other questions about sameness and difference within the group. There were significant age differences among the four: Stein was born in 1872, Martin in 1912, Johnston in 1929, and Rainer in 1934—generational divides that shaped Johnston's relationship to each. As she did with poet Guillaume Apollinaire, Johnston sometimes imagined Stein as something of a queer ancestor. Martin became an older role model, and Rainer, especially as Johnston and she aged, a peer. The fact that Martin and Rainer moved in different versions of largely white avant-garde New York worlds also factored into Johnston's relationships with them. Visiting Martin initially in New York's Coenties Slip, where Martin lived among what art historian Jonathan Katz has called a "queer family" of artists, many of whom were homosexuals, must have been notable to Johnston, who moved, like Rainer, through the more heteronormative (at least for women) downtown dance scene.[10]

A close reading of Johnston's writing about these women/lesbians/doorknobs and their (not so) quiet existences also rearranges Johnston's relationship to the term *lesbian*. In her arts criticism about lesbians, Johnston gets to be seen, ironically, as a writer first, and a lesbian second. Johnston often expressed frustration over how other labels obscured her desire to be primarily understood as a writer. When she was viewed as a critic, her writing was often seen as only in service to artists as opposed to being art itself, and when she was viewed as a lesbian feminist, her writing was often treated as a mere conduit for her politics. She constantly asked to be understood as a writer—a point she most prominently reiterated in her 1972 appearance on the *Dick Cavett Show*. Cavett introduced her as a "women's liberationist" and "lesbian feminist"—both labels Johnston told Cavett she willingly accepted, but to which she added that she also wanted "to be identified as a writer."[11] Reading Johnston as a writer of lesbian arts criticism, as I do in this chapter, offers no clear definition of *lesbian* but instead suggests what lesbian criticism might do: let women decide for themselves who they are, how they get described, and how their work is to be approached.

• • •

THE STORY OF Martin-as-doorknob arrives via a lengthy essay by Johnston about visiting the artist at her secluded home in northern New Mexico, a trip Johnston calls a "pilgrimage." The essay (originally published as two *Voice* columns) discusses the grids Martin is best known for painting—what Johnston calls "mystical geometries." The descriptions in the packed, utterly un-skimmable writing always arise from stories of Johnston being alongside Martin: the pair sitting next to one another looking at Martin's paintings in her Coenties Slip loft or Johnston following Martin through sagebrush to get to the edge of a canyon to catch a New Mexico sunset. On that walk to the canyon, Martin tells the story of why she left New York—a story Johnston says she partially knows. But she doesn't ask Martin any questions: "it isn't necessary to clarify everything or anything." Another type of silhouette emerges, not of an artist alone, but (as Johnston thought of them) of two women alongside one another, joined by art and practices of looking. It is not sameness that brings them together; they don't even agree on a definition of *woman*. It is a shared admiration of and interest in being people who might be called *women*, who might be called *lesbians*, who might be called *queer*, and who are working at making ways to see and be seen at the edge of the known.

Writing Lesbian Style: Gertrude Stein

In a May 1971 *Voice* column, Jill Johnston recounted the morning after her raucous appearance at the Town Hall event where she shut down Norman Mailer. She writes that she "woke up . . . laughing for an hour over events" and then left the bed in which she awoke to return to her own, where she climbed in to find she was not alone.[12] Her copy of Gertrude Stein's *Selected Writings* was tucked next to her pillow. Opening the book, she rereads Stein's first line: "I always wanted to be historical," and then Stein's announcement that she will return to America only once she has become a lion. Stein and her writing prove to be auspicious bedmates for Johnston that morning, reminders of another lesbian who had taken space and imagined fantastic transformations (see figure 4.1). The day after Johnston announced that "all women are lesbians except those who don't know it . . . yet," Johnston writes that she lies next to Stein and wonders: Could Gertrude Stein be her mother?[13]

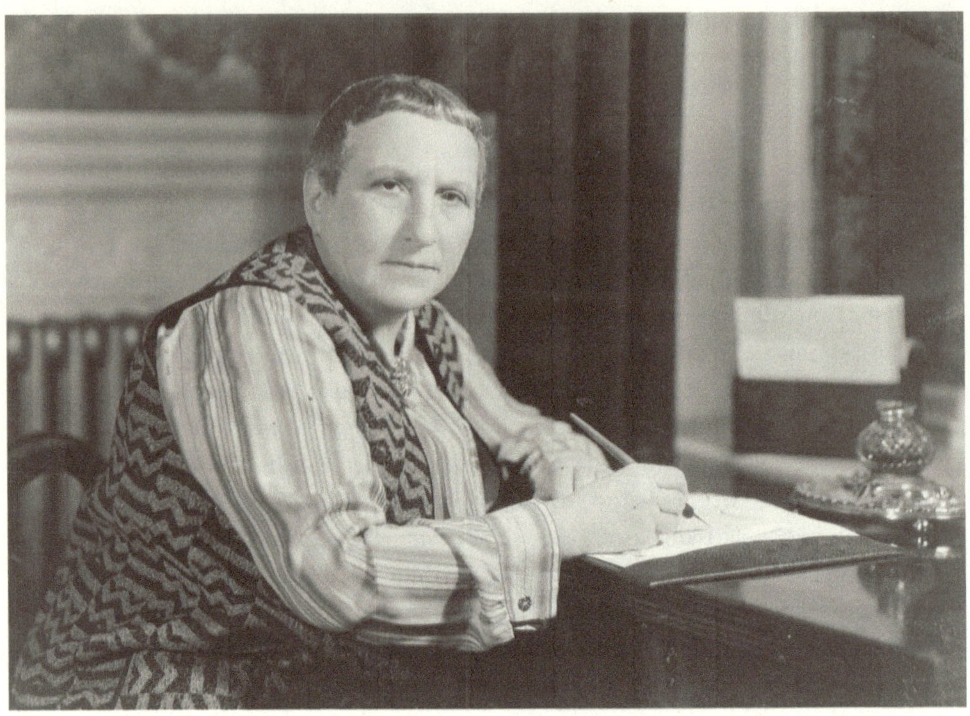

4.1 Gertrude Stein writing, 1936. Photo by Hulton Archive via Getty Images.

Alongside and *produced by*: both seem apt ways to characterize Johnston's relationship to Stein, a writer who reinvented language, planned to become a lion, and, eventually, became a lesbian icon despite not being all that compelled by the label *lesbian*. In twenty years of writing for the *Voice*, Johnston mentions Stein in almost thirty columns, often at great length. If Johnston's *Voice* columns were a regular dinner party, Stein was her most frequent guest.

Stein first appears in the column as Johnston examines a frequent phenomenon in dance in the early 1960s, the repetition of choreographic material with small differences. To help readers understand how this "method of circularity" hones an audience's perception, Johnston makes her first-ever Stein reference, comparing choreographer Aileen Passloff's use of repetition to the writer's.[14] A year later, Johnston notes a similar choreographic strategy in Yvonne Rainer's *Three Seascapes*, and again turns to Stein for explanation, this time at length. In this 1962 mention, Johnston explains that it is not just that Rainer and Stein deploy repetition through similar devices, but that they do so with similar aims, working to simultaneously create a "sense of familiarity" and a challenge to the audience/reader.[15] Discussing the overlap she sees in Rainer's and Stein's work, Johnston borrows language from Stein again—and also, again, notes that Stein is in her bed, though this time the book with which Johnston sleeps is Stein's *Lectures in America*. Johnston quotes directly from Stein, beginning with the phrase "began and kept on being," language that, in its play with time and sound, itself makes Johnston's point. In what Johnston called *repetition* and what Stein would likely have called *insistence*, change and continuity can co-occur: a hum continues as it is also slightly revised and reanimated by the hummer. Stein used *insistence* to describe how repeating patterns with slight variances evoke the "always alive . . . organic and animate," rather than "a mechanical quality" that she thought *repetition* usually connoted.[16] With Stein in her writing, in her bed, and on her tongue, Johnston can explain what produces the compelling liveliness in Rainer's otherwise "analytic, reductive" choreography (as Sally Banes once described Rainer's work).[17]

Stein re-emerges in Johnston's column in 1964, again alongside Rainer. Now it's Rainer's *Dialogues*, a trio made for Deborah Hay, Judith Dunn, and Rainer, that Johnston sees as resembling Stein's writing. In Johnston's estimation, Rainer and Stein insist on "style and the material mutually activat[ing] each other."[18] Both women made structure and content mutually constitutive—a quality that will eventually emerge in Johnston's writing, too. By referencing Stein and Rainer together, she builds a distinctly female bridge between the modern (Stein) and the postmodern (Rainer), inserting both women into an artistic coterie usually dominated by men. Rainer's "stopping, changing, growing, loving, flowing, thinking, and becoming" exist alongside "[Jasper] Johns' flag and [Andy] Warhol's soup cans and Rauschenberg's goat"—and "Stein's rose" is all these artists' queer modernist antecedent.

Stein seems to inspire Johnston's approach to writing as much as Stein offers her a way to think about others' art. Stein is the lesbian echo in Johnston's prose, perhaps best exemplified in a review of Judson artist Robert Morris's performance *21.3*. As Johnston describes the work's complex relationship between process and product, her writing creeps toward placing "style and material" into a feedback loop, just as she had noticed in Stein and Rainer's work. To capture the effect Morris creates, Johnston's language flips quickly, multiple times, between the words *process* and *product*, so much so that the two words almost seem to merge. Johnston then knowingly marks her linguistic play, with its collision of the visual, sonic, and kinesthetic ("I'm turning some verbal cartwheels myself here") and its play with time ("I might be having a better time now than I had at the concert").[19] Johnston is emerging as not only a critic but also a writer—and as another artist whose choices become more apparent when seen through the frame of Stein's.

From a twenty-first-century vantage point, Stein seems an obvious comparison with Johnston, but, in the early 1960s, when Stein first appeared in Johnston's writing, she was relatively unknown. As Stein scholar Wendy Steiner has noted, few read or studied Stein after her death in 1946. Only in the late 1970s, when feminist literary scholars "insisted the canon be widened," did Stein return to the broader readership she had had in the United States in the 1930s and 1940s, when she toured the country delivering the talks that became *Lectures in America*.[20] By frequently citing Stein in her widely read column, Johnston helped return Stein to greater circulation, hoisting her from the past into Johnston's queer present.

By the late 1960s, Stein is less a lesbian echo and more a lesbian wink in Johnston's writing. Johnston begins her 1969 column "Casting for 69" with what at first seems a random reference to Stein, recalling a discussion with friend and writer Ann Wilson about the size of Stein's head. Immediately after mentioning Stein, however, Johnston makes her first (albeit oblique) reference in the *Voice* to having a girlfriend. She describes posing for sculptor George Segal on a mattress amid a pile of rumpled bedsheets with her "friend," Polly, and Johnston reports Segal will title the work "Girlfriends."[21] If one reads the column and is aware of Johnston's soon-to-come lesbian activism, the reality of the relationship in the scene seems blatantly obvious. At the time, however, Stein is the only knowing observer. Maybe that's why her head is so big.

Quickly, things get less subtle. The word *dyke*—a pejorative in the wrong mouth but a sexy and bold word in the right one—first appears in Johnston's column in reference to Stein. The writer is no longer just a random big head but is now a "big dyke."[22] The announcement is both clear and not. Johnston writes that "people say Gertrude Stein is a big dyke," a slight sidestep of confirmation ("people say"). Johnston continues to skirt around Stein's sexuality as she muses over photographs of a young Stein, "any ordinary American buxom Jewish college girl," and photographs of an older Stein, where Johnston says she looks "aggressive," a shift she attributes to Stein's "collaboration" with Alice Toklas—who some readers would have recognized as Stein's female partner.[23] In another column, a little more than a year later, Johnston writes about enjoying listening to recordings of Stein reading aloud in her "stately cadence rich Brahmin sophistication even deep sexy mellifluous incredible voice."[24] Some of what Johnston and Stein share remains unconfirmed, but it's getting awfully easy—and pleasurable—to recognize.

Lesbian readers likely finally got their confirmation of Johnston's sexuality in a January 1971 column that also featured Stein. The column, "The Wedding," one of Johnston's lushest pieces of writing, celebrates the marriage of lesbian musician Pauline Oliveros to Lin Barron six months prior and mirrors the iterative nature of coming out. Johnston first writes about the wedding itself, alternating between descriptions of the ceremony held beneath a series of ocean cliffs between Los Angeles and San Diego and Johnston's recent amorous night in Los Angeles with an opera singer. Johnston peppers her descriptions with interjections that reference growth and change: Greek mythological figure Daphne's transformation into a tree and the supposed fertility of the ground on the island of Lesbos. Of the former, a result of Daphne trying to escape the god Apollo, Johnston writes, "She knew herself changed, and rooted in earth, and safe from pursuit as the blood in her body flowed down to become sap and her limbs and the flesh and the flowing hair become branches and leaves."[25] This seems like how a writer whose approach to prose has been forged by dance might (should?) describe coming out. And then, in a moment that gets excruciatingly close to announcing her own sexuality, Johnston writes, "The difference between the generations between say ours and Gertrude's is merely one of great pride in announcement."[26] Readers in the know will understand that "Gertrude" references Stein and that "our" generation is the group to which Oliveros and Johnston belong, the lesbians whose adult lives straddled Stonewall.

Stein's name practically functions a stand-in for *lesbian* in the description of the ceremony and the events that surrounded it. Oliveros is a "musical Gertrude Stein," a comparison that Oliveros scholar Martha Mockus notes many critics made at the time, usually largely based on visual appearance but also in reference to Oliveros's just-shy-of-public lesbianism.[27] Johnston's column erased all doubt about Oliveros's sexuality. The musician was grateful for the announcement, writing to Johnston after it was published to thank her for "bringing us [Oliveros and Barron] all the way out via your column and the reading on campus here and your encouraging me to dress the way I liked. It has made a lot of difference to me."[28] Again Stein had helped Johnston get where she—and now other women—needed to be. Coming out is a social act, made possible and safer through lesbian adjacencies. The world might condemn you, but others will accompany you, offering a hand (or head) and a soft landing.

Over the next months and years, Stein remains a regular character in Johnston's discussions of lesbianism, in her column and in public. But Johnston's most extended engagements with her always eventually return to

Stein's resistance to treating language as straightforward in its relationship to representation. In the spring of 1972, in her lengthiest discussion of Stein, Johnston wonders, Is Stein's insistence on obscurity, another quality Johnston shared with her, a hallmark of a lesbian style?

In one of dance studies' foundational texts, *Reading Dancing: Bodies and Subjects in Contemporary American Dance* (1988), Susan Foster argues for style as an essential category for studying American concert dance and defines style as a choice (or series of choices) that "impl[y] a background of alternatives rejected in favor of some feature of movement that lends distinctiveness to, by signifying an identity for, its bearer."[29] According to Foster, style allows individuals to distinguish themselves from others *and* situate themselves in a group or tradition.[30] Johnston understands style, particularly what she calls Stein's "lesbian style," as Foster does: a strategy that simultaneously marks one's individuality *and* one's community or lineage. Johnston begins her discussion of Stein's style with a list of lesbians and their overlapping relationships: "Natalie Barney (L'Amazone) who was at one time the lover of Romaine Brooks who painted a portrait of Lady Una Troubridge who was the lover of Radclyffe Hall."[31] This web of lesbian connections renders each woman, particularly Barney and Brooks, as distinct individuals, and emphasizes each woman's lesbianism as producing a number of overlapping relationships. To describe oneself or another as a lesbian is to make a demand of and for the self *and* of and with others. As Sara Ahmed writes in her reconsideration of lesbian feminism for the twenty-first century, "I write as a lesbian. I write as a feminist. This is an individual claim but also a claim I make for others."[32]

Via Stein, Johnston surfaces another point about "lesbian style." Might the two women share a lesbian style of writing—a style that sets each apart and also marks their association as lesbians? If there can be such a thing as an emphatic maybe, then that is Johnston's answer. In her column "Stein: Affectionately Obscene Poetry," Johnston investigates possible connections between Stein's and her own approaches to writing, as she remembers reading Stein's novel *Things as They Are* (1950) while in California for Oliveros's wedding. The posthumously published book's discussion of intimacies among women and one woman's recognition of her disinterest in conventional gender roles leads Johnston to ask if there was an "intimate connection between [Stein's] stylistic obscurities and her domestic lesbian arrangement."[33] Did the "necessity of obscurity" help Stein become "the mother of invention?" Johnston refuses any connection between Stein's "stylistic obscurity" and the closet, and instead credits Stein's playful navigation of her identity as a woman who lived outside the conventions of femininity with her artistic innovations. In Johnston's reading, "not only was Stein not hiding behind pseudonyms or fiction but what there was of it in her work was a celebration of lesbianism!"

In that 1972 column, Johnston launched—in a newspaper—nothing short of a close reading of Stein as queer lesbian semiotician, a writer bending language away from any clear, singular referent. She argues that Stein undertook a play with "obscurity" to continuously re-orient her readers, accentuating what language could produce rather than what it represented. According to Johnston, Stein, all at once, presented a word as though referring to a person and then obscured that relationship in order to produce new possibilities of relation between the original referent and language. Johnston argued that Stein thus created a "celebration of lesbianism" that "often had nothing whatever to do with the thing being represented."[34]

What Johnston tracks in Stein's writing parallels what literary scholar Laura Frost calls "Stein's tickle," the way her "somatic, acoustic language and her erratic and rhythmic cadences" involve the "susceptible reader" in "her circuit of pleasure."[35] Frost terms this kinesthetic effect of reading Stein a "tickle" because it arises from Stein's "contrast between tedium or disorientation and moments of intensity or excitement," a "sliding scale of pleasure to irritation."[36] Readers of Johnston's column knew this scale well; they survived it and felt compelled to return to it each week her column appeared. In letters to the editor, readers often compared Johnston to Stein, particularly as they attempted to make sense of Johnston's use of punctuation (or lack thereof). The comparisons were apt. Stein's discussion of commas in her "Poetry and Grammar" could have been a description of Johnston's writing in its style, content, and effect: "A long complicated sentence should force itself upon you, make you know yourself knowing it and the comma, well at the most a comma is a poor period that it lets you stop and take a breath but if you want to take a breath you ought to know yourself that you want to take a breath."[37] Johnston rarely used commas, but directed most of her displeasure toward the paragraph, an "aversion" she compared to Stein's feelings about commas. Johnston imagined that if she ever wrote a "history of english literature" (Stein's description of her "Poetry and Grammar"), it would end "in a critique of the paragraph." Johnston explained, "For me the paragraph is an archaic device predicated on the notion of separable categories of thought and information. The world from beginning to end is one paragraph and insomuch as there is no observable end or beginning."[38] Stein tickled Johnston across time.

A week after writing "Stein: Affectionately Obscene Poetry," Johnston got worried. She knew readers were too quick to create "separable categories," despite her calls for the opposite. Had she done to Stein what she was always annoyed when people did to her: see a lesbian and miss the writer? Had she, by linking "Stein's stylistic obscurity" with the writer's "sexual life," not done "justice to the scope of Stein's motivations as an artist" and instead provided an opportunity for people to misread her? [39] In the next week's column, Johnston underscored that being "unreadable" or "obscure" might be a signal of a lesbian style in writing but that such style was not merely a reaction against patriarchy or heteronormativity. As she put it, writing about herself in relationship to Stein, "i enjoy my obscurities for various aesthetic and mischievous and ambitious reasons and although I may once have worked on coded systems to cover myself sexually i had and still have other reasons as I said for sometimes being unreadable."[40] Johnston, like Stein, required her readers to do the work. No referent—and certainly not an easy categorization of the two writers' genders or sexualities—provides anything near a full explanation of either's work. Both refused writing as a practice that fixed meaning to a stable referent or origin. In their writing, *lesbian* becomes a verb, not a noun or adjective (forms of speech Stein hated). Verbs can "make mistakes" and be "mistaken . . . both as to what they do and how they agree or disagree with whatever they do."[41] As Stein and Johnston imagined how language could produce, rather than represent, a subject, they kept *lesbian* (and lesbians) in motion.

Writing the Body: Yvonne Rainer

The first time Yvonne Rainer (see figure 4.2) met Jill Johnston it was intense. In her 2006 autobiography, Rainer remembers meeting Johnston after a performance and feeling Johnston's gaze on her, "ever intent, the expression indicating detachment, calculation, and bemusement."[42] The details of Rainer's description suggest that she brought her own intensity to the exchange. She also felt a certain joy—and not just because Johnston had recently reviewed her work favorably. When Rainer looked at Johnston and felt Johnston return her gaze, she thought, "Now there's a creature as strange as I am."[43]

Johnston must have felt a similar affinity. She wrote about Rainer more than any other artist in her entire career; Rainer appears in Johnston's *Voice* column forty-plus times. In some ways, this extensive body of writing is relatively straightforward. Johnston was a critic who frequently saw Rainer's work throughout the 1960s, across many strains of experimentation.

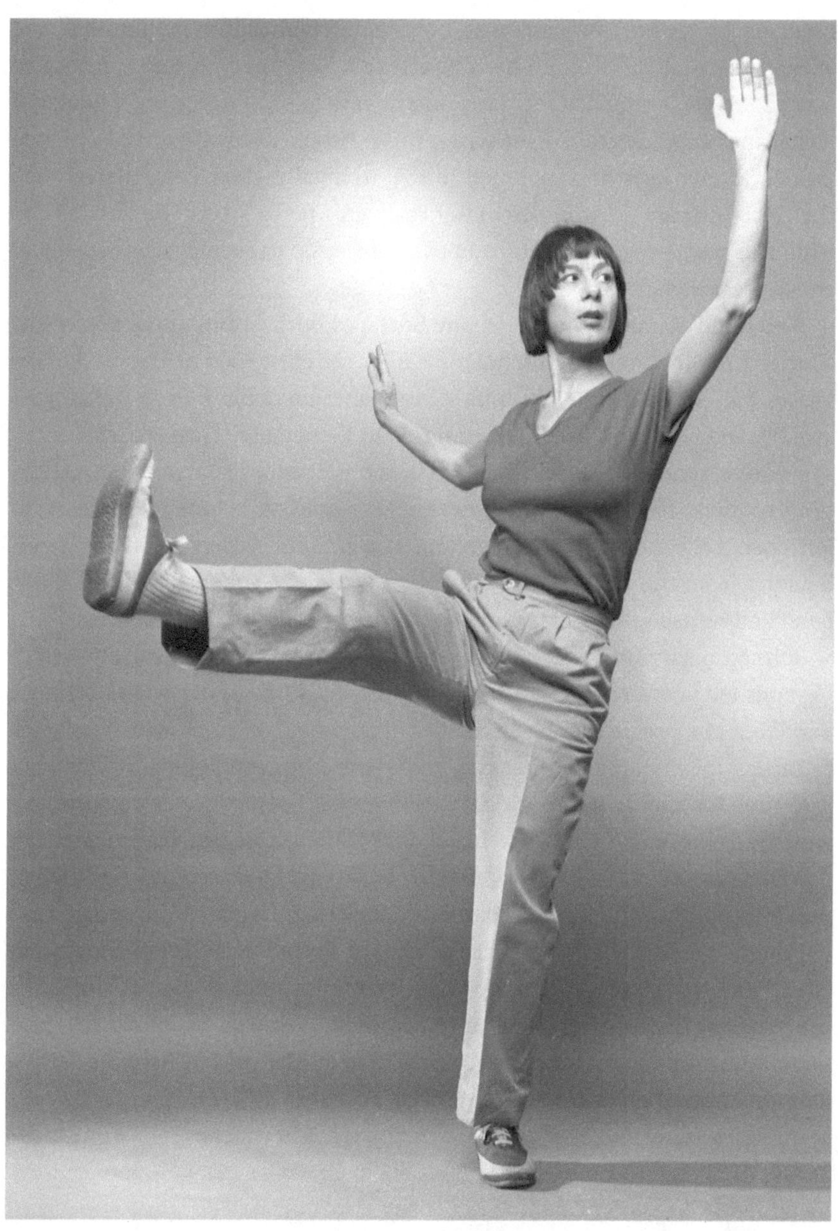

4.2 Yvonne Rainer dancing, 1982. Photo by Jack Mitchell via Getty Images.

Later, as Rainer became known as a filmmaker who addressed feminist and lesbian themes, the women became friends. Long past the time Johnston saw dance performances regularly, she always kept in touch with Rainer, if sometimes sporadically. As she writes in a personal note to Rainer from 1996 (which Rainer kept and included in the archival material she placed with the Getty Library), "After our call, I realized I feel a strong bond with you from the past—and a certain sadness over large gaps and disjunctures in communications."[44]

The bond Johnston names is one borne of both professional and social overlaps. Rainer knew what Johnston had done for her and her fellow Judson artists, naming Johnston "the inimitable champion of the Judson Dance Theatre."[45] And while Johnston's central role in Rainer's life then was as a critic, she also remembers the Jill Johnston of the 1960s for her raucous contributions to the social scene of the time. Rainer would often look up in whatever loft hosted the party after the performance and find Johnston upside down, hanging from the rafters.[46] Both women were experimenting with how to bend and refuse norms. That's much of what they saw in one another.

Johnston's writing about Rainer is a study in one woman closely watching another woman in public—a ubiquitous, daily phenomenon in the dance world but one rare in the then male-dominated field of dance criticism. Much as Rainer documented her first time looking at Johnston, Johnston found her first time looking at Rainer rather striking, too. Seeing Rainer perform in a work by Yoko Ono, Johnston writes that "Yvonne Rainer the dancer was nice to look at as she sat still on a chair, also as she did an 'exercise' in excruciating slow motion of bending the knees, contracting the abdomen, and grimacing the facial muscles."[47] If a reader wanted to find evidence of Johnston's attraction to women in her performance reviews, "nice to look at" might be the smallest indicator of such. In the context, however, of Johnston's hallmark attention to movement and the attention she paid to Rainer's skillful manipulation of repetition, "nice to look at" reads differently. It documents surprise, the unexpected pleasure Johnston takes in watching someone move in "excruciating slow motion." Something in Ono's staging of Rainer's movement and/or Rainer's execution of the slight movements caught Johnston off guard and captured her attention. From then on, Johnston's writing about Rainer is a study in one woman paying careful attention to the details of another woman's motion. What is striking about how Johnston's attends to Rainer is that her intense scrutiny does not trap Rainer in any one moment or position, but rather insists on watching her as a way to observe how Rainer and her work change. As Johnston writes about Rainer's 1963

Terrain: "The content is really something—but it is always the transformation that makes you care."[48]

To some degree, Rainer trained Johnston to watch this way through her choreographic interest in directing audiences to find new ways of experiencing performance. As Johnston put it in a pre-Judson review, Rainer intentionally created work that "we are not accustomed to looking at."[49] Johnston immediately loved the challenge Rainer posed to her audiences, even as she also worried the challenge might lead others to dismiss the then twenty-seven-year-old's choreography. This concern probably inspired Johnston's incorporation of Stein as comparison in her writing about Rainer early on, with Stein's language helping explain the choreographer's stringency and repetitive loops to readers. With help from Stein, Johnston led audiences toward a perhaps particularly lesbian version of what Holly Hughes and David Román have identified as a key offering of queer performance: teaching audiences new ways of seeing.[50]

While others might have needed help recognizing what Rainer was doing, Johnston fell fast—the beginning of a relationship via writing that, as Rainer puts it, "incurred a debt that I feel unequipped to repay in kind."[51] In late March 1962, Johnston declares Rainer "an important new phenomenon on the scene, not 'promising' but 'arrived,'" pointedly refusing the developmental narratives that infantilize younger artists and artists from marginalized groups.[52]

A year later, however, Johnston's fervor over Rainer falls into a different critical trap. She can't help celebrating what she sees as Rainer's genius by way of elevating her over artists of both the present and the past. In the 1963 review, Johnston proclaims Rainer "the most independent choreographer of this particular scene [Judson]," creating a hierarchy among artists even as what Johnston most lauded about Judson were its attempts to eliminate hierarchy. Johnston then places Rainer in lineages of female modern dance royalty, describing Rainer as "the greatest thing since Isadora crossed the Atlantic, or St. Denis saw that Egyptian cigarette poster, or say other important moments you can think of in the lives of several astonishing ladies a few decades ago."[53] Rainer is now among the "great women of modern dance."

Being compared to modern dance matriarchs like Isadora Duncan or Ruth St. Denis might be a compliment for some, but Johnston quickly disapproves of her rhetoric. In another column on Rainer she publicly reprimands herself for the comparisons, considering herself guilty of "dabbling in a notorious occupational absurdity of critics" of using the past to measure art of the present. This does not temper Johnston's praise but rather serves as a public reminder that the critic's job is to follow artists' development, to be with an artist and their artwork in the present moment. Johnston underscores this point, writing, "If I had to say Miss Rainer would be the next anything, I'd say she would be the next Yvonne Rainer."[54] Foreseeing that there would be multiple iterations of Rainer's art making (and there were), as a critic, Johnston wanted to move with the unfolding layers, not calcify individual moments.

There was, however, a choreographer with whom Johnston thought Rainer should be compared: her other favorite, Merce Cunningham. While Johnston technically compares the two, it's more like she places the two choreographers beside one another, a parallelism of man and woman as equals. In Johnston's estimation, Rainer and Cunningham produce work that resembles the other's, as though they share "imperceptible communications in a common climate."[55] As discussed in chapter 1, many critics initially dismissed Cunningham, arguing that his early work thrived only because of his performance charisma, not his choreographic innovation. Johnston disagreed, seeing Cunningham—as she later did Rainer—as someone who did not separate dancing from choreography and excelled at both. To Johnston, Rainer, like Cunningham, was an artist with "choreographic ambitions" that reached far beyond "looking good in a dance of one's own."[56] In a 1960 review, Johnston lauded Cunningham for bringing "us back to the reality that dancing concerns dancing, and that movement in itself can be more expressive than when it is once removed as a vehicle for cerebral intention."[57] Three years later, Johnston makes a similar claim about Rainer, championing her for approaching dancing as "facts not . . . idealized commentaries" and thus avoiding seeming to "pretend to mean" and using the body to create a symbol of an idea or emotion.[58] She also saw Rainer as extending Cunningham's interest in chance procedures, noting that he had focused on the "indeterminate" as a catalyst for performance, whereas Rainer "transpos[ed] the chance operation into the actual performance of the dance."[59] Rainer constantly transformed herself, as well as the tenets of dance that came before her, and Johnston was the attentive reporter tracking the new developments.

Johnston ventured that Rainer's unending transformations resulted from her ability to create "a viable contract between guidelines supplied by the choreographer and performers alert and imaginative enough to be existing under any circumstances."[60] Dynamic relationships, not choices made by individuals, produced constant action. Johnston arrived at this idea by treating Rainer's work almost as a journalist might approach an assigned beat: she saw each of Rainer's works many times and practically saw everything Rainer made. Of the various works that eventually resulted in Rainer's best-known piece, *Trio A*, Johnston covered at least two work-in-progress versions; solo, trio, and evening-length versions; and iterations in New York; Washington, DC; and Connecticut. She saw *Parts of Some Sextets*, a work best known for inspiring Rainer's statement "No Manifesto" (1965), at least four times, twice in New York and twice in Hartford, Connecticut. Across these many returns, Johnston tracked how Rainer built upon past investigations and asked new questions in a manner Johnston described as an "accretion."[61] Johnston approached Rainer as Jill Dolan imagines feminist critics should, sympathetic but not sycophantic, attending to how a work moves into the world with varied meanings and audiences.[62]

Johnston's feminist approach to Rainer's work is also queer in its refusal to equate transformation with linear progress. Johnston's writing zigs and zags with Rainer and is replete with Johnston's signature use of juxtapositions that are almost contradictions. She describes Rainer's contribution to the first Judson evening, her work *Ordinary Dance*, as a "poetry of facts."[63] Of Rainer's 1964 *Dialogues*, a piece where talking and dancing co-occur without ever syncing, Johnston writes that the performance's "controlled insanity" presents "emotions as facts," a welcome departure from past generations' presentations of "idealized commentaries on the human condition."[64] Rainer satisfies Johnston's interest in disruption and redirection.

In other moments, Johnston's writing about Rainer feels flat, bordering on dull—especially in comparison to the dizzying sensibility she brings to most of her criticism. This could be Johnston mirroring Rainer's affectively flat approach to choreography, or it could be evidence of the ways writer and critic were in a dynamic relationship. It sometimes seems that Johnston does the written equivalent of thinking out loud, trying to catch up to Rainer in public, on the page. Writing about *Terrain*, Johnston admits to being puzzled but frames that as a positive. Once she's "confused," Johnston has "more fun," even "get[s] a little weak." Rainer requires her to play with how to orient to the work, moving among seeing "so clearly" to "retreating" or "having it [the dance] retreat from me." Watching, Johnston is in a tussle between seer and seen and celebrates never being able to "locate the actual connection between a signal and its referent."[65] To watch (and to write about) Rainer is to be in motion.

The confusion Johnston experiences watching *Terrain* so fascinates her that she returns to the piece in a column weeks later, writing the sentence I cannot seem to help repeating throughout this book: "The content is really something—but it is always the transformation that makes you care."[66] The statement is notable for many reasons, but particularly for its pronouns. Johnston, a writer never wary of the first person—being the *I*—chooses the second person *you*. She addresses her readers, again helping them find a way to be with Rainer's challenge to audiences. Rainer scholar and art historian Carrie Lambert-Beatty has argued that Johnston was among the most comfortable with the complexity of seeing, a concern Lambert-Beatty describes as the force that "charged so much of [the 1960's] performance experimentation: an alternating current of pleasure in and resistance to dance's inaccessibility to vision."[67] Regular readers of Johnston's columns could be affirmed in their possible discomfort in watching Rainer's work, even as Johnston often tried to teach them that they already had the skills to watch subtle or mundane choreography. In one of her more poetic responses to Rainer, Johnston writes, "I can tell you how and when my bed or icebox is more important to me than my wallpaper, and I can tell you how I might love my wallpaper if it were better looking, and I can imagine how important wallpaper must be to those who manufacture it."[68] Presenting everything as of equal import does not render it all equally important but rather requires an audience to make choices and rearrange elements, to bring tactics of living and navigating one's world into the theater with them. With Johnston's writing as aid, readers/audiences could find reasons to continue meeting the demands Rainer made of them, seeking the experience of being with the transformations that Johnston so relished.

Rainer's famous (infamous?) work *Trio A* was the apex of what enraptured Johnston about Rainer. It most realized Rainer's skill at "jamming avenues of expectation [in a manner that] creates a deprivation requiring efforts to discover new routes of involvement."[69] What Johnston most appreciated about *Trio A* led others, most notably then *New York Times* dance critic Clive Barnes, to dismiss Rainer in the cruelest terms possible. Seeing Rainer's work on a 1966 bill at Judson, Barnes describes the program as a "total disaster" of "total nothingness," merely "pitiful, adolescent caterwauling."[70] Writing about a 1969 evening of work by Rainer, Meredith Monk, and Twyla Tharp, Barnes describes Rainer as "bland and innocuous," and Rainer and Monk as "a disgrace to the name of dancing."[71] He also admits he left the concert early, deeming it too "boring." Barnes is unwilling to "discover [the] new routes of involvement" these women required of audiences, and the gendered language in his screeds reveals his resistance as at least partially fed by sexism. Rainer and Monk are "self-appointed casual priestesses" offering "hysterical studies in boredom," whereas the male choreographers he compares them to are "genuinely adventurous." (The only woman included in the "adventurous" list is Judith Malina of the Living Theatre, and she only gets in via marriage, as one of "the Becks," her husband's surname.) Barnes's sexism continues in his muted apology published a few weeks later.[72] He writes that he's received letters "spring[ing] to the defense" of Monk and Rainer, whom he refers to as "the two ladies chiefly under fire." He then goes on to say he has discussed why the two were on the bill he saw with the evening's four producers—all of whom just happened to be men. Barnes reports that the male quartet, all "friends of mine," apologized for the program, claiming none had seen Rainer's work before that night. It was 1969. Rainer had been making significant work for almost a decade.

It's a good thing Yvonne Rainer had Jill Johnston. Barnes, as the *Times* dance critic, had inarguably the most prominent platform from which to discuss dance, but the detailed attention Johnston brought to Rainer cemented (perhaps overly so) Rainer's position in dance history. Johnston tracked the evolution of *Trio A* into *The Mind Is a Muscle* like "a baby whose birth you attended and subsequently watched in its expanding versions of itself," a watching over time that has helped make *Trio A* perhaps the most iconic dance of the postmodern era.[73] Johnston cares about the work, partially because she is challenged by it. "Wow this has become a complicated dance," she writes in 1969. She works to describe the piece's "innumerable focal changes [that] are always, with maybe one or two exceptions, up, down, side, diagonal or back, never directly at the audience."[74] For Johnston, a woman being complicated is not a reason to leave early; it's a reason to stay and to look more closely.

Johnston also recognizes Rainer's refusals of audience engagement, as Rainer "consciously . . . withdraw[ing] that contact which is the performer's traditional trade-tool of seductive involvement."[75] She surmises this partially from paying close attention and partially from reading Rainer's "No Manifesto," a statement written by Rainer while making *Parts of Some Sextets* and published in the academic journal *TDR/The Drama Review*. Rainer's refusal to meet the audience's gaze will later be described as an explicitly gendered, even feminist choice, a reading bolstered by the 1978 film of the work made by dance historian Sally Banes, which captures Rainer in *Trio A*, her lone female body refusing now not just the audience but also the camera's eye. Yet, long before dance historians and theorists in the academy began to watch dance in ways inspired by feminist theory, particularly feminist film theory, Johnston watches Rainer closely and recognizes how the choreography and choreographer are "repelled by certain entertainment values in the theatre, including I presume her own seductive exertions."[76] Johnston must have had

Rainer in mind when, in 1970, she applauded the women of the dance world who had dismantled the idea that the only reason a "lady" would be onstage would be to "exhibit her charms, her grace and deportment, her bodily attributes, her seductive powers, in the formally sanctioned theatre of a man's license for approved general voyeurism."[77] Watching Rainer guided Johnston toward central tenets of feminism, years before, as Johnston put it, "the feminists found her."[78] Though maybe the feminists had found each other earlier, in that moment Rainer met Johnston's gaze and realized there was "a creature as strange as I am."

Writing Friendship: Agnes Martin

Jill Johnston once described Agnes Martin, writing, "She's extremely handsome and she has the most brilliant twinkling blue eyes and her body is full and she's very solidly there yet shy and a little retreating at the same time" (see figure 4.3).[79] Martin's paradoxical sense of solidity plus shy retreat must have been entrancing to the bombastic Johnston. The structure of her description of the painter—the many *ands*—also suggests that more aspects of Martin's complexity came into Johnston's view as the two kept company with one another. Johnston makes no attempt to hide her admiration, even awe, for Martin, a person with whom Johnston found great resonance, despite their many differences.

Johnston always admired Martin, first for her paintings and then for her way of living, especially how Martin handled her diagnosis of schizophrenia—a diagnosis Johnston shared. Martin seems to have occupied a singular space for the younger lesbian. In the obituary she wrote for Martin in *Art in America*, Johnston called Martin "the only great woman I ever knew personally, an otherworldly woman with a magnificent aura and a fiercely independent nature."[80] Martin also had a certain fondness for Johnston, telling her during a 1973 visit Johnston made to Martin's remote home on the Pastorales mesa in New Mexico, that she admired Johnston because, of all those who ever came to visit her, only Johnston avoided being "very conventional."[81]

Johnston first wrote about Martin in a 1965 *ARTnews* piece, a short review of a show the artist had in New York. Johnston would go on to regularly mention Martin in twenty columns over the years, including two in 1973 that record Johnston's extended trip to visit Martin in New Mexico, one of many Johnston made over many decades and a journey she always referred to as a

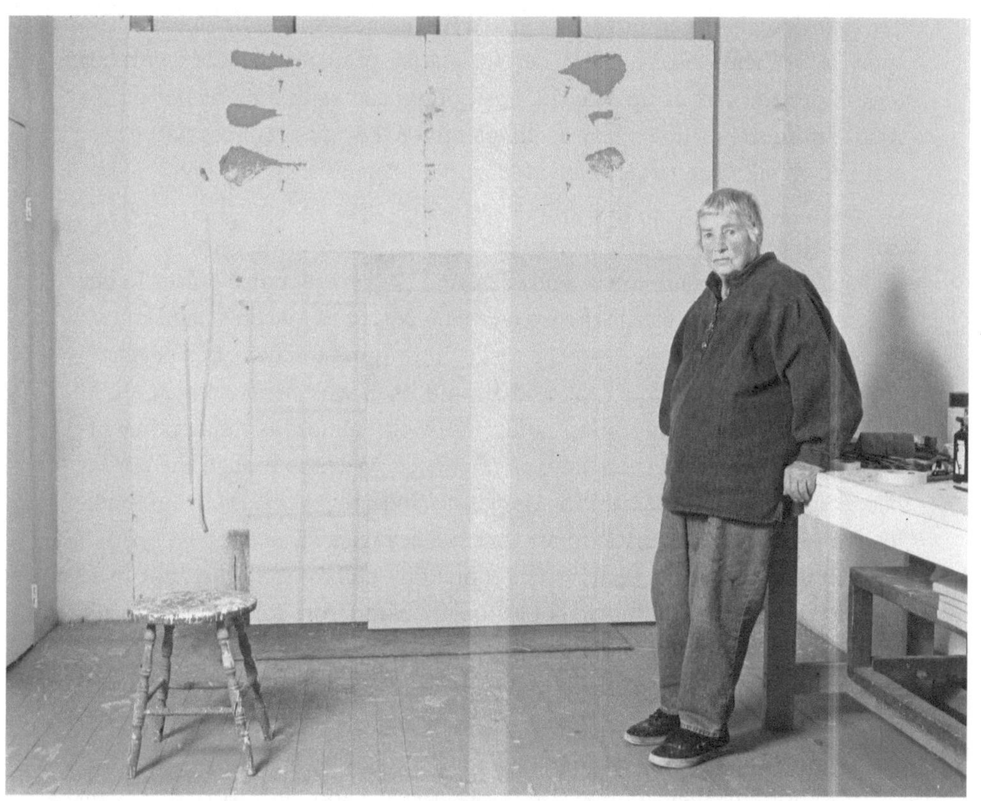

4.3 Agnes Martin in her New Mexico studio, 2004. © Michele Mattei.

"pilgrimage."[82] The word choice seems apt, as Johnston's feelings about Martin bordered on reverence. Johnston kept two letters from Martin framed on a wall in her home. The woman accustomed to being the one producing words held Martin's writing close and high.

Johnston came to know Martin through her paintings. She first saw them in 1964 at the Elkon Gallery in New York and immediately called her friend, curator Richard Bellamy, to ask why he wasn't showing the paintings Johnston found so extraordinary. *ARTnews* then assigned her to review a 1965 show of Martin's, and Johnston leveraged the assignment to get an invitation to see Martin's work privately in her Coenties Slip loft before it traveled to the gallery. Writing about that first visit, Johnston provides a tremendous number of physical details, not what one might expect from a visit supposedly made to look at paintings. She describes how Martin kept pulling back her then-long hair and how she carried her paintings, one by one, to "the spot," where she would make "a certain gesture of hiking the work with her foot under the canvas up into the position on the nails sticking out of the wall" before sitting down next to Johnston for the "quiet concentrated ceremonial ritual" that was looking at Martin's—"agnes's"—paintings.[83] From the start, Johnston's relationships to art and artist overlapped, a triangulation produced by two people looking.

Johnston's emphasis on the physical and the reverent also pulses in her writing about the paintings themselves. She describes Martin's hand-drawn grids as "absurdly simple—yet the result is the quiet intensity of a perfectly contained image that moves in and around itself without moving at all."[84] The paintings are "penetrating" and "suffusing," almost as though they literally pierce or spread their viewer.[85] Johnston writes as though the border between herself and the paintings is porous, initiating her into the intersubjective relationship of critic to art that she evangelized as the best form of criticism—discussed in chapter 1 as Johnston's call for critics to shift from "seeing" to "entering." Martin got a similar charge from Johnston's writing. In one of her letters to Johnston, one of those hanging in Johnston's home, Martin writes, "It is so pleasant and easy to fly when I read what you write. Every word is flying."[86] "The content is really something—but it is always the transformation that makes you care."

In addition to their mutual admiration for one another's work, Johnston and Martin had a particular bond centered around their shared diagnosis of schizophrenia. Johnston said it was "fairly safe" for the two to talk about "insanity" as they agreed "that nobody knows anything about it except the insane."[87] Martin appears for the first time in Johnston's *Voice* column in a cluster of pieces from 1969, a time when Johnston made a cross-country road trip after realizing she "had lost [her] mind again" and needed to elude "any authorities who might once again throw me in the bins."[88] As part of her road trip/escape, she tries to seek out Martin, seemingly in hopes of finding respite or advice from a person who had been sympathetic and helpful in past instances of what Johnston called her "breakups" (as opposed to *breakdowns*).[89] Johnston writes that she looks for Martin first in California and then New Mexico. Johnston had heard that Martin had just built a home in the latter place—her first home since 1967, when she had left New York after ending a relationship with a woman to begin two years of nomadic life, which ended when Martin had her most severe "psychotic episode" to date.[90] On the road in 1969, Johnston probably did not know about Martin's recent episode, but knew that Martin had, with Thalia Poons, "rescued" Johnston from her second mental "breakup." (The first had been a year earlier and had landed Johnston in a series of psychiatric wards.) Camping with Johnston and Poons, Martin had once sat naked on a rock midriver in a "Rubenesque position" and predicted Johnston's "difficult future," inevitable breakdowns/breakups to come.[91] Finding Martin while fighting off another breakup would have meant finding a powerful kindred spirit.

Martin and Johnston, however, shared not just a mental health diagnosis but also a perspective on the state of psychiatric medicine in the United States. Both had been swept into what historian of psychiatry Jonathan Metzl has described as the "benzodiazepine craze," a period from 1965 to 1979 when doctors diagnosed large numbers of women with schizophrenia and overprescribed drugs like Thorazine to many.[92] When Johnston called Martin and Poons as her 1966 breakup began, Martin encouraged her to take all the Thorazine she had on her—a sign that Martin must have thought Johnston was in an extreme state, since otherwise Martin, like Johnston, resisted the medicalization of their conditions. Both refused psychiatric terminology their entire lives. Martin called her difficult periods "trances," a parallel with Johnston's language of "breakup."[93] Both women also knew that medical language like *schizophrenia* locates an issue within an individual person, isolating and then pathologizing a set of behaviors, rather than understanding mental differences as "figured in and through . . . other categories of difference," as theorist Alison Kafer proposes in her book, *Feminist, Queer, Crip*.[94] Psychiatry then imposes social norms on the individual person, and, as Johnston put it, "helps people 'adjust' to their roles in the self denying hierarchical structures of scarcity oriented work-pressed society and to lock them up if they couldn't."[95] This was all the more true for women. As Metzl charts, women were often overprescribed medications like Thorazine if they expressed that they were struggling to meet society's gendered expectations.[96] Psychiatry diagnosed women like Martin and Johnston as the problem; they disagreed.

Martin and Johnston also both knew that as much as the medicine that doctors prescribed could flatten one's sense of the world, there was a worse psychiatric sentence: being committed into the "hospital-prison system," as Johnston called it.[97] In a letter to Johnston, Martin wrote that mental institutions were "dead wrong" and, echoing Johnston on the mental health complex, that they merely turned people "back to the conventionality that drove them insane."[98] Martin must have been one of the few people who could directly empathize with Johnston's horrific experiences in 1965 (and again in 1966) of being "locked into a gray walled dungeon with no way out and shot full of paraldehyde and 1000 mgs of Thorazine and locked into a cell within the dungeon a room containing a peestained mattress and the dents of bludgeoning heads and trust up to a bed and laced up into a straight jacket and left to die for the night I did and I've never been the same since."[99]

Having experienced such, both grew interested in the antipsychiatry movement of the 1960s. Johnston was particularly drawn to the writing of R. D. Laing, whose 1967 book *The Politics of Experience* she described as "a belated vindication against our censure and invalidation" in psychiatric hospitals. Laing proposed that instead of being locked in the "dungeons" of mental hospitals, those with diagnoses of schizophrenia or psychosis should be allowed to live together without locked doors or antipsychotic meds, a vision Laing enacted in London's Kingsley Hall from 1965 to 1970—an arrangement Johnston called a "freakout house" in a column where she wrote about visiting Laing in 1973, the same year she first visited Martin in New Mexico.[100]

Martin proposed what Johnston found to be a better version of antipsychiatry. Instead of the forced isolation core to "psychiatric treatment," Martin advocated for different forms of "isolation" as "cure" to "madness."[101] In the solitude she found through painting and living in the desert, Martin found her cure. To Johnston, she was "the only woman we know who escaped completely," who found her own spot in the "bewilderness."[102] Martin often encouraged Johnston, her friend and to some degree mentee, to find her own ways to withdraw from the world. She praised Johnston for being "unconventional" and "so far out" but pressed her to go further, to become completely "independent," a day Martin said she was "worried" that Johnston might not reach but that she thought she could, a transformation Martin told Johnston she was "looking forward to . . . with excitement."[103] Though Johnston never really withdrew as Martin did, she understood why Martin had done so. Visiting Martin in New Mexico a few years later, Johnston felt deep appreciation for Martin's choice and her advice. She wrote that Martin was "better off in the desert throwing mud at her adobe and polishing her green truck" than she, Johnston, was, "going around meeting hundreds of strange women."[104] Amid these "strange women," Martin and her paintings were, for Johnston, "a bellwether in a stormy world."[105]

Approaches

Johnston's interest in Martin's art and her overlap with Martin in terms of navigating mental health diagnoses were entrées to their connection, but it was Martin's role in Johnston's life as someone she admired and listened to that led to the women's deepest connections. If Stein provided a frame through which Johnston could see others' work, and Rainer and Johnston felt a mutuality of ever-developing strangeness, Martin was the person who helped Johnston see herself and constantly reorient herself to the world. Or as Johnston put it in a 1975 column, "agnes is not a friend i hasten to add. she's a force, an elemental invisible monument with arms pointing in all directions at the crossroads."[106]

Knowing Martin's importance to Johnston seemed to require my own pilgrimage to New Mexico in order to complete this book, so, in 2021 and again in 2023, I traveled to northern New Mexico where Johnston visited Martin. Before Martin passed away in 2004, she built a quiet monument to the solitude she so valued in Taos's Harwood Museum of Art. The monument takes the form of an octagonal room at the back of the museum filled with large works by Martin painted especially for the space: seven paintings for the room's seven walls. (The room's eighth side is an open door.) All the paintings are acrylic on linen and feature slight variations of soft, yet somehow also bright, blue and white stripes.

Each day I am in Taos, I go to the Martin room, often sitting on one of the four small bright yellow Donald Judd–designed benches that mark the room's center. Every visit I notice something new in the paintings: the subtle differences in Martin's brush strokes, how the whites and blues meet and overlap. Sometimes I reread Johnston's two long 1973 pieces about visiting Martin. As I face the painting directly across from the room's entrance, a work titled *Perfect Day*, I am reminded of the 1997 documentary about Martin, *Agnes Martin: With My Back to the World*, a title that comes directly from Martin.[107] It is her description of how painting allowed her to orient to the world. The Martin room at the Harwood, where I sit with my back to the room's door, fosters the sense of solitude that perhaps approaches the feeling that painting brought Martin.

As I sit longer, my awareness of the open door behind me fades away, and I realize why Johnston used terms like "suffuse" to describe Martin's geometries. The room's octagonal shape means that six of the paintings directly face another painting, and whatever travels between those paintings crosses the room's center, where the benches are and where I sit. Solitude gives way to the subtle force of exchange. Eventually I grow curious about the paintings' titles, partially because Johnston says Martin often asked her about titles when she visited the Coenties Slip loft in the 1960s.[108] Johnston says that she was never sure why Martin wanted to talk about titles but that the conversations allowed her to sense more of what was present in Martin's grids. I look at the titles. Seated with my back to the door, I look directly at *Perfect Day* and am between three other pairings. *Lovely Life* faces *Ordinary Happiness. Love* faces *Innocence.* And *Friendship* faces *Playing*. Sitting among these pairings, I am reminded of—I feel—just how many ways women might come together, might touch across time.

• • •

JILL JOHNSTON'S WRITING about Agnes Martin, Gertrude Stein, and Yvonne Rainer leaves a breadcrumb trail to the writer Johnston would become once her time as a regular columnist came to an end. The writing is also a capacious and messy summation of what Johnston saw writing, particularly criticism, to be: a form of approach. Criticism was a way to describe the unruly experiences of encountering others through art. As a writer Johnston chronicled how she approached art; approached artists; approached women, particularly lesbians; approached bodies; and approached all of life with a sense of fullness, disruption, and excess. Her goal was neither full comprehension nor complete attachment, neither announcement nor confirmation. Jill Johnston's goal was to write of force and of motion. To read her is to experience the impact of words on bodies, the impact of bodies on words, and all that moves in the spaces between.

EPILOGUE

Last Sentences

I'm not clear on the purpose of settling the past unless we go back to invent it but I'm not keen on writing myself into the future either.
—Jill Johnston, *Village Voice*, 1972

In 1988, at an intimate dinner at Kate Millett's home, Jill Johnston asked Millett, "When did you know it had all come down for you, Kate? When did it all fall apart?"[1] In essence, the question was, How did Johnston's fellow gay, female celebrity activist and writer know that the end of the movements that had forged the two women's activism—radical feminism and gay liberation—had come to an end?

Johnston already knew how she would answer the question. She even kind of knew how Millett would. In the audiotape of the dinner, which Millett placed into her official archive, Johnston, Millett, and the third dinner guest, Johnston's wife-to-be Ingrid Nyeboe, had been swirling around the idea of how to recognize the end for quite some time. Johnston knew *an* end had come when Clay Felker, best known for the slick version of New Journalism he fostered as editor of *New York Magazine*, bought the *Voice* and became her editor in 1974. Talking to Millett, Johnston remembers Felker calling and telling her, "You can't continue to do what you're doing." He was emphatic, even belligerent. She tells Millett she remembers not just what he said but what the phone call and his tone meant she had to do: "Hold the phone out here [away from her body] because otherwise [her] ears would have deafened." Felker's admonition—even more than a decade later—seemed clear in instruction, import, and impact, despite him not having named what exactly it was Johnston had to stop doing. For the male editor, hers was a writing that dared not speak its name.

In thinking about Millett's trajectory through the 1970s, Johnston strikes a more congratulatory tone. She credits Millett with having "extracted" from the feminists (who Johnston calls "those goddamn people") a commitment to support gay liberation. Johnston's positivity, however, is short-lived. A back-and-forth between the more hopeful Millett and Johnston ensues.

JOHNSTON: I didn't think we won at all.

MILLETT: We didn't lose. I think we won, and we're still winning on it.

[Johnston laughs, big and open—almost as big and open as she laughs earlier in the night when the two discussed if either could pull off a blazer, become "blazer dykes," as Johnston puts it.]

JOHNSTON [to Nyeboe]: Kate thinks we won; I think we lost.

The end is now more the moment of accounting—of who won, who lost, or, as both Millett and Johnston eventually settle on, who survived. With survival as their measure of liberation and its effects, both women shift their verb tenses from past to present. They agree: "We're surviving." Millett, however, adds a caveat: "But half the time we don't even believe in better days."

The tape captures all their equivocations. Both women are invested in what it documents. They frequently check that it's running and adjust the recorder's position in the room. Despite their attentions, several times throughout the night the recording cuts out abruptly. The machine is unreliable. But every time Johnston and Millett get it working again.

• • •

I'M SITTING IN a restaurant in the college town where I live, talking with a colleague, mentor, and friend who's been following my progress on this book. (It's 2019, and I've already been working on it for several years.) She asks when I'm going to be done. I can tell the correct answer is "soon." Even though I've been researching and writing the book consistently, I know I'm not that close to the end. A little ashamed, I confess this to her.

As I walk home, I try to figure out why the question of when the book will be done bothered me so much, including landing on my body like a half-hearted punch. I'm an academic; we can say we're "finishing" something for years! I turn onto the block where I live, and the answer surfaces: I don't ever want this project to end. But maybe it won't really end—Johnston's writing has produced my own, perhaps even produced me in some ways. Her writing, as action and object, forged a space for other women, other lesbians, other writers to produce themselves, including me.

• • •

AMONG THE MANY lessons gleaned from a close reading of Jill Johnston's writing is this: an ending is not the end. She regularly closes her columns with a collection of sentences that seem to open outward to the world. In many cases, Johnston's conclusions, often a series of short sentences that almost resemble a poem, read less like a summation, or even the common newspaper structure of concluding with less important sentences that can be jettisoned depending on available space, and more like the closing lines of a sonnet. Instead of an ending, Johnston offers a turn.

It's useful to think of Johnston's approach to the closings of writing much like an English sonnet, a poetic form built of dense quatrains of shifting rhyme and content that conclude with an unexpected final two lines in the form of a couplet. Poet and scholar Carl Phillips has called these last lines the English sonnet's "most rebellious component," a throwing off of sonic and formal expectations to guide a reader "toward dispersion, sonically, even as it structurally aims to deploy an argument that leads to something like conclusion or proof."[2] In a sonnet's closing lines, there can be both continuity and dispersal. One of many examples of a similar tension in Johnston's writing comes in her early 1969 column titled "Tell Me the Weather." The piece first reads as a compression of news from various artists' lives, particularly how their work shifts in, after, or through travel. As the piece continues, Johnston shifts to focusing on her own travels, namely, a journey through a snowstorm with friend Ann Wilson to a ski slope in New Hampshire. On arrival, Johnston reviews the skiers much as she would dancers, and then recounts a conversation with an eight-year-old skier about how one might learn to ski.

As is common in Johnston's writing, "Tell Me the Weather" unfolds with the rhythm of its content. To read it is to feel something of what it would be like to drive through a snowstorm or launch into a not-quite-in-control trip down a blue slope. Johnston invites the reader to peer through density as momentum gathers. And then, in one of her sonnet-like turns, the column concludes:

> Back-and-forth with an "eight-year-old skier" about the "right" way to ski down a slope. I asked her if you have to learn how to fall. Naturally. And what's the object in learning how to fall? She didn't know. She was just certain there was a correct way to fall and someone had to show you how. One time I fell out of bed and split a cartilage in my knee. Maybe she's right. But I dunno, I just don't fall out of bed anymore. And I don't recall taking a lesson to fall off my first roof into a deep snow just for the helluvit.[3]

The short (for Johnston) sentences slam on the reader's brakes, leaving the gathered momentum to send the reader pinging in multiple directions, a sensibility heightened by the dialogic format. There is a shift from earlier, more general statements about action (dancing or skiing) toward the individual body, represented by the *I* and in cartilage and joints. And there is a slightly illogical almost proverb: "And I don't recall taking a lesson to fall off my first roof into a deep snow just for the helluvit"—a statement that feels like a lesson but that isn't meant to offer a clear direction. It's a laugh and a bit of restlessness.

"Tell Me the Weather" appears in Johnston's 1971 collection *Marmalade Me*, a volume that can be, quite entertainingly, read through each column's last sentences. Most columns in the volume are ones Johnston wrote from 1964 to 1970 as she experimented with what a column about performance could be. These last sentences come in many forms but always provide a sense of spiraling outward, a handoff to a reader to go elsewhere (if not necessarily forward). Sometimes that instruction toward travel comes almost literally. Many of Johnston's closing sentences reference transportation, planes or cars. Sometimes the travel is more poetic—even intersubjective—as in the case of a column about poetry events curated by Hannah Weiner. Johnston closes the piece by writing, "I should've known me when I was you, then I would've been me. I wish I'd known you when I wasn't me and I would've been you. If there are as many minds as there are heads, there are as many lovers as there are hearts. Riding the image as though it were a breaking wave."[4] Boundaries are dissolving, and motion is everywhere.

Play is also key to these nonending endings. The way that performance, as a live, time-based form, can never be truly summarized often influences Johnston's last sentences. For instance, she concludes her 1966 review of a Robert Whitman Happening—one of her most innovative assessments of how time works in performance with its visceral insistence on keeping the reader in time with Johnston as spectator—writing that she heard "a finale noise box interpreting the sounds of the swamp [which] Simone (Whitman) told me it was more truly the sound of paper crackling through the trees in the wind. At that point I couldn't have cared less."[5] Much as is the case with "Tell Me the Weather" and its splitting knee cartilage, Johnston's specificity grounds the reader in a sensorial image but then provides the sense that specificity is both necessary and beside the point. The specific is a launch pad to dream from, not to categorize and be encased by. Jill Johnston's last sentences are invitations to linger or float, not to figure everything out.

Finally, Johnston's endings often emphasize the sensorial. They are meant to be felt as much as read. She accomplishes this through building momentum via rhythm but also through irreverence. The closing of her 1968 "The Holy Hurricane," itself a column in which Johnston reflects on how performances conclude, is among the best examples of this and among the most overtly sonnet-esque in its closing sentences:

> Yes the place becomes a holy mess. A holy hurricane of blood. A riot of red. A holocaust of bodies. This is a catechism and a cataclysm. The baptism by fire. The remembrance of things past. The resurrection and the life. "Drink of it, all of you, for this is my blood of the covenant, which is poured out for the many for the forgiveness of sins." This is the eye of insanity of the dissolution of boundary. A consummation devoutly to be wished. Inferno Purgatorio Paradise.[6]

An ending can be, Johnston demonstrates, exactly as she imagines at the beginning of "The Holy Hurricane": a "dam [that] breaks a private pond [and] becomes a public ocean."[7]

• • •

I STAND AT the corner of New York's Twenty-Third Street and Fifth Avenue, with Ingrid Nyeboe, Jill Johnston's wife; Ingrid's now-wife, painter Louise Fishman; and a playwright friend I have cajoled into joining us. We await the arrival of the dykes already marching from Bryant Park uptown—those who began this year's Dyke March, part of the fiftieth anniversary of Stonewall. There are looming rainclouds, but our little crew is undeterred. I had been nervous earlier but (with a little prodding from a friend) had asked Ingrid and Louise if we could walk together. They had not minded me joining them, and now we're on the corner, a "private pond" turning into a "public ocean." Louise wears a T-shirt adorned with the cover image from Esther Newton's book *Margaret Mead Made Me Gay*. (Esther and Louise were once lovers, now close friends.) Ingrid tells me she's wearing the shirt she wore the first time she walked in a Dyke March with Jill.

The first marchers come into sight: a row of dykes in wheelchairs. Just ahead of this first wave, clusters of marshals run single file along where street meets sidewalk, reminding everyone waiting to join the march to do so only after the wheelchairs have passed. We will go at the pace they set for us. As the wheelchair users approach our intersection, heading south along Fifth Avenue, another group of marshals—a younger group, it seems—link hands and walk across the intersection's eastern and western sides. As is Dyke March practice, no permission has been sought to be in public space; this is a protest, not a parade. The women who are marshals stand shoulder to shoulder and form the barricade that protects marchers from approaching traffic. Police are present (if contentiously so), but it is literally lesbian adjacency that keeps us safe, marking these streets, this intersection, as queer lesbian space.

With the lesbian human barricades now in place, the first wave of marchers in sight, and more people now visible just behind those in wheelchairs, the energy in the air feels ready to burst. But then, everything stops. Just as the last wheelchair rolls into place, tens, maybe hundreds, of fists rise into the air, and there is silence so complete it is loud.

I stare. Not a voyeur's stare but a stare that is the visual equivalent of thirstily gulping down water. Wanting to take in every last dyke before me, I witness their choreography, their offered protection, their multitude. They are looking at us and offering an invitation to look, to be seen. To see the wheelchairs and the knee scooters, the shaved heads and the long hair, the trans liberation flags with their pink, white, and blue stripes. There are a lot of us, and there are lots within that *us*. "Hello all you sexes. We're too good to be true."[8]

The cement curb beneath my feet almost seems to be moving. It's actually the soon-to-be marchers around me that I feel. Those of us waiting on the sidewalk are becoming a group, an edged curb the first marchers pass that will soon be absorbed into the protest, falling in behind the wheelchairs. Now part of the march, my little group falls into our own line: Ingrid to my left, with Louise to her left; my friend to my right.

We walk in the middle of the street, heading downtown, a vantage point that, for me, is one full of perspectives forged by dance. Though I have lived in New York briefly and visited often, I lay no claim to being a New Yorker—an identity readily apparent by how slowly I walk amid the fast step of real New

Yorkers on their city's sidewalks. New York to me is purely about dance and writing. The buildings that edge Fifth Avenue and loom on the horizon beyond I see in tandem with George Balanchine's ballets and Edwin Denby's writing about people alongside architectural verticality. I love watching all these people in public urban space because I learned about the intricacies of so-called pedestrian movement from studying postmodern dance and Johnston's and Deborah Jowitt's writing about how walking and running are just as graceful and intricate as pirouettes. And I map the city through its performance spaces, knowing that Lincoln Center and the Met, where Jill saw the balletic spectacles she so intelligently lampooned, are behind me, and her beloved Judson Church and myriad downtown art galleries are ahead of me. Walking in a New York City street doesn't just remind me of dance; to me, it's inseparable from it.

The various scales surrounding us, of the city and of the marchers, shuffle our order and my sense of perspective: Louise is now next to me, and though she is much shorter than me, I have the sense she's leaning down to tell me something. "We were so scared in 1970." I realize she's talking about that first march, Stonewall's first anniversary. Louise leans into me again, making sure I heard: "We were so scared in 1970." I heard her, and I hear her again, even as we walk by the windows of corporate store after corporate store, painted with rainbow flags.

Any chance at a midprotest conversation about what Louise has shared is swallowed by the samba band we now walk behind. Their volume provides the odd sense of solitude urbanscapes can. I scan the crowd ahead and behind. There are two samba bands. A few people with babies strapped to their chests. Many marchers now topless. Some have tape over their nipples, and others have the telltale curved lines left from top surgery. One of the topless marchers has "freedom" scrawled in black marker across their chest. Louise leans up/down again to remark, with a wink, "There are a lot of beautiful women here." In the crowd and in her comment, *beautiful* feels big, open, and sexy. Good to walk among and with and be.

The march finally arrives at Washington Square Park. I'm struck that there is no final speaker, no rally—marching together was the thing. My friend has to take off. Ingrid and Louise say their goodbyes and head to meet another friend for dinner, a lesbian who is a judge who cannot walk in the protest due to her position but who has walked alongside on the sidewalk the whole time.

I'm alone now, so I crawl up the edge of the park's famous arch to watch the waves continue to come and then splinter into smaller groups around the park. I watch. I wonder if this is why Jill used to climb into the rafters at parties, as Yvonne Rainer told me she did. It's fun to climb up above; it's also a good spot to watch from. I can now see those still coming down the avenue, and also I realize I recognize a number of the marchers now scattered around the park. Lesbian scholars whose work inspired my own and who are cited in this book casually chat with one another. Two of my favorite lesbian performers greet a lesbian comedian's small dog. Most of those I recognize are older than me, though not all. I'm buoyed by all the ways I'm in the middle, surrounded by political lesbians, and, at forty-one, have plenty of people to look up to and plenty to be pushed by.

It's not lost on me as I stand on the arch's side that Judson Church is just behind me—the place that through association is probably most responsible for Johnston's relative fame, even as all the lesbians around me probably know her more for *Lesbian Nation* than for her dance criticism. But the two aren't all that far apart. Four blocks up, as we crossed the busy intersection at Fourteenth Street, the marshals had done their thing for the last time in the march: linking hands and then stretching themselves across the wide street. The lines of marshals to the east stood still as we crossed—Louise just ahead of me, Ingrid just behind. As I turned my head to the right, to the west, that line of marshals began a sloppy kick line, a leisurely, perhaps intentional reenactment of the apocryphal kick line done by those at Stonewall as they faced off with cops in 1969. Queers fed up with having their congregating and dancing policed. Among all these queers, these lesbians marching and dancing, across time and space, I know it's OK for this book to end. We'll still be here, writing sentences that turn and turn again.

SCORES FOR JILL

Feel the shoulders around you.
Lean. Just enough.
Find what you need.
Enter.

Dance with a partner, any way you both want.
Holler from the audience.
Claim the lineage you need.
Read with your whole body.
Leave before it's over.

Turn and turn again.

NOTES

PREFACE

1. Deborah Hay, discussion with author, April 2017.

2. Adeyemi, "Beyond 90°," 14.

3. Adeyemi, "Beyond 90°," 15.

4. Jill Johnston, 1972–73, box 52, folder 743, Phyllis Birkby Papers, Sophia Smith Collection of Women's History, Smith College, Northampton, MA.

5. Taylor, *Archive and the Repertoire*, 16.

6. "Helen Ansell," in "Jill Johnston Exposed," special issue, *Culture Hero: A Fanzine of the Starts of the Super World* (1970), n.p. Accessed at Sallie Bingham Center for Women's History and Culture, Rubenstein Library, Duke University, Durham, NC.

7. Joan E. Biren/JEB, quoted in Povitz, "To See," 667.

8. Jill Johnston, "Non Noto," *Village Voice*, March 20, 1969, 20.

9. In her slide show/performance *The Dyke Show*, Joan E. Biren/JEB riffed on degrees of confirmation offered by lesbian images, including categories like "unmistakable lesbian" or "only plausibly lesbian." Quoted in Povitz, "To See," 674.

10. Jill Johnston, "Teach Your Angels Karate," *Village Voice*, September 23, 1971, 44.

11. Ingrid Nyeboe, personal communication with author, January 13, 2021.

12. Katz, *Hide/Seek*, 51.

13. Jennifer Doyle, quoted in Katz, *Hide/Seek*, 18.

INTRODUCTION

Portions of this introduction appeared in "'Not Yet and Elsewhere': Locating Lesbian Identity in Performance Archives, as Performance Archives," in "Outing Archives, Archives Outing," special issue, *Contemporary Theatre Review* 31, nos. 1–2 (2021), 34–50, https://doi.org/10.1080/10486801.2021.1878504.

1. This was the name of the archive at the time Johnston worked there. In 1964 it became the Jerome Robbins Dance Division.

2. Johnston, *Mother Bound*, 78.

3. Arondekar et al., "Queering Archives," 214–16. Nyong'o's notion of queering the archive arises from braiding together the theories of Black studies scholar Saidiya Hartman and queer studies scholar Heather Love, among others.

4. Johnston, *Mother Bound*, 91.

5. Wolf, "Desire in Evidence," 345.

6. Jagose, *Lesbian Utopics*, 1–2.

7. Davis, *Blues Legacies*, 22.

8. Jagose, *Lesbian Utopics*, 5.

9. This series of questions about lesbian identity reimagined via Johnston flows from Valerie Traub's provocations about lesbian historiography: "What if 'the lesbian' did not allude or lead to epistemological surety, but rather to the obstacles, difficulties, and recalcitrance of knowledge relations?" *Thinking Sex*, 286.

10. Jill Johnston, "Going Down with Peggy and Janice," *Village Voice*, July 5, 1973, 23.

11. Vivian Gornick, "Lesbians and Women's Lib: 'In Any Terms She Shall Choose,'" *Village Voice*, March 18, 1971, 5, 8.

12. Freeman, *Time Binds*, 13–14.

13. In Arondekar et al., "Queering Archives," 217.

14. Dinshaw, *Getting Medieval*, 1, 12.

15. Dinshaw, *Getting Medieval*, 16.

16. I use "Jill" as I speculate on her actions as a person, and "Johnston" when I refer to her writing and criticism.

17. Horst, "Review: American Dance Festival," 97.

18. Morris, *Game for Dancers*, 17–18.

19. Johnston, *Mother Bound*, 91.

20. Johnston, "Thoughts," 102.

21. Johnston, "Thoughts," 102.

22. Johnston, "Modern Dance," 56.

23. Hegedus and Pennebaker, *Town Bloody Hall*.

24. Monroe, "'Oh No!,'" 244; and Cvetkovich, "White Boots."

25. Johnston, *Mother Bound*, 91.

26. There were female dance critics in the United States before Johnston, notably Edna Ocko, Margaret Lloyd, and Doris Hering, though most critics writing for publications with broad circulation were men. Dance critics at leftist, Jewish, and Black newspapers tended to be women. (Thank you to Hannah Kosstrin for helping me think about this.) For more on Ocko, see Garafola, "Writing on the Left."

27. Johnston, *Mother Bound*, 91.

28. McAuliffe, *Great American Newspaper*, 268–70.

29. Johnston, "Thoughts," 102.

30. Jill Johnston, "Robert Whitman," *Village Voice*, September 8, 1966, 10.

31. Battcock, introduction to *Marmalade Me*, 12.

32. Jill Johnston, "Waring-Rainer," *Village Voice*, May 6, 1965, 15, 26.

33. Diane Fisher to Jill Johnston, undated, box 6, Jill Johnston Literary Archives, New York, NY (hereafter JJLA).

34. Jill Johnston, "Holy Christometer," *Village Voice*, December 19, 1968, 35.

35. Ad, *New York Times*, November 16, 1969, BR61.

36. Jill Johnston, "Come Seven," *Village Voice*, May 15, 1969, 26, 30.

37. Ad, *New York Times*, November 16, 1969, BR61.

38. I have redacted last names from all fan mail sent personally to Johnston. J. to Jill Johnston, March 15, 1971, box 7, JJLA.

39. G. to Jill Johnston, June 18, 1969, box 7, JJLA.

40. Jill Johnston, "Lois Lane Is a Lesbian," *Village Voice*, March 4, 1971, 9.

41. Johnston, *Lesbian Nation*, 50.

42. Johnston, *Lesbian Nation*, 72.

43. Johnson, "Black Culture," 192.

44. Johnston, "Mad for Her."

45. For more on the changing demographics of New York City, particularly the Village, see Andersson, "'Wilding.'" For more on performance spaces and their impact on racial demographics in New York City, see Foulkes, "Streets and Stages."

46. Jill Johnston, "Dyke Nationalism and Heterosexuality," *Village Voice*, October 12, 1972, 21.

47. Moraga, "Entering the Lives."

48. Manning, "Race in Motion," 237.

49. Chaleff, "Activating Whiteness," 72.

50. Hesford, *Feeling Women's Liberation*, 73.

51. Jagose, *Inconsequence*, 3–4.

52. Springer, *Living for the Revolution*, 3.

53. Dinshaw, *Getting Medieval*, 49.

54. Jill Johnston, entry for August 8, 1974, journal, JJLA.

55. In Hegedus and Pennebaker, *Town Bloody Hall*.

56. Croft, "Lesbian Echoes."

57. Garcia, "'Don't Leave Me, Celia!,'" 204.

58. Koestenbaum, *Queen's Throat*, 132–47.

59. Castle, *Apparitional Lesbian*, 202.

60. Castle's argument shares much with dance theorist Susan Foster's assessment of how modern dance functioned via a structured closet—a structure essential to the ascendancy of gay men in midcentury US American modern dance: the generation with whom Johnston studied (Limón) and whom she lauded in her writing (Cunningham). See Foster, "Closets Full of Dances."

61. Jill Johnston, "Lois Lane Is a Lesbian (2)," *Village Voice*, March 11, 1971, 21.

62. Jill Johnston, "Stein: Affectionately Obscene Poetry," *Village Voice*, May 4, 1972, 25, 28; and Jill Johnston, "Avocados and Rainstorms," *Village Voice*, May 11, 1972, 52, 54, 56.

63. Johnston, "Agnes Martin: Surrender and Solitude," in *Gullibles Travels*, 277.

64. Translation: "One woman's horse is another woman's doorknob," with thanks to Peggy McCracken for her translation assistance with this Johnston-esque point.

65. Echols, *Daring to Be Bad*, 211. For a discussion of transphobia and the role of trans women in 1970s lesbian feminism, see Heaney, "Women-Identified Women."

For more on the exclusion of Black lesbians from lesbian feminism (even for a figure as well known as Audre Lorde), see Musser, "Re-membering Audre."

66. Cvetkovich, *Archive of Feelings*, 242. Writing about her work documenting lesbian and queer history with Proyecto ContraSIDA por Vida, a nonprofit HIV-prevention agency located in the Mission District of San Francisco, Latina queer theorist Juana María Rodríguez notes that the "untidy" nature of queer archives, which I find so charming in the Johnston papers at the Herstory Archives, is not always seen as charming for "communities of color [who] are so often under attack, [already] marked as a collective hot mess." In Arondekar et al., "Queering Archives," 214–15.

67. Note by "Carol," Jill Johnston folder, Lesbian Herstory Archives, New York, NY.

68. Note by anonymous, Jill Johnston folder, Lesbian Herstory Archives.

69. Note by anonymous, Jill Johnston folder, Lesbian Herstory Archives.

70. Fishman passed away in 2021, and the fact she will not be able to read this book is one of the few regrets I have about this project.

71. Stacey, *Star Gazing*, 145.

72. Ingrid Nyeboe, Skype interview with author, December 2, 2017.

73. Halberstam, *Queer Art of Failure*, 11.

74. Ad, *Village Voice*, March 25, 1971, 14.

75. Jill Johnston, "Take Me Disappearing," *Village Voice*, December 14, 1967, 33.

76. Ingrid Nyeboe, email to author, January 12, 2023. Johnston and Nyeboe did extensive research regarding Johnston's birth, including accessing passenger lists for Olive and Jill's passage across the Atlantic, which listed both under the surname Crowe, Olive's maiden name. In the United States, both lived with the surname Johnston, a name Olive eventually made legal for each.

77. Johnston, *Mother Bound*, 14.

78. Johnston, *Mother Bound*, 46.

79. Johnston, *Mother Bound*, 56–59.

80. "Cyril F. Johnston," *New York Times*, April 1, 1950, 14; and Johnston, *Mother Bound*, 66–67.

81. Johnston, *Mother Bound*, 66.

82. Ingrid Nyeboe, interview with author, September 29, 2016.

83. Cvetkovich, "Sexual Trauma/Queer Memory," 372.

84. Johnston, *Mother Bound*, 2.

85. Jill Johnston, entry for June 6, 1974, journal, JJLA.

86. Johnston, entry for June 6, 1974.

87. Johnston, *Mother Bound*, 70.

88. Johnston, *Mother Bound*, 73.

89. Johnston, *Mother Bound*, 75.

90. Johnston, "How Dance Artists," 2. All quotations are from this page until otherwise noted.

91. Johnston, *Mother Bound*, 81.

92. Johnston, *Mother Bound*, 87.

93. Johnston, *Mother Bound*, 98–99.
94. Johnston, "Mad for Her," 25–26.
95. Miles Bellamy, interview with author, July 2017.
96. Johnston, *Mother Bound*, 114.
97. Nyeboe, interview with author, September 29, 2016.
98. Jill Johnston, "Holy Hurricane," *Village Voice*, March 21, 1967, 31–32.

CHAPTER 1. SHE WAS A CRITIC

1. Johnston, preface to *Marmalade Me*, 13.
2. Muñoz, *Cruising Utopia*, 126.
3. Muñoz, *Cruising Utopia*, 121.
4. Muñoz, *Cruising Utopia*, 105.
5. Johnston, "Holy Hurricane," in *Marmalade Me*, 130.
6. Johnston, "Holy Hurricane," in *Marmalade Me*, 130.
7. Johnston, "Holy Hurricane," in *Marmalade Me*, 130.
8. Moi, "Ambiguity and Alienation," 112. Moi notes this concern as central to Simone de Beauvoir's *The Second Sex* (1949), a book Johnston's journals reveal she frequently reread across her life and that she likely encountered when it was first translated into English in 1953, two years before she began her career as a critic.
9. Jill Johnston, "Romantic Dancers," *Village Voice*, August 22, 1963, 14.
10. Muñoz, *Cruising Utopia*, 127.
11. Johnston, "Firestorm on Christopher Street," xxvii.
12. Dolan, *Feminist Spectator as Critic*, xxiv.
13. Jill Johnston, "Judson '64: I," *Village Voice*, January 21, 1965, 12, 19.
14. Gardiner et al., "Interchange on Feminist Criticism"; and Kolodny, "Dancing through the Minefield."
15. Geoffrey Hendricks and Sur Rodney Sur, interview with author, January 5, 2017.
16. Horst, "Review: American Dance Festival," 97.
17. Jill Johnston, "Judson Speedlimits," *Village Voice*, July 25, 1963, 10.
18. "On Husbandry," 100.
19. Sabin, "Merce Cunningham," 25.
20. Soares, *Louis Horst*, 200.
21. Johnston, "Thoughts," 101.
22. Johnston, "Modern Dance," 55.
23. Johnston, "Critics' Critics," in *Marmalade Me*, 100.
24. Johnston, "Critics' Critics," in *Marmalade Me*, 102.
25. In her essay "The Modern Dance—Directions and Criticisms" (1957), Johnston first names description as the critic's key task, explicitly arguing for "description" to replace "indictment." "Modern Dance," 55.
26. Clive Barnes, "Dance: Critic's Credo," *New York Times*, September 12, 1965, x25; and Johnston, "Critics' Critics," in *Marmalade Me*, 101.
27. Conner, quoted in Daly, review, 185.

28. Martin, *Modern Dance.*

29. Daly, review, 188.

30. Hamilton, *Just around Midnight*, 4.

31. Gruen, quoted in Sichel, "Criticism without Authority," 96.

32. Jill Johnston, "Write about Face," *Village Voice*, date unknown, 1975.

33. Whitehead, "Expressing Life through Loss," 282.

34. Deborah Hay, discussion with author, April 2017.

35. Banes, "Jill Johnston," 3.

36. Hendricks and Sur interview.

37. Jean Robinson, "New Happenings at the Reuben," *Village Voice*, June 16, 1960, 13.

38. Jill Johnston, "New 'Happenings' at the Reuben," *Village Voice*, June 23, 1960, 13.

39. Jill Johnston, "James Waring and Co.," *Village Voice*, January 5, 1961, 9.

40. Morris, *Game for Dancers*, 19.

41. Johnston, "Judson Speedlimits."

42. Meredith Monk, interview with author, January 2019.

43. Lambert-Beatty, *Being Watched*, 38–39.

44. Jill Johnston, "Mon Levinson," *ARTnews*, March 1965, 17.

45. Jill Johnston, "Claes Oldenburg," *ARTnews*, January 1962, 47.

46. Jill Johnston, "Being beyond Doing," *Village Voice*, June 2, 1975, 33. Numerous sources, including Johnston herself, have said her association with the *Voice* began in 1959, but I have not found her byline in the paper until February 1960. She may have been hired in 1959 but remained unpublished until 1960.

47. McAuliffe, *Great American Newspaper*, 13.

48. Jill Johnston, entry for June 16, 1974, journal, Jill Johnston Literary Archives, New York, NY.

49. Jacobs, *Death and Life*, 51–54.

50. Anderson, "'Wilding,'" 275.

51. Edmund White, quoted in Anderson, "'Wilding,'" 265.

52. Manning, *Modern Dance, Negro Dance*, xvi, 23.

53. Johnston, *Mother Bound*, 115–17.

54. Carolee Schneemann, discussion with author, August 2018.

55. McAuliffe, *Great American Newspaper*, 130.

56. "Pomare Goes to Germany," *Village Voice*, June 22, 1961, 9; "Langston Hughes to Read," *Village Voice*, July 20, 1961, 1; and Norman Mailer, "Mailer to Hansberry," *Village Voice*, June 8, 1961, 11.

57. Jill Johnston, "Mr. Ailey," *Village Voice*, December 21, 1961, 15.

58. Jill Johnston, "Central Park," *Village Voice*, September 20, 1962, 9.

59. DeFrantz, *Dancing Revelations*, 181.

60. Jill Johnston, "Katherine Dunham," *Village Voice*, November 8, 1962, 9.

61. Manning, "Modern Dance, Negro Dance," 502; and Dee Das, *Katherine Dunham.*

62. Musser, *Between Shadows and Noise*, 43–44.

63. Johnston, "Katherine Dunham," 9.

64. Johnston, "Romantic Dancers," 14.

65. Johnston, "Judson '64: I," 12.

66. Jill Johnston, "Democracy," *Village Voice*, August 23, 1962, 9.

67. Banes, *Democracy's Body*, xviii.

68. Banes, *Democracy's Body*, xviii.

69. Johnston, "Judson '64: I," 12.

70. Johnston, "Judson '64: I," 19.

71. Halberstam, *Queer Art of Failure*, 11.

72. Jill Johnston, "Fresh Winds," *Village Voice*, March 15, 1962, 14.

73. Steve Paxton, interview with Don McDonagh, March 31, 1979, Jerome Robbins Dance Division, New York Public Library.

74. Mattingly, *Shaping Dance Canons*, 68.

75. Mattingly, *Shaping Dance Canons*, 68.

76. Letter exhibited in PEPOSA, José Álvarez Colón's interactive installation on the history of improvisation in Puerto Rican experimental dance. Hidrante Gallery, San Juan, Puerto Rico, 2023.

77. Hay, discussion.

78. Schneemann, discussion.

79. Yvonne Rainer, discussion with author, June 2017.

80. Rainer, discussion.

81. Banes, "Jill Johnston," 3–9.

82. Johnston, "Democracy," 9.

83. Jill Johnston, "From Lovely Confusion to Naked Breakfast," *Village Voice*, July 18, 1963, 12.

84. Jill Johnston, "Cunningham in Connecticut," *Village Voice*, September 7, 1961, 4.

85. Daly, review, 188.

86. Monk, interview.

87. Sontag, "Against Interpretation," 14.

88. Lorde, "Uses of the Erotic," 53.

89. Quoted in Moser, *Sontag*, 398.

90. Sontag, *Reborn*, 221.

91. Moser, *Sontag*, 173. The other was the *Partisan Review*, where Sontag had dreamed of writing since she was a child and where, also in 1964, she published "Notes on Camp." See Moser, *Sontag*, 64–65.

92. McAuliffe, *Great American Newspaper*, 131.

93. Jill Johnston, "Anybody Dying of Love," *Village Voice*, October 14, 1971, 25.

94. Rollyson and Paddock, *Susan Sontag*, 99–100.

95. Rollyson and Paddock, *Susan Sontag*, 100.

96. Sontag, "Against Interpretation," 13.

97. Sontag, "Against Interpretation," 13.

98. Lorde, "Uses of the Erotic," 54.

99. Johnston, "Cunningham in Connecticut," 4.

100. Jill Johnston, "Take Me Disappearing," *Village Voice*, December 14, 1967, 33.

101. Sontag, "Happenings," 273.
102. Sontag, "Happenings," 265.
103. Many thanks to Hannah Kosstrin for pointing this out to me.
104. Jill Johnston, "Allan Kaprow," *ARTnews*, Summer 1961, 61.
105. Sontag, "Interview," 26.
106. Lorde, "Uses of the Erotic," 59.
107. Rollyson and Paddock, *Susan Sontag*, 154.
108. McRobbie, "Modernist Style," 2.
109. Rainer, discussion.
110. Johnston, *Mother Bound*, 87; Johnston, preface to *Marmalade Me*, 13.
111. Johnston, *Mother Bound*, 64.
112. Johnston wrote this in 1980, almost a decade before Judith Butler would first offer her now-ubiquitous theory of gender performativity in 1988 in *Theatre Journal*, "Performative Acts and Gender Constitution: An Essay in Phenomenology and Feminist Theory."
113. Johnston, *Mother Bound*, 117.
114. Sontag, *Reborn*, 180–81.
115. Susan Sontag, quoted in Haslett, "Other Susan Sontag."
116. Johnston, *Mother Bound*, 64, 69–70.
117. Johnston, *Mother Bound*, 69–70.
118. Johnston, *Mother Bound*, 88.
119. Johnston, *Mother Bound*, 117.
120. Sontag, "Thirty Years Later," 312.
121. Jill Johnston, "Inside 'Originale,'" *Village Voice*, October 1, 1964, 6, 16; and Jill Johnston, "The Artist in a Coca-Cola World," *Village Voice*, January 31, 1963, 7, 24.
122. Johnston, "Fluxus Fuxus," in *Marmalade Me*, 74.
123. Johnston, preface to *Marmalade Me*, 15.
124. Johnston, preface to *Marmalade Me*, 14.
125. Deborah Jowitt, who wrote about dance occasionally for the *Voice* when Johnston was unavailable—sometimes due to hospitalization—took over the title "Dance" at the paper.
126. Jill Johnston, "Communications," *Village Voice*, November 4, 1965, 6, 8, 10.
127. Johnston, "Judson '64: I," 12.

INTERRUPTION 1. UP ON THE ROOF

1. Jill Johnston, "Non Noto," *Village Voice*, March 20, 1969, 50.
2. Picard, quoted in Sichel, "Criticism without Authority," 96; Krasinski, "Jill Johnston," 175; and Sichel, "Criticism without Authority," 69.
3. Deborah Hay, discussion with author, April 2017.
4. Jackson, *Social Works*, 89.
5. Johnston, *Mother Bound*, 142.
6. Jill Johnston, "Inside 'Originale,'" *Village Voice*, October 1, 1964, 6, 16.
7. Johnston, *Paper Daughter*, 96.

8. Doyle, Flatley, and Muñoz, introduction, 4.

9. Jill Johnston, "Credo Qui Absurdism," *Village Voice*, November 28, 1968, 31.

10. Doyle, Flatley, and Muñoz, introduction, 4–5.

11. Jill Johnston, "Yvonne Rainer: I," *Village Voice*, May 23, 1963, 17.

12. D. Schwartz, "*Sleep*." Giorno was also a close friend of Johnston's. She called him when she began seeing what she thought were "visions" in August 1965. Johnston watched him transition from "a preppie living on the Upper East Side who worked on Wall Street to an offbeat poet under the influence of Andy Warhol and William Burroughs." *Paper Daughter*, 21. For more on the role of repetition in *Sleep*, see Joseph, "Play of Repetition."

13. Johnston, "Yvonne Rainer: I," 17.

14. Jill Johnston, "Yvonne Rainer: II," *Village Voice*, June 6, 1963, 18.

15. Jill Johnston, "New 'Happenings' at the Reuben," *Village Voice*, June 23, 1960, 13.

16. Carolee Schneemann, interview with author, August 2018.

17. Rawls, "Herko Dialogues"; Muñoz, *Cruising Utopia*, 147–68; and Aramphongphan, "Real Professionals?"

18. Aramphongphan, "Real Professionals?," 1.

19. This question, whether a woman can be more than a phallic extension of a man in a balletic pas de deux, is crystallized in Foster, "Ballerina's Phallic Pointe."

20. Jill Johnston, "Judson Speedlimits," *Village Voice*, July 25, 1963, 10. In *Binghamton Birdie*, Herko also wore a superhero T-shirt with a made-up insignia that spelled out "Judson," a campy disruption of the memorialization already forming around Judson. See Muñoz, *Cruising Utopia*, 159.

21. Sontag, "Notes on Camp," 10.

22. Johnston, "Non Noto," 50.

CHAPTER 2. SHE WAS AN AUDIENCE

Epigraph source: Jill Johnston, "Not in Broad Daylight," *Village Voice*, November 21, 1968, 32–33.

1. Johnston, *Paper Daughter*, 85.

2. Jill Johnston, "The Object," *Village Voice*, May 21, 1964, 12.

3. Johnston, *Mother Bound*, 159.

4. Jill Johnston, "Jack Moore," *Village Voice*, March 8, 1962, 14.

5. Johnston, "Jack Moore," 14.

6. Jill Johnston, "Judson '64: I," *Village Voice*, January 21, 1965, 12, 19.

7. Allen Hughes, "'Living Dolls' and Literature," *New York Times*, August 22, 1965, x9.

8. Johnston, "New American Modern Dance," 193.

9. Jill Johnston, "Judson '64: II," *Village Voice*, January 28, 1965, 11.

10. Jill Johnston, "Cultural Gangsters," *Village Voice*, June 6, 1968, 33.

11. Jill Johnston, "The Unhappy Spectator," *Village Voice*, October 17, 1968, 34–35.

12. Johnston, "Unhappy Spectator," 34.

13. Janet Solinger, oral history interview with Marc Pachter, October 7, 2005, Archives of American Art, Smithsonian Institution, https://www.aaa.si.edu/collections/interviews/oral-history-interview-janet-w-solinger-12579#transcript.

14. David Bourdon, untitled essay, in "Jill Johnston Exposed," ed. Les Levine, special issue, *Culture Hero: A Fanzine of the Stars of the Super World* (1970), n.p. I consulted this source at the Sallie Bingham Center for Women's History and Culture, Rubenstein Library, Duke University, Durham, NC.

15. Johnston, *Paper Daughter*, 58.

16. Johnston, *Paper Daughter*, 178.

17. Johnston, *Paper Daughter*, 195.

18. Johnston, *Paper Daughter*, 178.

19. Jill Johnston, entry for July 11, 1979, journal, Jill Johnston Literary Archives, New York, NY.

20. Johnston, *Paper Daughter*, 1, 8, 18, 19, 24, 29, 32, 43, 84, 142, 148, 153, 178, 188, 222, 223, 232, 233, 242, 244.

21. Jill Johnston, "Take Me Disappearing," *Village Voice*, December 14, 1967, 33.

22. Jill Johnston, "Judson Speedlimits," *Village Voice*, July 25, 1963, 10; and Jill Johnston, "New 'Happenings' at the Reuben," *Village Voice*, June 23, 1960, 13.

23. Johnston, "Unhappy Spectator," 34.

24. Jannarone, *Artaud and His Doubles*, 80.

25. Jannarone, *Artaud and His Doubles*, 75.

26. Jannarone, *Artaud and His Doubles*, 91.

27. The connections were explored in *Judson Dance Theater: The Work Is Never Done*, curated by Ana Janevski and Thomas Lax, Museum of Modern Art, New York, September 2018–February 2019.

28. Judith Malina and Julian Beck, quoted in Jannarone, *Artaud and His Doubles*, 13.

29. Malina and Beck, quoted in Jannarone, *Artaud and His Doubles*, 13.

30. Deleuze and Guattari, *Thousand Plateaus*.

31. Jill Johnston, "Boiler Room," *Village Voice*, March 29, 1962, 14.

32. Johnston, *Paper Daughter*, 29.

33. Johnston, "Boiler Room," 14.

34. Allan Kaprow, quoted in Jill Johnston, "(Response to Allan Kaprow)," *Village Voice*, July 26, 1962, 10.

35. Johnston, "(Response to Allan Kaprow)," 10.

36. Jannarone, *Artaud and His Doubles*, 88.

37. Banes, "Jill Johnston," 3.

38. Crano, "Haptic Spectatorship," 57.

39. Johnston, *Mother Bound*, 127.

40. Jannarone, *Artaud and His Doubles*, 2.

41. Jill Johnston, "Horses Teeth," *Village Voice*, December 11, 1969, 35.

42. Kreutzer, "Mediating and Disrupting," 142. While many second-wave feminists, like Johnston, were drawn to and championed Moorman, George Maciunas of Fluxus actually publicly denounced Moorman for, in his view, being too willing to do what the male members of Fluxus, including Paik, asked.

43. Johnston, *Paper Daughter*, 192-93.

44. Jill Johnston, "Over His Dead Body," *Village Voice*, March 28, 1968, 19–20.

45. Jill Johnston, "Dancing Is a Dog," *Village Voice*, November 2, 1967, 16.

46. Johnston, "Ship Ahoy!," in *Marmalade Me*, 110–11.

47. Jill Johnston, "The Artist in a Coca-Cola World," *Village Voice*, January 31, 1963, 24.

48. Johnston, *Paper Daughter*, 192–93.

49. Johnston, "Fluxus Fuxus," in *Marmalade Me*, 74.

50. Krasinski, "Jill Johnston," 175.

51. Jill Johnston, "Over His Dead Body," 19–20.

52. Johnston, "Dancing Is a Dog," 16.

53. Johnston, *Paper Daughter*, 136.

54. Jill Johnston, "Hello Young Lovers," *Village Voice*, September 19, 1968, 34.

55. Sedgwick, *Touching Feeling*, 2, 8.

56. Sedgwick, *Touching Feeling*, 8.

57. G. Stein, "Composition as Explanation," 25. For more on the relationship between Stein's "continuous present" and dance, see Aguiar and Queiroz, "From Gertrude Stein."

58. Johnston's writing does what one of her favorite choreographers, Merce Cunningham, argued in 1952 was dance's "most fortunate" attribute, that "space and time cannot be disconnected." Cunningham, "Space, Time and Dance," 150–51.

59. Jill Johnston, "New Exposure," *Village Voice*, April 27, 1967, 13.

60. Johnston, "Paxton's People," in *Marmalade Me*, 137.

61. Johnston, "Hello Young Lovers," 34.

62. Johnston, "Hello Young Lovers," 34.

63. Savran, "'You've Got That Thing,'" 534.

64. Savran, "'You've Got That Thing,'" 536.

65. Hughes and Román, introduction, 5.

66. Kirsch, *Gertrude Stein*, 67.

67. Johnston, "Hello Young Lovers," 34.

68. Sedgwick, "Queer and Now," 8.

69. Sedgwick, "Queer and Now," 8.

70. Alwood, *Straight News*, 90.

71. Shelley, *We Set the Night*, 112.

72. Shelley, *We Set the Night*, 138.

73. Jill Johnston, "Any Time," *Village Voice*, November 7, 1968, 25, 36.

74. Johnston, "Hello Young Lovers," 34.

75. Nussbaum, "Rebirth."

76. De Veaux, *Warrior Poet*, 314.

77. Muñoz, "Race, Sex," 153.

78. Brooks, *Liner Notes*, 245.

79. Lorde, *Zami*, 186.

80. Lorde, *Zami*, 203.

81. Lorde, *Zami*, 89, 97, 182.

82. Lorde, “Pirouette,” 106.
83. De Veaux, *Warrior Poet*, 85.
84. Faderman, *Odd Girls*, 173.
85. De Veaux, *Warrior Poet*, 85.
86. Jill Johnston, “Danscrabble,” *Village Voice* August 15, 1968, 23.
87. Johnston, “Danscrabble,” 23.
88. De Veaux, *Warrior Poet*, 248–49.
89. Lorde, “Master’s Tools,” 112.
90. Brooks, *Liner Notes*, 251.
91. Johnston, “Hello Young Lovers,” 34.

INTERRUPTION 2. BORN OF PAPER

1. Julie Bindel, “Jill Johnston Obituary,” *Guardian*, October 11, 2020, https://www.theguardian.com/world/2010/oct/11/jill-johnston-obituary.
2. Elaine Woo, “Jill Johnston Dies at 81; Author of ‘Lesbian Nation,’” *Los Angeles Times*, September 26, 2020, https://www.latimes.com/local/obituaries/la-me-jill-johnston-20100926-story.html.
3. William Grimes, “Jill Johnston, Critic Who Wrote ‘Lesbian Nation,’ Dies at 81,” *New York Times*, September 21, 2010, https://www.nytimes.com/2010/09/21/arts/21johnston.html.
4. Phelan, *Mourning Sex*, 16.
5. Phelan, *Mourning Sex*, 2.
6. Johnston, *Paper Daughter*, 131, 139.
7. Jill Johnston, “Not in Broad Daylight,” *Village Voice*, November 21, 1968, 34.
8. Johnston, *Paper Daughter*, 58.
9. Johnston, *Paper Daughter*, 131.
10. D. W. Winnicott coined the term *transitional object* in 1951 to describe an object that offers a sense of security during a period of transition from a bond with the mother.
11. Johnston, *Paper Daughter*, 198.
12. Johnston, *Paper Daughter*, 198.
13. Johnston, *Paper Daughter*, 43.
14. Johnston, *Paper Daughter*, 141, 148.
15. S. Schwartz, “‘We’ll See You,’” 1.
16. Johnston, *Paper Daughter*, 132.
17. Johnston, *Paper Daughter*, 131.
18. Shattuck, *Banquet Years*, 256.
19. Shattuck, *Banquet Years*, 36–37.
20. Apollinaire, “Zone,” in *Zone*, 3–16 (translation by Ron Padgett).
21. Jill Johnston, “Light Years Away,” *Village Voice*, October 3, 1968, 14.
22. Read, introduction, ix.
23. See Apollinaire, *Calligrammes* (translation by Ann Hyde Greet).
24. Jill Johnston, “Survival Plan Number One,” *Village Voice*, May 18, 1972, 25.
25. Shattuck, *Banquet Years*, 256–57; and Read, introduction, ix.

26. Johnston, *Paper Daughter*, 104.
27. Ingrid Nyeboe, interview with author, October 1, 2016.
28. Johnston, *Paper Daughter*, 153.
29. Johnston, *Paper Daughter*, 153.
30. Cvetkovich, "Sexual Trauma/Queer Memory," 372.
31. Johnston, "Not in Broad Daylight," 32, 33.
32. Jill Johnston, "Helas," *Village Voice*, May 8, 1969, 21, 30.
33. Jill Johnston, "Summore Treasures," *Village Voice*, August 6, 1969, 27.

CHAPTER 3. SHE WAS A LESBIAN FEMINIST

Portions of this chapter appeared in "'I'm Gay,' She Never Said," *Brooklyn Rail*, June 2017, https://brooklynrail.org/2017/06/dance/Im-gay-she-never-said; and " Lesbian Echoes in Activism and Writing: Jill Johnston's Interventions," in *Futures of Dance Studies*, edited by Susan Manning, Janice Ross, and Rebecca Schneider (Madison: University of Wisconsin Press, 2020), 117–34.

1. Hunter and Patterson, foreword, ix.
2. Johnston, *Lesbian Nation*, 134; and Johnston, *Paper Daughter*, 140.
3. Johnston, "Dance Quote Unquote," 104.
4. Johnston, *Lesbian Nation*, 87.
5. Johnston, *Lesbian Nation*, 7.
6. Suzanne BeVier, email to author, December 12, 2022.
7. Jill Johnston, "Movement Schmoovement," *Village Voice*, November 11, 1971, 49, 52; Jill Johnston, "Delitism, Stardumb, and Leadershit," *Village Voice*, December 14, 1972, 29.
8. Johnston, "Was Lesbian Separatism Inevitable?," 141.
9. Hesford, *Feeling Women's Liberation*, 120. All quotations from this page until otherwise noted.
10. The notion of the postmodern lesbian as a constantly morphing figure parallels thinking done in the 1990s by primarily literary theorists about a related term, the *lesbian postmodern*. This work had twin projects. It was "an attempt to demand the recognition of lesbian visibility in the postmodern terrain vis-à-vis cultural production," and also a consideration of how "a postmodern aesthetic with its valorization of difference, sexual plurality, and gender blurring/blending . . . assists lesbian cultural production." See Doan, preface, x. The latter emphasis more closely aligns with the question of the lesbian postmodern as presented by Johnston in the 1970s and in Hesford's understanding of postmodernism in that period.
11. For more on the ways in which, in the decades after World War II, "the homosexual-heterosexual binary . . . continued to rely on a Black-white racial axis for articulation," see Jones, *Ambivalent Affinities*, 5.
12. Faderman, *Odd Girls*, 11.
13. See Gutterman, *Her Neighbor's Wife*, 11–13.
14. Enke, *Finding the Movement*, 6.

15. Chauncey, *Gay New York*, 2. Chauncey's temporal focus, the late nineteenth century until World War II, is also a period, as legal historian Margot Canaday has argued, when gay men, as opposed to gay women, were more surveilled because "male perverts mattered so much to the state because male citizens did." Canaday, *Straight State*, 13.

16. Johnston, *Lesbian Nation*, 150.

17. Jill Johnston, "Hasten Slowly," *Village Voice*, July 16, 1970, 17–18.

18. Jill Johnston, "Dance Journal," *Village Voice*, September 24, 1970, 31.

19. Johnston, *Mother Bound*, 131.

20. Johnston, "Dance Journal," 31. All quotations from this page until otherwise noted.

21. Sally Banes has described this phenomenon of female performers exceeding and critiquing sexist narratives in plots through their performance, and Stacy Wolf has described a similar strategy in musical theater. See Banes, *Dancing Women*, 8–9; and Wolf, *Changed for Good*, 8.

22. Echols, *Daring to Be Bad*, 158, 190.

23. Rosen, *World Split Open*, 160. Despite a *New York Times* article reporting otherwise, no actual fire was set (a choice made to comply with local ordinances). The imagined image of bra-burning was more indicative of media fantasy than radical feminist reality.

24. Echols, *Daring to Be Bad*, 93–95.

25. Rosen, *World Split Open*, 300.

26. "the woman identified woman," in "the woman identified woman drafts and other papers," Ellen Shumsky Papers, Sophia Smith Collection of Women's History, Smith College, Northampton, MA. See "'The Woman Identified Woman,' drafts and final version, 1970," Five College Compass Digital Collections, https://compass.fivecolleges.edu/islandora/object/smith:1354803. The drafts included in Ellen Shumsky's papers demonstrate the ways in which the manifesto was intended to describe a gendered system of power, as opposed to elevating the category of lesbian.

27. The Radicalesbians made their proposed definition of *lesbian* palatable for a larger straight female audience by displacing the term in their manifesto's title, in hopes that "the woman identified woman" (which could misread as transphobia from a twenty-first-century standpoint) would be less threatening to heterosexual women. Echols, *Daring to Be Bad*, 216.

28. Atkinson, "Lesbianism and Feminism," 11.

29. Atkinson, "Lesbianism and Feminism," 11.

30. Atkinson also had an expansive definition of lesbianism as a "commitment, by choice, full-time of one woman to others of her class that is called lesbianism." "Lesbianism and Feminism," 12.

31. Millett, *Flying*, 15.

32. Hesford, *Feeling Women's Liberation*, 28.

33. Hesford, *Feeling Women's Liberation*, 28.

34. Jill Johnston, "New 'Happenings' at the Reuben," *Village Voice*, June 23, 1960, 13.

35. Johnston's lesbian echo might be grouped with José Muñoz's larger concept of queerness as "anticipatory illumination," a concept that he draws from philosopher Ernst Bloch and characterizes as ways in which queerness, particularly as a form of hope, manifests as a "surplus of both act and meaning," a quality both "open, indeterminate," and the "being singular plural of queerness." *Cruising Utopia*, 3, 15.

36. Jill Johnston, "Of This Pure but Irregular Passion," *Village Voice*, July 2, 1970, 29.

37. Getsy, "Spectacle of Privacy," 117.

38. Jane O'Wyatt, email to author, October 10, 2022.

39. Johnston, "Of This Pure but Irregular Passion," 29–30.

40. Warner, *Acts of Gaiety*, 116–17.

41. "Briefly Noted," *Ladder* 15, nos. 1 and 2 (October–November 1970), 26.

42. Jill Johnston, "The Crooked Road to the Center," *Village Voice*, September 10, 1970, 35.

43. "New Victory in an Old Crusade," *Time*, August 24, 1970, 10–12; and Charlotte Curtis, "Women's Liberation Gets into the Long Island Swim," *New York Times*, August 10, 1970, 32.

44. "New Victory," 10–12.

45. Jill Johnston, "Bash in the Sculls," *Village Voice*, August 13, 1970, 10.

46. Gloria K. Schuch, "The Story of the J," letter to the editor, *Village Voice*, May 13, 1971, 4.

47. Johnston, "Bash in the Sculls," 10.

48. Johnston, "For an Improper Person," *Village Voice*, November 19, 1970, 44.

49. Johnston, "Bash in the Sculls," 11.

50. Johnston, "For an Improper Person," 43–44.

51. Michael Durham (text) and Grey Villet (photographs), "A Direct Assault on Laws and Customs," *Life Magazine*, December 31, 1971, 64–69.

52. Faderman, *Odd Girls*, 225; Hesford, *Feeling Women's Liberation*, 5; and Echols, *Daring to Be Bad*, 264, 382.

53. D'Emilio and Freedman, *Intimate Matters*, 323.

54. Johnston, *Lesbian Nation*, 100.

55. Gever, *Entertaining Lesbians*, 5.

56. Gever, *Entertaining Lesbians*, 5.

57. Jill Johnston, "Movement Schmoovement," *Village Voice*, November 11, 1971, 52.

58. Jill Johnston, entry for December 15, 1974, journal, Jill Johnston Literary Archives, New York, NY (JJLA).

59. Millett, *Sexual Politics*, 10–12.

60. Millett, *Sexual Politics*, 315. *Harper's* introduced Mailer's "The Prisoner of Sex" by writing that "no [other] writer in America could have illuminated," as they say Mailer has, the "underlying issues raised [by women's liberation]." Mailer, "Prisoner of Sex," 41.

61. Johnston, *Lesbian Nation*, 32.

62. Warner, *Acts of Gaiety*, 119.

63. Jill Johnston, "Germaine and Guillaume in Baltimore," *Village Voice*, April 22, 1971, 31–32.

64. Warner, *Acts of Gaiety*, 121.

65. Rosalyn Drexler, "Theatre for Ideas: A Night of Lib and Let Lib: What Happened to Mozart's Sister?," *Village Voice*, May 6, 1971, 28.

66. Johnston, *Lesbian Nation*, 27.

67. Johnston, *Lesbian Nation*, 27.

68. All descriptions of and quotations from the event are drawn from Hegedus and Pennebaker, *Town Bloody Hall*. Johnston published her essay in the *Voice* a week later. See "On a Clear Day You Can See Your Mother," *Village Voice*, May 6, 1971, 37, 40, 46.

69. "woman identified woman," Shumsky papers. Johnston respected the Radicalesbians greatly, describing them as "the most radical people I knew" and crediting member Lois Hart with introducing her to feminism when both were involved in the Gay Liberation Front. Yet Johnston thought that the Lavender Menace actions "didn't work anyway since the media always distorted everything." Johnston, *Lesbian Nation*, 23.

70. Kuppers, "Vanishing in Your Face," 51, 54.

71. Warner, *Acts of Gaiety*, 121.

72. Rosen, *World Split Open*, 160.

73. Olsson, *Black Power Mixtape*.

74. Davall, "To Pee."

75. Jagose, *Inconsequence*, 3.

76. Johnston, "Dance Journal," 31–32, 49.

77. Gutterman, *Her Neighbor's Wife*, 15.

78. Foster, "Choreographies of Gender," 6.

79. Butler, "Performative Acts," 519.

80. Foster, "Choreographies of Gender," 6.

81. Andrew Sarris, "Heteros Have Problems Too (1)," *Village Voice*, February 4, 1971, 6. In *The Art of Confession*, Christopher Grobe has argued that the confessional performance is an invention of post–World War II American culture.

82. Andrew Sarris, "Heteros Have Problems Too (2)," *Village Voice*, February 11, 1971, 10.

83. "Drafts," box 5, JJLA; and Jane O'Wyatt, email to author, October 10, 2022.

84. Jill Johnston, "Lois Lane Is a Lesbian," *Village Voice*, March 4, 1971, 9.

85. Susan Sands, "Tumbling After," letter to the editor, *Village Voice*, March 18, 1971, 80.

86. Jill Johnston, "Lois Lane Is a Lesbian (2)," *Village Voice*, March 11, 1971, 28.

87. Johnston, "Lois Lane Is a Lesbian (2)," 21.

88. Jill Johnston, "Who Is the Father of Her Child?," *Village Voice*, June 24, 1971, 29.

89. Johnston, "Who Is the Father," 29.

90. Johnston, "Delitism, Stardumb, and Leadershit," 29.

91. Bertha Harris, "Lesbian/Feminist Parley: Closing the Label Gap," *Village Voice*, December 28, 1972, 15. All quotations are from this source until otherwise noted.

92. Johnston, "Delitism, Stardumb, and Leadershit," 30.

93. Johnston, "Comingest Womanifesto," 89.

94. Johnston, "Comingest Womanifesto," 90.

95. Johnston, *Paper Daughter*, 78–79.

96. Johnston, "Comingest Womanifesto," 92.

97. Johnston's *Lesbian Nation* should be seen as a forerunner to ACT UP's coinage of Queer Nation almost two decades later, an example of a lineage queer theorist Heather Love has said has been done too little: recognizing how feminist movements have shaped queer action. Love, "Introduction to 'Rethinking Sex.'"

98. A. Stein, *Sex and Sensibility*, 3–4.

99. A. Stein, *Sex and Sensibility*, 2. All quotations are from this page until otherwise noted.

100. Dolan, *Feminist Spectator as Critic*, xvi.

101. Hesford, *Feeling Women's Liberation*, 120. Riffing on Benedict Anderson's "imagined communities," Lauren Berlant and Elizabeth Freeman have described the work of Johnston, Monique Wittig, and Judith Butler's *Gender Trouble* as seeking to create "safe spaces of lesbian political theory outside the political public sphere." While their emphasis on lesbian feminist organizing as a space of imagination aligns with my reading of Johnston's *Lesbian Nation*, their categorizing of the book as a "separatist" tract fully aligns with neither Johnston's position in the book nor her understanding of herself relative to lesbian organizing of the early 1970s when lesbian separatism was but one aspect of lesbian feminism. As Sara Warner notes, Berlant and Freeman's disregard for the actual content of Johnston's proposal "reinforce(s) numerous misconceptions about lesbian feminism." See Berlant and Freeman, "Queer Nationality," 168; and Warner, *Acts of Gaiety*, 4, 126.

102. Jill Johnston, "Gayer than Thou," *Village Voice*, December 2, 1971, 39.

103. Jill Johnston, "Lesbians, (Wo)men, Faggots, Witches, Etc.," *Village Voice*, June 21, 1973, 31.

104. Provitola, "TERF or Transfeminist," 389.

105. Provitola, "TERF or Transfeminist," 389; and Disch, introduction.

106. Johnston, "Was Lesbian Separatism Inevitable?," 141. Careful historical scrutiny of the histories and discourses that produced lesbian feminism is very much what Valerie Traub has called for in lesbian history, "investigating the cultural conditions that render [versions of queer women] culturally salient at particular moments." *Thinking Sex*, 86.

107. Jill Johnston, "Schizofrenzier than Thou," *Village Voice*, May 25, 1972, 48.

108. Echols, *Daring to Be Bad*, 216.

109. Shumsky, "Radicalesbians," 17.

110. Audio recording, January 3, 1972, Dick Cavett Show Archive, Cavalier Films, Los Angeles, CA.

111. Johnston had a similar experience with an interviewer in Canada, as cap-

tured in the film *Jill Johnston. . . . October 1975* (directed by Kay Armatage and Lydia Wazana) and analyzed by Warner, "Gay Old Time."

112. Jill Johnston, "'Judson '64: I," *Village Voice*, January 21, 1965, 12.

113. See iLAND, *Field Guide*, 2. iLAND is an artistic entity well suited to be adjacent to Johnston due to its emphasis on collectivity and the group's roots in Monson's history as a choreographer and activist passionate about lesbian and queer issues.

114. iLAND, *Field Guide*, 2.

115. McAuliffe, *Great American Newspaper*, 161.

116. Johnston, *Lesbian Nation*, 154.

117. For criticism of *Lesbian Nation*, see Marilyn Webb, "Books: The Self That Jill Built," *Village Voice*, May 31, 1973, 27–28. For how the book spawned collectives, see Littel, "Game of Lesbian Imagination"; and Ross, *House That Jill Built*.

118. Johnston, "Like Grendel and Beowulf Somehow," *Village Voice*, February 15, 1973, 88.

119. Johnston, "Like Grendel and Beowulf Somehow," 33.

120. Johnston, "Like Grendel and Beowulf Somehow," 88.

121. Jill Johnston, "The Venus Flytrap of Feminism," *Village Voice*, May 10, 1973, 28.

122. If this was the case, it was despite the ostracism many lesbians experienced in hippie countercultures, especially Woodstock. Remembering her brief stop at Woodstock, Esther Newton wrote, "In this groupiest of heterosexual scenes, I felt terrified. . . it was their world, we just tried to survive it." *My Butch Career*, 132.

123. Millward, "*Lesbian Nation* and Black Nationalism," 51.

124. Shelley, *We Set the Night*, 140.

125. Millward, "*Lesbian Nation* and Black Nationalism," 51.

126. Johnston, *Lesbian Nation*, 80.

127. Vider, *Queerness of Home*.

128. Johnston, *Lesbian Nation*, 80.

129. Johnston, *Lesbian Nation*, 80.

130. Ti-Grace Atkinson, "Our Country 'Tis of She," letter to the editor, *Village Voice*, June 21, 1973, 98.

131. For more on how radical movements in the 1960s often worked in parallel, see Jones, *Ambivalent Affinities*.

132. Jill Johnston, "Dyke Nationalism and Heterosexuality," *Village Voice*, October 12, 1972, 21.

133. Millward, "*Lesbian Nation* and Black Nationalism," 51.

134. Clarke, "Lesbianism," 136.

135. Clarke, "Lesbianism," 136.

136. Clarke, "Lesbianism," 136.

137. iLAND, *Field Guide*, 2.

138. Newton, *My Butch Career*, 165.

139. Vider, *Queerness of Home*, 119.

140. Thompson, "Urgent," 31.

141. Phyllis Birkby, *Dykes at Jill's Weekend, Upstate* N.Y., date unknown, Phyllis Birkby Papers, Sophia Smith Collection of Women's History, Smith College,

Northampton, MA. For this and other Birkby films, see "Films of Phyllis Birkby," Sophia Smith Collection, Smith College, https://media.smith.edu/departments/ssc/birkby/birkby_playlist.html.

142. Schweighofer, "Land of One's Own," 489.

143. Jill Johnston, "Lois Lane Is a Lesbian (3)," *Village Voice*, March 25, 1971, 27–28, 38.

144. Schweighofer, "Land of One's Own," 495.

145. Schweighofer, "Land of One's Own," 495.

146. Combahee River Collective, "Black Feminist Statement," 232.

147. Jill Johnston, "Unidentified Flying Information," *Village Voice*, August 31, 1972, 16, 18. Johnston was accused by the *New York Times* of being racist at a recent organizing meeting for an upcoming feminist action; Laurie Johnston, "Women's Group to Observe Rights Day Here Today," *New York Times*, August 25, 1972, 40.

148. In a 1972 letter to Johnston, Jefferson wrote, "You're an amazing woman and I love your columns more and more for such diverse observations/remembrances/evocations etc." Margo Jefferson to Jill Johnston, July 24, 1972, box 6, Margo Jefferson folder, JJLA.

149. Margo Jefferson to Jill Johnston, August 15, 1974, box 6, Margo Jefferson folder, JJLA.

150. Smith and Smith, "Across the Kitchen Table," 121, 120.

151. Johnston, "Lois Lane Is a Lesbian," 9.

152. Jill Johnston, "The Second Sucks and the Feminine Mystake," *Village Voice*, January 6, 1972, 26.

153. Bassi and LaFleur, "Introduction," 324.

154. Tompkins, "Ball Busters."

155. Johnston, *Lesbian Nation*, iii.

156. Johnston, *Lesbian Nation*, 156.

157. Timmie Thornton, "Dress Reversal," letter to the editor, *Village Voice*, July 20, 1972, 61, 63.

158. Thornton, "Dress Reversal."

159. Timmie to Jill Johnston, February 20, 1972, box 7, JJLA.

160. Lew to Jill Johnston, January 19, 1972, box 7, JJLA.

161. Bornstein, *Gender Outlaw*, 5.

162. Ahmed, *Living a Feminist Life*, 214.

163. Ahmed, *Queer Phenomenology*, 1–2.

164. Jill Johnston, "Writing into the Sunset," *Village Voice*, September 7, 1972, 41.

INTERRUPTION 3. WE CAN HEAR YOU: READING WITH THE BODY

Epigraph source: Alix Danu, "Come All Ye Faithful," letter to the editor, *Village Voice*, July 6, 1972, 4.

1. Bonnie to Jill Johnston, April 17, 1971, box 7, Jill Johnston Literary Archives, New York, NY (JJLA).

2. Peter to Jill Johnston, undated, box 7, JJLA.

3. Margaret to Jill Johnston, August 18, 1970, box 7, JJLA.

4. Elizabeth Freeman poses this mode of engagement as the opposite of engaging hoping to confirm belief or to complete "damaged wholes." *Time Binds*, 13–14.

5. Jameson, quoted in Freeman, *Time Binds*, 11. Freeman builds on Jameson's comment to imagine a queering of time where one's body is "intelligible only through its encounter with other bodies."

6. Jill Johnston, "Lois Lane Is a Lesbian," *Village Voice*, March 4, 1971, 9.

7. Johnston, "Lois Lane Is a Lesbian," 10.

8. Jill Johnston, "Lois Lane Is a Lesbian (3)," *Village Voice*, March 25, 1971, 27–28, 38.

9. Johnston, "Lois Lane Is a Lesbian (3)," 27.

10. Wittig, *Straight Mind*, 25.

11. Johnston, "Lois Lane Is a Lesbian (3)," 27.

12. McAuliffe, *Great American Newspaper*, 20, 149.

13. McAuliffe, *Great American Newspaper*, 149.

14. Sue E. Brueggeman, "Booby Trip," letter to the editor, *Village Voice*, March 25, 1971, 4, 36.

15. Barbara Wilson, "Scarlet Letter," letter to the editor, *Village Voice*, May 13, 1971, 4.

16. Brueggeman, "Booby Trip," 4, 36.

17. William Perley, "Les Toil," letter to the editor, *Village Voice*, May 25, 1972, 82, 84; and Jim Mcgahan, "When It Pours He Reigns," letter to the editor *Village Voice*, January 3, 1974, 4. The most egregious, obviously misogynist, and homophobic attacks on Johnston came in a series of 1972 essays by downtown actor Julie Bovasso, who calls Johnston "a very busy professional lesbian," a category Bovasso says is "very sad people or very busy people, usually too sad to be busy or too busy to be sad." A week later, Bovasso complains lesbians are mad at her for attacking Johnston and calls on Johnston to save her from her "mysterious, murderous friends." See Julie Bovasso, "Answering Jill Johnston on a Few Points," *Village Voice*, August 31, 1972, 17; and Julie Bovasso, "Open Letter to My Would-Be Executioners," *Village Voice*, September 7, 1972, 50, 58.

18. Pearl Rebuck, "They Stoop to Conk'er," letter to the editor, *Village Voice*, September 14, 1972, 4.

19. The letter was from Kenneth Pitchford, a leader of the Effeminist movement, a group of men professing allyship to women. "The Effeminist Mystique," letter to the editor, *Village Voice*, July 20, 1972, 4, 61.

20. Jane Hamilton, "What Are You Trying to Say?," letter to the editor, *Village Voice*, June 27, 1974, 97.

21. Dave Cripps, "Tumbling After," letter to the editor, *Village Voice*, July 25, 1974, 4.

22. Suntan to Jill Johnston, August 31, 1972, box 7, JJLA.

23. Jill Johnston to Kate Millett, [n.d.], 1973, box 7, JJLA.

24. Marilyn Webb, "The Self That Jill Built," *Village Voice*, May 31, 1973, 27–28.

25. Elizabeth Campbell, "Letter to the Editor: Webb Fete," *Village Voice*, June 7, 1973, 4.

26. Lillian Faderman tracks a rise, during World War II, in women who understood themselves as lesbians being drawn to military service. See *Odd Girls*, 120, 126.
27. Linda to Jill Johnston, January 31, 1972, box 7, JJLA.
28. Joy to Jill Johnston, October 13, 1971, box 7, JJLA.
29. Jeanine Tesori and Lisa Kron, "Ring of Keys," in *Fun Home*, n.p.
30. Cecilia to Jill Johnston, July 27, 1972, box 7, JJLA.
31. Cynthia to Jill Johnston, February 4, 1972, box 7, JJLA.
32. Jill Johnston, "The Wedding," *Village Voice*, January 14, 1971, 33–34.
33. Unsigned letter to Jill Johnston, July 8, 1971, box 7, JJLA.
34. Georgia to Jill Johnston, May 14, ca. 1971, box 7, JJLA.
35. Kathy to Jill Johnston, undated, box 7, JJLA.
36. Carol to Jill Johnston, November 9, 1971, box 7, JJLA.
37. Florence to Jill Johnston, undated, box 7, JJLA.
38. Unsigned letter to Jill Johnston, May 3, 1972, box 7, JJLA.
39. Freeman, *Time Binds*, 11.
40. Jocelyn to Jill Johnston, September 26, 1971, box 7, JJLA.
41. Joan to Jill Johnston, undated, box 7, JJLA.
42. Deborah to Jill Johnston, February 7, 1972, box 7, JJLA.
43. Unsigned letter to Jill Johnston, May 12, 1971, box 7, JJLA.
44. Jean to Jill Johnston, July 6, 1970, box 7, JJLA.
45. B. to Jill Johnston, August 24, 1971, box 7, JJLA.
46. M. to Jill Johnston, April 26, 1971, box 7, JJLA.
47. Joan to Jill Johnston, July 10, 1971, box 7, JJLA.
48. Mona to Jill Johnston, April 9, 1971 box 7, JJLA.
49. S.E. to Jill Johnston, September 17, 1971, box 7, JJLA.
50. Elana to Jill Johnston, February 1, 1972, box 7, JJLA.
51. Jean to Jill Johnston, May 17, 1971, box 7, JJLA.
52. Mona to Jill Johnston, June 4, 1971, box 7, JJLA.
53. Mona to Johnston, June 4, 1971.
54. Donna to Jill Johnston, February 17, 1972, box 7, JJLA.
55. Shannon to Jill Johnston, April 26, 1971, box 7, JJLA.
56. Pat to Jill Johnston, July 11, 1972, box 7, JJLA.
57. Sandy to Jill Johnston, December 5, 1972, box 7, JJLA.
58. S.E. to Jill Johnston, July 6, 1972, box 7, JJLA; and MD to Jill Johnston, August 13, 1972, box 7, JJLA.
59. Joan Gregg, "Voice in the Wilderness," letter to the editor, *Village Voice*, February 14, 1974, 75.

CHAPTER 4. SHE WAS A WRITER

1. Grace Glueck, "Hiding behind the Flag," *New York Times*, February 9, 1997, 3.
2. Johnston, *Jasper Johns*, 14–15.
3. Katz, *Hide/Seek*.
4. Johnston, "Tracking the Shadow."

5. Glueck, "Hiding behind the Flag"; and Winter, "Personality Profiles," 423.

6. Cook, "Doorknob in the Desert," 34.

7. Dolan, *Feminist Spectator as Critic*, xxxvii.

8. Bridgman, *Gertrude Stein in Pieces*.

9. Johnston, "Agnes Martin: Surrender and Solitude," in *Gullibles Travels*, 277.

10. Katz, "Agnes Martin," 118.

11. Audio recording, January 3, 1972, Dick Cavett Show Archives/Cavalier Films, Los Angeles, CA.

12. Jill Johnston, "I Suppose She Was Born," *Village Voice*, May 13, 1971, 41.

13. Hegedus and Pennebaker, *Town Bloody Hall*.

14. Jill Johnston, "Aileen Passloff," *Village Voice*, March 9, 1961, 7.

15. Jill Johnston, "Fresh Winds," *Village Voice*, March 15, 1962, 13–14.

16. Gertrude Stein, quoted in Frost, *Problem with Pleasure*, 80.

17. Banes, *Democracy's Body*, xviii.

18. Johnston, "Pain, Pleasure, Process," *Village Voice*, February 27, 1964, 9.

19. Johnston, "Pain, Pleasure, Process," 9.

20. Steiner, introduction, xxi. Steiner does note that artists were always reading Stein.

21. Jill Johnston, "Casting for 69," *Village Voice*, January 9, 1969, 27, 35. The pattern of grouping lesbians together with Stein as a lesbian bat signal continues as Stein appears in a column Johnston writes about a visit to Agnes Martin in New Mexico, Jill Johnston, "Pubis Est Veritas," *Village Voice*, March 6, 1969, 31–33, 36.

22. Jill Johnston, "Come Seven," *Village Voice*, May 15, 1969, 26, 30.

23. Johnston, "Come Seven," 26, 30.

24. Jill Johnston, "Hasten Slowly," *Village Voice*, July 16, 1970, 18.

25. Johnston, "The Wedding," *Village Voice*, January 14, 1971, 33–34.

26. Johnston, "Wedding," 34.

27. Johnston, "The Wedding," 33–34; and Mockus, *Sounding Out*, 183.

28. Quoted in Mockus, *Sounding Out*, 78.

29. Foster, *Reading Dancing*, 76. Style arises, argues Foster, from three sources: "the quality with which the movement is performed, the characteristic use of parts of the body, and the dancer's orientation in the performance space." *Reading Dancing*, 77.

30. Foster, *Reading Dancing*, 78, 87.

31. Jill Johnston, "Stein: Affectionately Obscene Poetry," *Village Voice*, May 4, 1972, 25.

32. Ahmed, *Living a Feminist Life*, 214.

33. Johnston, "Stein," 25.

34. Johnston, "Stein," 25.

35. Frost, *Problem with Pleasure*, 87.

36. Frost, *Problem with Pleasure*, 80, 66–67.

37. G. Stein, "Poetry and Grammar," 221.

38. Jill Johnston, "Survival Plan Number One," *Village Voice*, May 18, 1972, 56.

39. Jill Johnston, "Avocados and Rainstorms," *Village Voice*, May 11, 1972, 54.

40. Johnston, "Avocados and Rainstorms," 54.

41. G. Stein, "Poetry and Grammar," 211–12.

42. Rainer, *Feelings Are Facts*, 289.

43. Rainer, *Feelings Are Facts*, 289.

44. Jill Johnston to Yvonne Rainer, box 17, folder 55, Yvonne Rainer Papers, Getty Library, Los Angeles.

45. Rainer, *Feelings Are Facts*, 289.

46. Yvonne Rainer, interview with author, June 12, 2017.

47. Jill Johnston, "Life and Art," *Village Voice*, December 7, 1961, 10, 14.

48. Johnston, "Yvonne Rainer: II," *Village Voice*, June 6, 1963, 18.

49. Johnston, "Fresh Winds," 13.

50. Hughes and Román, introduction.

51. Rainer, *Feelings Are Facts*, 291.

52. Jill Johnston, "Boiler Room," *Village Voice*, March 29, 1962, 14.

53. Jill Johnston, "Judson Concerts #3, #4," *Village Voice*, February 28, 1963, 9.

54. Jill Johnston, "Yvonne Rainer: I," *Village Voice*, May 23, 1963, 17.

55. Jill Johnston, "To Whom It May Concern," *Village Voice*, May 30, 1968, 29, 30.

56. Jill Johnston, "Pickled Alive," *Village Voice*, July 28, 1966, 7.

57. Jill Johnston, "Old Hat and New in Connecticut," *Village Voice*, September 8, 1960, 10.

58. Johnston, "Pain, Pleasure, Process," 15.

59. Johnston, "Yvonne Rainer: I," 17.

60. Jill Johnston, "Judson '64: I," *Village Voice*, January 21, 1965, 12.

61. Johnston, "Judson '64: I," 12, 18.

62. Dolan, *Feminist Spectator as Critic*, 120–21.

63. Jill Johnston, "Democracy," *Village Voice*, August 23, 1962, 9.

64. Johnston, "Pain, Pleasure, Process," 15.

65. Johnston, "Yvonne Rainer: I," 17.

66. Johnston, "Yvonne Rainer: II," 18.

67. Lambert-Beatty, *Being Watched*, 70.

68. Jill Johnston, "Waring—Rainer," *Village Voice*, May 6, 1966, 26.

69. Jill Johnston, "Rainer's 'Mind Is a Muscle,'" *Village Voice*, June 2, 1966, 13.

70. Clive Barnes, "Dance: Village Disaster: Concert of Old and New Works at Judson Church Unveils Just One Minor Talent," *New York Times*, January 11, 1966, 20.

71. Clive Barnes, "Blue Movies? Ho Hum," *New York Times*, February 16, 1969, D20.

72. Clive Barnes, "Critic's Concern—And Ford's," *New York Times*, March 2, 1969, D35.

73. Jill Johnston, "Rainer's Muscle," *Village Voice*, April 18, 1969, 29.

74. Johnston, "Rainer's 'Mind Is a Muscle,'" 13.

75. Johnston, "Rainer's 'Mind Is a Muscle,'" 13.

76. Johnston, "Rainer's 'Mind Is a Muscle,'" 13.

77. Jill Johnston, "Dance Journal," *Village Voice*, September 24, 1970, 31–32, 49.

78. Johnston, *Paper Daughter*, 140.

79. Jill Johnston, "Agnes Martin: Surrender and Solitude," *Village Voice*, September 13, 1973, 30, 32, 33.

80. Johnston, "Agnes Martin: 1912–2004," *ARTnews/Art in America*, March 2005, 41.

81. Johnston, "Agnes Martin: Surrender and Solitude," *Village Voice*, 32.

82. Johnston, "Agnes Martin: Surrender and Solitude," *Village Voice*, 30.

83. Johnston, "Agnes Martin: Surrender and Solitude," in *Gullibles Travels*, 268–69.

84. Jill Johnston, "Agnes Martin," *ARTnews*, April 1965, 10.

85. Johnston, "Agnes Martin," *ARTnews*, 10.

86. Agnes Martin to Jill Johnston, undated; scan provided by Ingrid Nyeboe, in email to author, October 3, 2017.

87. Jill Johnston, "Agnes Martin (2): 'Of Deserts and Shores,'" *Village Voice*, September 20, 1973, 39.

88. Johnston, "Mad for Her," 26.

89. Rainer, *Feelings Are Facts*, 292.

90. Princenthal, *Agnes Martin*, 147.

91. Johnston, "Agnes Martin: 1912–2004," 42.

92. Metzl, "'Mother's Little Helper,'" 240–43.

93. On Martin's use of the word *trances*, see Jill Johnston, "Off to the Bewilderness," *Village Voice*, November 9, 1972, 29.

94. Kafer, *Feminist Queer Crip*, 17.

95. Johnston, "R. D. Laing: The Misteek of Sighcosis," in *Gullibles Travels*, 234.

96. Metzl, "'Mother's Little Helper,'" 240–43.

97. Jill Johnston, "R. D. Laing: The Misteek of Sighcosis," *Village Voice*, November 30, 1973, 16.

98. Agnes Martin to Jill Johnston, January 27, 1974; scan provided by Ingrid Nyeboe, in email to author, October 3, 2017.

99. Johnston, "R. D. Laing," *Village Voice*, November 30, 1973, 16.

100. Johnston eventually decided Laing was a "chauvinist" who encouraged those around him to be "sycophants." "There'll Awe Ways Be an England," *Village Voice*, March 8, 1973, 30.

101. Martin to Johnston, January 27, 1974.

102. Jill Johnston, "Babbling into Yr Shopping Bag," *Village Voice*, April 12, 1973, 32; and Johnston, "Off to the Bewilderness," 29.

103. Martin to Johnston, undated; and Martin to Johnston, January 27, 1974.

104. Johnston, "Agnes Martin (2)," 39.

105. Johnston, "Agnes Martin: 1912–2004," 41.

106. Jill Johnston, "Already Moribund," *Village Voice*, May 12, 1975, 28.

107. *Agnes Martin: With My Back to the World*, Mary Lance, dir., 2002.

108. Johnston, "Agnes Martin: Surrender and Solitude," 269.

EPILOGUE. LAST SENTENCES

Epigraph source: Jill Johnston, "Could I Have a Light," *Village Voice*, September 28, 1972, 19.

1. Kate Millett and Jill Johnston, box AV8 c. 1, Kate Millett Papers, Sally Bingham Center for Women's History and Culture, Rubenstein Library, Duke University, Durham, NC.

2. Phillips, “Whose Sonnet?,” 206.
3. Johnston, “Tell Me the Weather,” in *Marmalade Me*, 238.
4. Johnston, “Marmalade Me,” in *Marmalade Me*, 100.
5. Johnston, “Robert Whitman,” in *Marmalade Me*, 104.
6. Johnston, “Holy Hurricane,” in *Marmalade Me*, 132.
7. Johnston, “Holy Hurricane,” in *Marmalade Me*, 130.
8. Jill Johnston, “Hello Young Lovers,” *Village Voice*, September 19, 1968, 34.

BIBLIOGRAPHY

ARCHIVES

Archives of American Art. Smithsonian Institution, Washington, DC.

Phyllis Birkby Papers. Sophia Smith Collection of Women's History, Smith College, Northampton, MA.

Dick Cavett Show Archive. Cavalier Films, Los Angeles, CA.

Jerome Robbins Dance Division. New York Public Library, New York, NY.

Jill Johnston Literary Archive. New York, NY (JJLA).

Lesbian Herstory Archives. New York, NY.

Kate Millett Papers. Sallie Bingham Center for Women's History and Culture, Rubenstein Library, Duke University, Durham, NC.

Yvonne Rainer Papers. Research Collections, Getty Library, Los Angeles, CA.

Ellen Shumsky Papers Sophia Smith Collection of Women's History, Smith College, Northampton, MA.

INTERVIEWS AND CONVERSATIONS

Unless otherwise noted, interviews were conducted in person.

Bellamy, Miles. Interview with author, July 2017.

Hay, Deborah. Interview with author, April 2017.

Hendricks, Geoffrey, and Sur Rodney Sur. Interview with author, January 5, 2017.

Nyeboe, Ingrid. Interview with author, September 29, 2016.

Nyeboe, Ingrid. Interview with author, October 1, 2016.

Nyeboe, Ingrid. Skype interview with author, December 2, 2017.

Monk, Meredith. Skype interview with author, January 2019.

Rainer, Yvonne. Interview with author, June 12, 2017.

Schneemann, Carolee. Interview with author, August 2018.

Abbott, Sidney, and Barbara Love. *Sappho was a Right-On Woman*. New York: Stein and Day, 1972.

Adeyemi, Kemi. "Beyond 90°: The Angularities of Black/Queer/Women/Lean." *Women and Performance* 29, no. 1 (2019): 1–16. https://doi.org/10.1080/0740770X.2019.1571861.

Aguiar, Daniella, and João Queiroz. "From Gertrude Stein to Dance: Repetition and Time in Intersemiotic Translation." *Dance Chronicle* 38, no. 2 (2015): 204–32. https://doi.org/10.1080/01472526.2015.1043801.

Ahmed, Sara. *Living a Feminist Life*. Durham, NC: Duke University Press, 2017.

Ahmed, Sara. *Queer Phenomenology: Orientations, Objects, Others*. Durham, NC: Duke University Press, 2006.

Alwood, Edward. *Straight News: Gays, Lesbians, and the News Media*. New York: Columbia University Press, 1996.

Andersson, Johan. "'Wilding' in the West Village: Queer Space, Racism and Jane Jacobs Hagiography." *International Journal of Urban and Regional Research* 39, no. 2 (2015): 265–83. https://doi.org/10.1111/1468-2427.12188.

Apollinaire, Guillaume. *Calligrammes: Poems of Peace and War (1913–1916)*. Translated by Ann Hyde Greet. Berkeley, CA: University of California Press, 1980.

Apollinaire, Guillaume. *Zone: Selected Poems*. Translated by Ron Padgett. New York: New York Review of Books, 2015.

Aramphongphan, Paisid. "Real Professionals? Andy Warhol, Fred Herko, and Dance." *PAJ: A Journal of Performance and Art* 37, no. 2 (2015): 1–12. https://doi.org/10.1162/PAJJ_a_00255.

Armatage, Kay, and Lydia Wazana, dirs. *Jill Johnston. . . . October 1975*. Toronto: Canadian Film Distributors Film Center, 1977.

Arondekar, Anjali, Ann Cvetkovich, Christina B. Hanhardt, Regina Kunzel, Tavia Nyong'o, Juana María Rodríguez, and Susan Stryker. "Queering Archives: A Roundtable Discussion." *Radical History Review* 2015, no. 122 (2015): 211–31. https://doi.org/10.1215/01636545-2849630.

Artaud, Antonin. *Theater and its Double*. Translated Mary Caroline Richards. New York: Grove, 1958.

Atkinson, Ti-Grace. "Lesbianism and Feminism." In *Amazon Expedition: A Lesbian Feminist Anthology*, edited by Phyllis Birkby, Bertha Harris, Jill Johnston, Esther Newton, and Jane O'Wyatt, 11–14. New York: Times Change, 1973.

Banes, Sally. *Dancing Women: Female Bodies on Stage*. New York: Routledge, 2013.

Banes, Sally. *Democracy's Body: Judson Dance Theater, 1962–1964*. Durham, NC: Duke University Press, 1993.

Banes, Sally. "Jill Johnston: Signaling through the Flames." In *Writing Dancing in the Age of Postmodernism*, 3–10. Middletown, CT: Wesleyan University Press, 1994.

Bassi, Serena, and Greta LaFleur. "Introduction: TERFs, Gender-Critical Movements, and Postfascist Feminisms." *TSQ: Transgender Studies Quarterly* 9, no. 3 (2022): 311–33. https://doi.org/10.1215/23289252-9836008.

Battcock, Gregory. Introduction to *Marmalade Me*, by Jill Johnston, 9–12. New York: E. P. Dutton, 1971.
Beauvoir, Simone de. *The Second Sex*. 1949. New York: Vintage, 2011.
Bechdel, Alison. *Fun Home: A Family Tragicomic*. New York: Mariner Books Classics, 2007.
Berlant, Lauren, and Elizabeth Freeman. "Queer Nationality." In *The Queen of America Goes to Washington City: Essays on Sex and Citizenship*, edited by Lauren Berlant, 145–74. Durham, NC: Duke University Press, 1997.
Bornstein, Kate. *Gender Outlaw: On Men, Women, and the Rest of Us*. Updated ed. New York: Vintage, 2016.
Birkby, Phyllis, Bertha Harris, Jill Johnston, Esther Newton, and Jane O'Wyatt. *Amazon Expedition: A Lesbian Feminist Anthology*. New York: Times Change, 1973.
Bridgman, Richard. *Gertrude Stein in Pieces*. New York: Oxford University Press, 1970.
Brooks, Daphne. *Liner Notes for the Revolution: The Intellectual Life of Black Feminist Sound*. Cambridge, MA: Harvard University Press, 2021.
Butler, Judith. *Gender Trouble: Feminism and the Subversion of Identity*. New York: Routledge, 2006.
Butler, Judith. "Performative Acts and Gender Constitution: An Essay in Phenomenology and Feminist Theory." *Theatre Journal* 40, no. 4 (1988): 519–31. https://doi.org/10.2307/3207893.
Canaday, Margot. *The Straight State: Sexuality and Citizenship in Twentieth-Century America*. Princeton, NJ: Princeton University Press, 2009.
Carmichael, Stokely, and Charles V. Hamilton. *Black Power: The Politics of Liberation in America*. New York: Vintage, 1967.
Castle, Terry. *The Apparitional Lesbian: Female Homosexuality and Modern Culture*. New York: Columbia University Press, 1993.
Chaleff, Rebecca. "Activating Whiteness: Racializing the Ordinary in US American Postmodern Dance." *Dance Research Journal* 50, no. 3 (2018): 71–84. https://doi.org/10.1017/S0149767718000372.
Chauncey, George. *Gay New York: Gender, Urban Culture, and the Making of the Gay Male World, 1890–1940*. 2nd ed. New York: Basic Books, 1994.
Clarke, Cheryl. "Lesbianism: An Act of Resistance." In *This Bridge Called My Back: Writings by Radical Women of Color*, edited by Cherríe Moraga and Gloria E. Anzaldúa, 128–37. Watertown, MA: Persephone, 1981.
Combahee River Collective. "A Black Feminist Statement." In *Words of Fire: An Anthology of African-American Feminist Thought*, edited by Beverly Guy-Sheftall, 231–40. New York: New Press, 1995.
Cook, Roger. "Doorknob in the Desert: Agnes Martin's Queer Becoming." *Journal of Contemporary Painting* 2, no. 1 (2016): 21–38. https://doi.org/10.1386/jcp.2.1.21_1.
Crano, R. D. "Haptic Spectatorship and the Political Life of Cruelty, or, Antonin Artaud 'Signaling through the Flames.'" *Journal of Dramatic Theory and Criticism* 24, no. 2 (2010): 49–68. https://doi.org/10.1353/dtc.2010.0004.
Croft, Clare. "Lesbian Echoes: Jill Johnston's Political Embodiments." In *Futures*

of Dance Studies, edited by Susan Manning, Janice Ross, and Rebecca Schneider, 117–34. Madison: University of Wisconsin Press, 2020.

Cunningham, Merce. "Space, Time and Dance." *Trans/Formations* 1 (1952): 150–51.

Cvetkovich, Ann. *An Archive of Feelings: Trauma, Sexuality, and Lesbian Public Cultures*. Durham, NC: Duke University Press, 2003.

Cvetkovich, Ann. "Sexual Trauma/Queer Memory: Incest, Lesbianism, and Therapeutic Culture." *GLQ* 2, no. 4 (1995): 351–77. https://doi.org/10.1215/10642684-2-4-351.

Cvetkovich, Ann. "White Boots and Combat Boots: My Life as a Lesbian Go-Go Dancer." In *Dancing Desires: Choreographing Sexualities on and off the Stage*, edited by Jane C. Desmond, 315–48. Madison: University of Wisconsin Press, 2001.

Daly, Ann. Review of *First We Take Manhattan*; *Four American Women and the New York School of Dance Criticism*; *Marmalade Me*; and *Spreading the Gospel of the Modern Dance: Newspaper Dance Criticism in the United States, 1850–1934*. *TDR/The Drama Review* 43, no. 1 (1999): 184–90. https://doi.org/10.1162/dram.1999.43.1.184.

Davall, Irene. "To Pee or Not to Pee, Sexism at Harvard." *On the Issues Magazine*, Summer 1990. https://ontheissuesmagazine.com/feminism/to-pee-or-not-to-pee-sexism-at-harvard/.

Davis, Angela T. *Blues Legacies and Black Feminism: Gertrude "Ma" Rainey, Bessie Smith, and Billie Holiday*. New York: Vintage, 1999.

Dee Das, Joanna. *Katherine Dunham: Dance and the African Diaspora*. New York: Oxford University Press, 2017.

DeFrantz, Thomas. *Dancing Revelations: Alvin Ailey's Embodiment of African American Culture*. New York: Oxford University Press, 2004.

D'Emilio, John, and Estelle Freedman. *Intimate Matters: A History of Sexuality in America*. 3rd ed. Chicago: University of Chicago Press, 2012.

Deleuze, Gilles, and Félix Guattari. *A Thousand Plateaus: Capitalism and Schizophrenia*. Minneapolis: University of Minnesota Press, 1987.

De Veaux, Alexis. *Warrior Poet: A Biography of Audre Lorde*. New York: W. W. Norton, 2004.

Dinshaw, Carolyn. *Getting Medieval: Sexualities and Communities, Pre- and Postmodern*. Durham, NC: Duke University Press, 1999.

Disch, Lisa. Introduction to "1970s Feminism," edited by Lisa Disch. Special issue, *South Atlantic Quarterly* 114, no. 4 (2015): 697–98. https://doi.org/10.1215/00382876-3157078.

Doan, Laura. Preface to *The Lesbian Postmodern*, edited by Laura Doan, ix–xi. New York: Columbia University Press, 1994.

Dolan, Jill. *The Feminist Spectator as Critic*. 2nd ed. Ann Arbor: University of Michigan Press, 2012. https://doi.org/10.3998/mpub.5169198.

Doyle, Jennifer, Jonathan Flatley, and José Esteban Muñoz. Introduction to *Pop Out: Queer Warhol*, edited by Jennifer Doyle, Jonathan Flatley, and José Esteban Muñoz, 1–19. Durham, NC: Duke University Press, 1996. https://doi.org/10.1215/9780822397649-001.

Echols, Alice. *Daring to Be Bad: Radical Feminism in America, 1967–1975*. Minneapolis: University of Minnesota Press, 1989.

Enke, Finn. *Finding the Movement: Sexuality, Contested Space, and Feminist Activism*. Durham, NC: Duke University Press, 2007.

Faderman, Lillian. *Odd Girls and Twilight Lovers: A History of Lesbian Life in 20th Century America*. New York: Columbia University Press, 1991.

Firestone, Shulamith. *The Dialectic of Sex: The Case for Feminist Revolution*. New York: Farrar, Straus and Giroux, 2003.

Foster, Susan Leigh. "The Ballerina's Phallic Pointe." In *Corporealities: Dancing Knowledge, Culture and Power*, edited by Susan Leigh Foster, 1–25. London: Routledge, 1996.

Foster, Susan Leigh. "Choreographies of Gender." *Signs* 24, no. 1 (1998): 1–33. http://doi.org/10.1086/495316.

Foster, Susan Leigh. "Closets Full of Dances: Modern Dance's Performance of Masculinity and Sexuality." In *Dancing Desires: Choreographing Sexualities on and off the Stage*, edited by Jane C. Desmond, 147–207. Madison: University of Wisconsin Press, 2001.

Foster, Susan Leigh. *Reading Dancing: Bodies and Subjects in Contemporary American Dance*. Berkeley: University of California Press, 1988.

Foulkes, Julia. "Streets and Stages: Urban Renewal and the Arts after World War II." *Journal of Social History* 44, no. 2 (2010): 413–34. https://doi.org/10.1353/jsh.2010.0083.

Freeman, Elizabeth. *Time Binds: Queer Temporalities, Queer Histories*. Durham, NC: Duke University Press, 2010.

Frost, Laura. *The Problem with Pleasure: Modernism and Its Discontents*. New York: Columbia University Press, 2013.

Garafola, Lynn. "Writing on the Left: The Remarkable Career of Edna Ocko." *Dance Research Journal* 34, no. 1 (2002): 53–61. https://doi.org/10.2307/1478133.

Garcia, Cindy. "'Don't Leave Me, Celia!': Salsera Homosociality and Pan-Latina Corporealities." *Women and Performance* 18, no. 3 (2008): 199–213. https://doi.org/10.1080/07407700802495944.

Gardiner, Judith Kegan, Elly Bulkin, Rena Grasso Patterson, and Annette Kolodny. "An Interchange on Feminist Criticism: On 'Dancing through the Minefield.'" *Feminist Studies* 8, no. 3 (1982): 629–75. https://doi.org/10.2307/3177715.

Getsy, David J. "The Spectacle of Privacy: Geoffrey Hendrick's *Ring Piece* and the Ambivalence of Queer Visibility." *Art Bulletin* 104, no. 3 (2022): 117–45. https://doi.org/10.1080/00043079.2022.2036021.

Gever, Martha. *Entertaining Lesbians: Celebrity, Sexuality, and Self-Invention*. New York: Routledge, 2003.

Greer, Germaine. *The Female Eunuch*. London: MacGibbon and Kee, 1970.

Grobe, Christopher. *The Art of Confession: The Performance of Self from Robert Lowell to Reality TV*. New York: New York University Press, 2017.

Gutterman, Lauren Jae. *Her Neighbor's Wife: A History of Lesbian Desire within Marriage*. Philadelphia: University of Pennsylvania Press, 2019.

Halberstam, Jack. *The Queer Art of Failure*. Durham, NC: Duke University Press, 2011.

Hamilton, Jack. *Just around Midnight: Rock and Roll and the Racial Imagination*. Cambridge, MA: Harvard University Press, 2016.

Heaney, Emma. "Women-Identified Women: Trans Women in 1970s Lesbian Feminist Organizing." *TSQ: Transgender Studies Quarterly* 3, no. 1–2 (2016): 137–45. https://doi.org/10.1215/23289252-3334295.

Hegedus, Chris, and D. A. Pennebaker, dirs. *Town Bloody Hall: A Dialogue on Women's Liberation*. New York: Pennebaker Hegedus Films, 1979.

Hesford, Victoria. *Feeling Women's Liberation*. Durham, NC: Duke University Press, 2013.

Hoffman, Abbie. *Woodstock Nation*. New York: Vintage, 1969.

Hughes, Holly, and David Román. Introduction to *O Solo Homo: The New Queer Performance*, edited by Holly Hughes and David Román, 1–16. New York: Grove, 1998.

Hunter, Dianne, and Rena Patterson. Foreword to *Gullibles Travels: Writing by Jill Johnston*, ix–xi. New York: Links, 1974.

iLAND. *A Field Guide to iLANDING: Scores for Researching Urban Ecologies*. Brooklyn, NY: 53rd State, 2017.

Jackson, Shannon. *Social Works: Performing Art, Supporting Publics*. New York: Routledge, 2011.

Jacobs, Jane. *The Death and Life of Great American Cities*. New York: Vintage, 1992.

Jagose, Annamarie. *Inconsequence: Lesbian Representation and the Logic of the Sexual Sequence*. Ithaca, NY: Cornell University Press, 2002.

Jagose, Annamarie. *Lesbian Utopics*. New York: Routledge, 1994.

Jannarone, Kimberly. *Artaud and His Doubles*. Ann Arbor: University of Michigan Press, 2010.

Jennings, Rebecca, and Liz Millward. "Introducing Lesbian Nation." *Women's History Review* 31, no. 1 (2022): 1–7. https://doi.org/10.1080/09612025.2021.1954331.

Johnson, Imani Kai. "Black Culture without Black People: Hip-Hop Dance beyond Appropriation Discourse." In *Are You Entertained? Black Popular Culture in the Twenty-First Century*, edited by Simone C. Drake and Dwan K. Henderson, 191–206. Durham, NC: Duke University Press, 2020. https://doi.org/10.1215/9781478009009-013.

Johnston, Jill. "The Comingest Womanifesto." In *Amazon Expedition: A Lesbian Feminist Anthology*, edited by Phyllis Birkby, Bertha Harris, Jill Johnston, Esther Newton, and Jane O'Wyatt, 89–92. New York: Times Change, 1973.

Johnston, Jill. "Dance Quote Unquote." In *Reinventing Dance in the 1960s: Everything Was Possible*, edited by Sally Banes, 98–104. Madison: University of Wisconsin Press, 2003.

Johnston, Jill. "Firestorm on Christopher Street." In *Pride: Photographs after Stonewall*, edited by Timothy McDarrah, xxvii–xxix. 2nd ed. London: Zed Books, 2019.

Johnston, Jill. *Gullibles Travels: Writing by Jill Johnston*. Foreword by Dianne Hunter and Rena Patterson. New York: Links, 1974.

Johnston, Jill. "How Dance Artists and Critics Define Dance as Political." *Movement Research Performance Journal* (Fall 2009): 2–3.

Johnston, Jill. *Jasper Johns: Privileged Information*. New York: Thames and Hudson, 1996.
Johnston, Jill. *Lesbian Nation: The Feminist Solution*. New York: Simon and Schuster, 1973.
Johnston, Jill. "Mad for Her." In *A Woman like That: Lesbian and Bisexual Writers Tell Their Coming Out Stories*, edited by Joan Larkin, 18–27. New York: Avon Books, 1999.
Johnston, Jill. *Marmalade Me*. Introduction by Gregory Battcock. New York: E. P. Dutton, 1971.
Johnston, Jill. "The Modern Dance—Directions and Criticisms." *Dance Observer* 24, no. 4 (April 1957): 55–56.
Johnston, Jill. *Mother Bound*. New York: Alfred A. Knopf, 1983.
Johnston, Jill. "The New American Modern Dance." In *The New American Arts*, edited by Richard Kostelanetz, 162–93. New York: Collier, 1965.
Johnston, Jill. *Paper Daughter*. New York: Alfred A. Knopf, 1985.
Johnston, Jill. "Thoughts on the Present and Future Directions of Modern Dance." *Dance Observer* 22, no. 7 (August–September 1955): 101–2.
Johnston, Jill. "Tracking the Shadow: Jill Johnston on Jasper Johns." *Art in America*, October 1987, 128–43.
Johnston, Jill. "Was Lesbian Separatism Inevitable?" *Gay and Lesbian Review* 13, no. 2 (March–April 2006), 36–37.
Jones, Jennifer Dominique. *Ambivalent Affinities: A Political History of Blackness and Homosexuality after World War II*. Chapel Hill: University of North Carolina Press, 2023.
Joseph, Branden W. "The Play of Repetition: Andy Warhol's 'Sleep.'" *Grey Room* 19, no. 4 (2005): 22–53. https://doi.org/10.1162/grey.2005.1.19.22.
Kafer, Alison. *Feminist, Queer, Crip*. Bloomington: Indiana University Press, 2013.
Katz, Jonathan. "Agnes Martin and the Sexuality of Abstraction." In *Agnes Martin*, edited by Lynn Cooke, 93–120. New Haven, CT: Yale University Press, 2011.
Katz, Jonathan. *Hide/Seek: Difference and Desire in American Portraiture*. Washington, DC: Smithsonian Books, 2010.
Kirsch, Sharon J. *Gertrude Stein and the Reinvention of Rhetoric*. Tuscaloosa: University of Alabama Press, 2014.
Koestenbaum, Wayne. *The Queen's Throat: Opera, Homosexuality, and the Mystery of Desire*. New York: Da Capo, 1993.
Kolodny, Annette. "Dancing through the Minefield: Some Observations on the Theory, Practice and Politics of a Feminist Literary Criticism." *Feminist Studies* 6, no. 1 (1980): 1–25. https://doi.org/10.2307/3177648.
Krasinski, Jennifer. "Jill Johnston: The I of the Beholder." In *The Disintegration of a Critic*, edited by Fiona McGovern, Megan Francis Sullivan, and Axel Wieder, 173–87. New York: Sternberg, 2019.
Kreutzer, Evelyn. "Mediating and Disrupting the Flow: Classical Music Conventions in the Performance and Video Art of Nam June Paik and Charlotte Moorman." *Music, Sound and the Moving Image* 14, no. 2 (2020): 141–48.
Kuppers, Petra. "Vanishing in Your Face: Embodiment and Representation in Les-

bian Dance Performance." *Journal of Lesbian Studies* 2, no. 2–3 (1998): 47–63. https://doi.org/10.1300/J155v02n02_04.
Laing, R. D. *The Politics of Experience.* New York: Ballantine, 1967.
Lambert-Beatty, Carrie. *Being Watched: Yvonne Rainer and the 1960s*. Cambridge, MA: MIT Press, 2008.
Lance, Mary, dir. *Agnes Martin: With My Back to the World.* Corrales, NM: New Deal Films, 2002.
La Rocco, Claudia, and Jillian Pena. "The Herko Dialogues: Fred by Claudia and Jillian." *Critical Correspondence*, Movement Research, December 19, 2014. https://movementresearch.org/publications/critical-correspondence/the-herko-dialogues-fred-by-claudia-and-jillian/.
Levine, Les, ed. "Jill Johnston Exposed: A Life Dominated by Strange Arts, Consuming Desires, and Ego Eroticism." Special issue, *Culture Hero: A Fanzine of Stars of the Super World* (1970).
Littel, Noah. "Playing the Game of Lesbian Imagination: Radical Lesbian Feminist Organizing in the Dutch Lesbian Nation." *Women's History Review* 31, no. 1 (2022): 68–87. https://doi.org/10.1080/09612025.2021.1954335.
Lorde, Audre. "The Master's Tools Will Never Dismantle the Master's House." In *Sister Outsider: Essays and Speeches*, 110–13. 1984. New York: Crossing, 2007.
Lorde, Audre. "Pirouette." In *New Negro Poets, U.S.A.*, edited by Langston Hughes, 106. Bloomington: University of Indiana Press, 1964.
Lorde, Audre. "The Uses of the Erotic." In *Sister Outsider: Essays and Speeches*, 53–59. 1984. New York: Crossing, 2007.
Lorde, Audre. *Zami: A New Spelling of My Name*. Watertown, MA: Persephone, 1982.
Love, Heather. "Introduction to 'Rethinking Sex.'" *GLQ* 17, no. 1 (2011): 1–14.
Mailer, Norman. *An American Dream*. New York: Dial Press, 1965.
Mailer, Norman. "The Prisoner of Sex." *Harper's*, March 1971, 41–92.
Manning, Susan. "Modern Dance, Negro Dance, and Katherine Dunham." *Textual Practice* 15, no. 3 (2001): 487–502. https://doi.org/10.1080/09502360110070411.
Manning, Susan. *Modern Dance, Negro Dance: Race in Motion*. Minneapolis: University of Minnesota Press, 2004.
Manning, Susan. "Race in Motion: Modern Dance, Negro Dance, and Katherine Dunham." In *The Dance Studies Reader*, edited by Jens Giersdorf and Yutian Wong, 234–45. 3rd ed. London: Routledge, 2018.
Martin, Del, and Phyllis Lyon. *Lesbian/Woman.* San Francisco: Glide Publications, 1972.
Martin, John. *The Modern Dance*. New York: A. S. Barnes, 1933.
Mattingly, Kate. *Shaping Dance Canons: Criticism, Aesthetics, Equity*. Gainesville: University of Florida Press, 2023.
McAuliffe, Kevin Michael. *The Great American Newspaper: The Rise and Fall of the "Village Voice."* New York: Scribner's Sons, 1978.
McRobbie, Angela. "The Modernist Style of Susan Sontag." *Feminist Review*, no. 38 (Summer 1991): 1–19. https://doi.org/10.2307/1395374.
Metzl, Jonathan. "'Mother's Little Helper': The Crisis of Psychoanalysis and the

Milltown Resolution." *Gender and History* 15, no. 2 (2003): 228–55. https://doi.org/10.1111/1468-0424.00300.
Millett, Kate. *Flying*. Champaign: University of Illinois Press, 2000. First published 1974 by Knopf (New York).
Millett, Kate. *Sexual Politics*. New York: Columbia University Press, 2016.
Millward, Liz. "*Lesbian Nation* and Black Nationalism." *Women's History Review* 31, no. 1 (2022): 51–67. https://doi.org/10.1080/09612025.2021.1954334.
Mockus, Martha. *Sounding Out: Pauline Oliveros and Lesbian Musicality*. New York: Routledge, 2007.
Moi, Toril. "Ambiguity and Alienation in *The Second Sex*." *Feminism and Postmodernism* 19, no. 2 (1992): 96–112. https://doi.org/10.2307/303535.
Monroe, Raquel L. "'Oh No! Not This Lesbian Again': The Punany Poets Queer the Pimp-Ho Aesthetic." In *Queer Dance*, edited by Clare Croft, 243–62. New York: Oxford University Press, 2017. https://doi.org/10.1093/acprof:oso/9780199377329.003.0016.
Moraga, Cherríe. "Entering the Lives of Others: Theory in the Flesh." In *This Bridge Called My Back: Writings by Radical Women of Color*, edited by Cherríe Moraga and Gloria Anzaldúa, 18–21. 40th-anniversary ed. Albany, NY: SUNY Press, 2021.
Moraga, Cherríe, and Gloria Anzaldúa, eds. *This Bridge Called My Back: Writings by Radical Women of Color*. 40th-anniversary ed. Albany, NY: SUNY Press, 2021.
Morris, Gay. *A Game for Dancers: Performing Modernism in the Postwar Years*. Middletown, CT: Wesleyan University Press, 2006.
Moser, Benjamin. *Sontag: Her Life and Work*. New York: Ecco, 2019.
Muñoz, José Esteban. *Cruising Utopia: The Then and There of Queer Futurity*. New York: New York University Press, 2009.
Muñoz, José Esteban. "Race, Sex, and the Incommensurate: Gary Fisher with Eve Kosofsky Sedgwick." In *Reading Sedgwick*, edited by Lauren Berlant, 152–65. Durham, NC: Duke University Press, 2019. https://doi.org/10.1515/9781478005339-012.
Musser, Amber Jamilla. *Between Shadows and Noise: Sensation, Situatedness, and the Undisciplined*. Durham, NC: Duke University Press, 2024.
Musser, Amber Jamilla. "Re-membering Audre: Adding Lesbian Feminist Mother Poet to Black." In *No Tea, No Shade: New Writing in Black Queer Studies*, edited by E. Patrick Johnson, 346–61. Durham, NC: Duke University Press, 2016. https://doi.org/10.1215/9780822373711-018.
Newton, Esther. *Margaret Mead Made Me Gay*. Durham, NC: Duke University Press, 2000.
Newton, Esther. *My Butch Career: A Memoir*. Durham, NC: Duke University Press, 2018.
Nussbaum, Emily. "The Rebirth of the Feminist Manifesto." *New York Magazine*, October 28, 2011. https://nymag.com/news/features/feminist-blogs-2011-11/.
Olsson, Göran Hugo, dir. *Black Power Mixtape, 1967–1975*. New York: IFC Films, 2011.
"On Husbandry and the Modern Dance." *Dance Observer* 20, no. 7 (August–September 1953): 100.

Phelan, Peggy. *Mourning Sex: Performing Public Memories*. New York: Routledge, 1997.
Phillips, Carl. "Whose Sonnet? (A Transgression)." In *The American Sonnet: An Anthology of Poems and Essays*, edited by Dora Malech and Laura T. Smith, 201–6. Iowa City: University of Iowa Press, 2023.
Povitz, Lana Dee. "To See and Be Seen: In Conversation with JEB." *Feminist Studies* 44, no. 3 (2018): 666–98. https://doi.org/10.1353/fem.2018.0045.
Princenthal, Nancy. *Agnes Martin: Her Life and Art*. New York: Thames and Hudson, 2015.
Provitola, Blase A. "TERF or Transfeminist Avant la Lettre? Monique Wittig's Complex Legacy in Trans Studies." *TSQ: Transgender Studies Quarterly* 9, no. 3 (2022): 387–406. https://doi.org/10.1215/23289252-9836050.
Rainer, Yvonne. *Feelings Are Facts: A Memoir*. Cambridge, MA: MIT Press, 2006.
Rainer, Yvonne. "No Manifesto." 1965. In *1000 Manifestos*. https://1000manifestos.com/yvonne-rainer-no-manifesto/.
Rainer, Yvonne, dir. *Trio A*. Performed by Yvonne Rainer. New York: Sally Banes, 1978.
Read, Peter. Introduction to *Zone: Selected Poems*, by Guillaume Apollinaire, ix–xxv. New York: New York Review of Books, 2015.
Rollyson, Carl E., and Lisa Olson Paddock. *Susan Sontag: The Making of an Icon*. Jackson: University Press of Mississippi, 2016.
Rosen, Ruth. *The World Split Open: How the Modern Women's Movement Changed America*. New York: Penguin, 2006.
Ross, Becki L. *The House That Jill Built: A Lesbian Nation in Formation*. Toronto: University of Toronto Press, 1995.
Rubin, Jerry. *DO IT! Scenarios of the Revolution*. New York: Simon and Schuster, 1970.
Sabin, Robert. "Merce Cunningham and Dance Company." *Dance Observer* 21, no. 2 (February 1954): 25.
Savran, David. "'You've Got That Thing': Cole Porter, Stephen Sondheim, and the Erotics of the List Song." *Theatre Journal* 64, no. 4 (2012): 533–48. https://doi.org//10.1353/tj.2012.a494444.
Schwartz, David. "*Sleep*: Perchance to Dream." *Reverse Shot*, Museum of the Moving Image, April 10, 2019. http://www.reverseshot.org/features/2546/sleep_whitney.
Schwartz, Selby Wynn. "'We'll See You at the Barre!': Stretching Queer Sociality with Ballez." *Global Performance Studies* 4, no. 1 (2021). https://doi.org/10.33303/gpsv4n1a16.
Schweighofer, Katherine. "A Land of One's Own: Whiteness and Indigeneity on Lesbian Land." *Settler Colonial Studies* 8, no. 4 (2018): 489–506. https://doi.org/10.1080/2201473X.2017.1365410.
Sedgwick, Eve Kosofsky. "Queer and Now." In *The Routledge Queer Studies Reader*, edited by Donald E. Hall and Annamarie Jagose, 3–17. London: Routledge, 2013.
Sedgwick, Eve Kosofsky. *Touching Feeling: Affect, Pedagogy, Performativity*. Durham, NC: Duke University Press, 2003.
Shattuck, Roger. *The Banquet Years: The Arts in France, 1885–1918; Alfred Jarry, Henri Rousseau, Erik Satie, Guillaume Apollinaire*. New York: Harcourt Brace, 1958.

Shelley, Martha. *We Set the Night on Fire: Igniting the Gay Revolution*. Chicago: Chicago Review Press, 2023.

Shumsky, Ellen. "Radicalesbians." *Gay and Lesbian Review* 16, no. 4 (2009): 17–20.

Sichel, Jennifer. "Criticism without Authority: Gene Swenson, Jill Johnston and Gregory Battcock." PhD diss., University of Chicago, 2018.

Smith, Barbara, and Beverly Smith. "Across the Kitchen Table: A Sister-to-Sister Dialogue." In *This Bridge Called My Back: Writings by Radical Women of Color*, edited by Cherríe Moraga and Gloria Anzaldúa, 111–25. 40th-anniversary ed. Albany, NY: SUNY Press, 2021.

Soares, Janet Mansfield. *Louis Horst: Musician in a Dancer's World*. Durham, NC: Duke University Press, 1992.

Sontag, Susan. "Against Interpretation." In *Against Interpretation and Other Essays*, 3–14. New York: Picador, 2001.

Sontag, Susan. "Happenings: An Art of Radical Juxtaposition." In *Against Interpretation and Other Essays*, 263–73. New York: Picador, 2001.

Sontag, Susan. "Interview: On Art and Consciousness." *Performing Arts Journal* 2, no. 2 (1977): 25–32. https://doi.org/10.1162/1520281053850820.

Sontag, Susan. "Notes on Camp." *Partisan Review* 31, no. 4 (1964): 515–30.

Sontag, Susan. *Reborn: Journals and Notebooks, 1947–1963*. Edited by David Rieff. New York: Picador, 2009.

Sontag, Susan. "Thirty Years Later." In *Against Interpretation and Other Essays*, 102–10. New York: Picador, 2001.

Springer, Kimberly. *Living for the Revolution: Black Feminist Organizations, 1968–1980*. Durham, NC: Duke University Press, 2005.

Stacey, Jackie. *Star Gazing: Hollywood Cinema and Female Spectatorship*. London: Routledge, 1994.

Stein, Arlene. *Sex and Sensibility: Stories of a Lesbian Generation*. Berkeley: University of California Press, 1997.

Stein, Gertrude. "Composition as Explanation." In *Look at Me Now and Here I Am: Writings and Lectures, 1909–1945*, edited by Patricia Meyerowitz, 21–33. Baltimore: Penguin, 1974.

Stein, Gertrude. *Lectures in America*, Boston: Beacon, 1985.

Stein, Gertrude. "Poetry and Grammar." In *Lectures in America*, 208–46. Boston: Beacon, 1985.

Stein, Gertrude. *Selected Writings of Gertrude Stein*. Edited by Carl Van Vechten. New York: Random House, 1946.

Stein, Gertrude. *Things as They Are*. Pawlet, VT: Banyan Press, 1950.

Steiner, Wendy. Introduction to *Lectures in America*, by Gertrude Stein, ix–xxvii. Boston: Beacon, 1985.

Taylor, Diana. *The Archive and the Repertoire: Performing Cultural Memory in the Americas*. Durham, NC: Duke University Press, 2003.

Tesori, Jeanine, and Lisa Kron. *Fun Home*. New York: Samuel French, 2015.

Thompson, Sharon. "Urgent: The Lesbian Home Movie Project." *Journal of Lesbian Studies* 19, no. 1 (2015): 114–16. https://doi.org/10.1080/10894160.2015.959879.

Tompkins, Kyla Wazana. "Ball Busters and the Recurring Trauma of Intergenerational Queer/Feminist Life." *Bully Bloggers* (blog), February 20, 2016. https://bullybloggers.wordpress.com/2016/02/20/ball-busters-and-the-recurring-trauma-of-intergenerational-queerfeminist-life/.

Traub, Valerie. *Thinking Sex with the Early Moderns*. Philadelphia: University of Pennsylvania Press, 2016.

Vider, Stephen. *The Queerness of Home: Gender, Sexuality, and the Politics of Domesticity after World War II*. Chicago: University of Chicago Press, 2022.

Warner, Sara. *Acts of Gaiety: LGBT Performance and the Politics of Pleasure*. Ann Arbor: University of Michigan Press, 2012.

Warner, Sara. "A Gay Old Time: Jill Johnston, 1975." In *Theatres of Affect: New Essays in Canadian Theatre*, edited by Erin Hurley, 104–22. Toronto: Playwrights Canada, 2014.

Whitehead, Anna Martine. "Expressing Life through Loss: On Queens That Fall with a Freak Technique." In *Queer Dance: Meanings and Makings*, edited by Clare Croft, 281–90. New York: Oxford University Press, 2017. https://doi.org/10.1093/acprof:oso/9780199377329.003.0018.

Winter, David G. "Personality Profiles of Political Elites." In *The Oxford Handbook of Political Psychology*, edited by Leonie Huddy, David O. Sears, and Jack S. Levy, 423–58. 2nd ed. New York: Oxford University Press, 2013.

Wittig, Monique. *The Straight Mind and Other Essays*. London: Beacon, 1992.

Wolf, Stacy. *Changed for Good: A Feminist History of the Broadway Musical*. New York: Oxford University Press, 2011.

Wolf, Stacy. "Desire in Evidence." *Text and Performance Quarterly* 17, no. 4 (1997): 343–51. https://doi.org/10.1080/10462939709366198.

INDEX

www.ingramcontent.com/pod-product-compliance
Lightning Source LLC
La Vergne TN
LVHW091123080826
845145LV00008B/2020

* 9 7 8 1 4 7 8 0 3 1 0 5 5 *